STEPPING OUT INTO THE FIELD

A Field Work Manual for Social Work Students

JULIET CASSUTO ROTHMAN
The Catholic University of America

Allyn and Bacon
Boston London Toronto Sydney Tokyo Singapore

For my husband, Leonard,
in gratefulness
for his patience, love, and support
and
for the social workers
of the new millennium

STEPPING OUT INTO THE FIELD

TABLE OF CONTENTS

PREFACE

You are about to embark upon an exciting journey. You have already taken the preliminary steps — you have considered your interests, abilities, and concerns; you have selected to focus them on a career in social work, and you have applied and gained acceptance to a professional program. You have made a commitment — of time, effort, and financial resources — to your chosen career.

Most students feel pulled toward a career in social work from several directions. There is a commitment to caring for the poor, the oppressed, and the disadvantaged, and to helping others toward a meaningful and satisfying life. There is a concern for justice and fairness, and a sincere belief in the importance of upholding the highest values of our society. There is a love of people — all kinds of people in all kinds of circumstances. There is an enjoyment in relationships and a strong desire for human connection. There is a fascination with the way we each learn and grow, and a desire to know more about people. Perhaps you have always wanted to work with people. Surely, you have been told in many different circumstances that you have been helpful to someone, and that your help was valued and appreciated. This has given you confidence that you truly can be helpful to others.

When you have comforted someone in a crisis, helped someone to make a decision, or worked with someone on a long-standing problem, you have reached out with sincerity. You *knew*, intuitively, just the right things to say and do to be helpful. Over time, you learned that you could trust your intuition to assist you in working with others.

As you enter professional training, you will bring all of these wonderful qualities with you. You will learn to add others, just as wonderful and just as necessary. Knowledge of people and environments, skills in interviewing, assessing, and intervening, awareness of resources to meet the needs of others, familiarity with community support networks, the ability to use self professionally: these and many other new professional processes will complement and supplement the natural skill and intuition you have brought with you.

One of the primary ways in which students learn is through direct practice. Field work is the vehicle through which you will encounter your first clients, groups, and projects as a professional. You will learn professional roles, values, and practice skills and encounter a wide range of circumstances during the course of your field placement. Each experience will contribute to the development of the professional person that you are in the process of becoming.

You will spend many hours in your field work placement. You will learn many new things, and encounter unforeseen circumstances, people, and events. It is my hope that this book will serve as a reference, and that it can provide support as you begin to explore your chosen vocation.

The book is organized around the experiences you will encounter during the process of field work education in a chronological order. Unit One, entitled Preparing to Enter the Field, provides some of the essential information necessary to begin your field work experience: the place of field work in the curriculum, the faculty and field work instructors who will be working with you, an understanding of the difference between the personal and the professional, and a beginning discussion of professional values and responsibilities. Unit Two addresses some of the circumstances and tasks you will find during the first weeks of placement: familiarizing yourself with the agency, building a good working relationship with your field instructor and your colleagues, and preparing for those all-important first contacts with clients as a student professional.

Unit Three includes some of the special things that can assist you in developing and maintaining an excellent field work experience: working with your learning contract, utilizing and creating opportunities for "crossover learning" between school and field, developing your relationship with your liaison, and preparing for the evaluation process that is an integral part of professional learning. The Unit Four assists you to prepare for the separation that is inherent in every field work placement from the very beginning. Terminating with clients, with your field instructor, with colleagues, and with the agency that has provided the structure and support you have needed as you engaged in the learning process is a complex process, but one that can, in itself, present wonderful opportunities for professional and personal growth. Unit Five, entitled If Problems Occur, is meant to serve as a reference point for you if you encounter situations in your field placement that concern you, and as a guide in assisting you to resolve them quickly and comfortably.

As you step out into this new field, may you find it to be a rich and rewarding experience!

INTRODUCTION

You have chosen to join a very special profession: one with historical roots grounded firmly in the values of service and caring; one that meets the challenges of today's rapidly changing societal needs and conditions with strength and confidence; and one that will demand of you the very best that you can give of yourself.

One of the distinguishing marks of education for the service professions is the way in which classroom learning is supplemented and reinforced by concomitant practice. It is generally recognized that, although potentially ethically problematic, direct contact with the populations and with the kinds of problems the student will encounter in future practice are a necessary part of preparation for competent professional practice. In addition to the skills and theoretical knowledge necessary for direct work with clients, groups, organizations, and communities, students in the professions must also understand the value base, expected codes of conduct and behavior, modes of communication, and protocols of their chosen profession.

In medicine, as in nursing, classroom learning is supplemented by "rotations" of hospital and clinic duties. In the field of education, students must "practice teach" in the classroom as part of their preparation. In our profession, social work, students combine classroom instruction with time in the field, in a field work placement. Because it is in the nature of service professions to work with human beings, such "practice" must necessarily be with and through individuals, organizations, and groups in need of the services of that profession. Thus, like other student professionals, student social workers must go where the population is, and provide service through the institutions that exist within the community to meet individual and societal needs.

Studies have shown that students entering field work may experience some anxiety, self-doubt, and apprehension as they approach a part of the educational process that may be very different from prior learning experiences (*Journal of Teaching in Social Work* 7(2): 81-95. 1993). These feelings may be allayed by thoughtful preparation for the field, and a consideration of some of the goals and objectives of the field experience, as well as of the special strengths and personal characteristics that students bring with them into practicum.

It is, of course, expected and understood that you as a student are less experienced than a seasoned professional, and that you will be at first unable to provide the level of services that a graduate professional would provide. You should always remember that there are two conditions that help to mitigate the potential for unfairness and inequality in this arrangement. The first is that, in common with other students, you will be closely, carefully, and rigorously supervised. Decisions will be made in consultation with an experienced professional, who has the double responsibility of training you to become a competent professional and of ensuring optimal treatment to enhance the well-being of the clients and populations you will serve.

The second is that your interest and attention, the extra time that you will have available due to your reduced student caseload, and the sincerity with which you will be rendering service will work very effectively in ensuring that you provide excellent service to each of your clients. In approaching your field work experience, you should be assured that your efforts on behalf of clients can and will make an enormous difference in their lives from the very first day that you begin to work with them.

This field work book was designed to assist you to have a meaningful and productive experience during this vital part of your social work education. We will embark together on a journey that extends from the day that you enter your agency for the first time to your final day, and beyond to the reflective process that will help you to integrate your experience into your developing professional social work identity. It is hoped that each reader will find in these pages experiences and suggestions that will help to make this the wonderful opportunity for growth that it is.

Good luck — grow, learn, help others, and enjoy this wonderful new career that you have chosen!

ACKNOWLEDGMENTS

I would like to thank my colleagues at the National Catholic School for Social Service, whose enthusiasm, interest, and support for this project were invaluable. Dr. Christine Anlauf Sabatino and Dr. Betty Plionis shared many of their experiences in working with students in Practice courses, and offered suggestions for the integration of coursework and field experience. Both Dr. Barbara Bailey-Etta, who served as Director of Field during most of my information-gathering and reflecting process, and Mrs. Loretta Vitale Saks, the current Director of Field, offered suggestions, shared forms and processes, and offered practical suggestions for guiding students through the field work process.

I would also like to thank my students, in the classroom and in the field, whose willingness to share special experiences, successes, concerns, and problems enabled me to enrich this book with many personal accounts and to more fully grasp the field work process through their eyes.

UNIT ONE

PREPARING TO ENTER THE FIELD

This first Unit will focus on familiarizing you with the way in which field work fits into the overall professional education process, and will offer some general concepts and principles to assist you in understanding the structure of the field work experience.

Chapter 1 explores field work in the context of the curriculum of professional social worker training, so that you can begin to place this part of your education into its broader framework. The Council on Social Work Education, the national body that oversees schools and programs in social work, assumes a major role in developing the structure of your field work program, and works closely with each school in developing both requirements and opportunities for field experiences.

As you enter the field, you will be guided and supported by a number of people at your school and in your agency. Your field work education team is introduced in Chapter 2. The members of your team will in all likelihood remain the same, and carry the same functions, throughout the course of your internship. Generally field education teams include representatives of the Field Work office, such as the Director and field liaison, representatives of your agency, such as your field instructor and agency director, and academic faculty, such as advisers, practice or methods instructors, and field work seminar instructors.

Chapter 3 will assist you in preparing for your new role as a social work professional, by distinguishing between your identity as a private individual and your identity as a social worker. In Chapter 4, we will be discussing some of the kinds of professional responsibilities and expectations that you may encounter during the course of your practicum. These will be related directly to the Code of Ethics of the National Association of Social Workers, which both develops guidelines and sets professional standards for both professional social workers and social work students.

CHAPTER ONE

THE PLACE OF FIELD WORK IN THE SOCIAL WORK CURRICULUM

Your school's curriculum has been designed to assist you in achieving your professional education goals. Careful thought and planning have created a framework that will ensure that you may learn not only competent practice skills, but also theoretical knowledge and professional judgment. Educational material designed to encourage the development of a professional social work value base and a commitment to ethical practice has been incorporated as well. Although all schools provide a strong generalist foundation for practice, you will also find many opportunities throughout the course of your studies to develop special skills and pursue particular areas of interest.

A. The Role of the Council on Social Work Education
The national body that oversees professional education in social work is the Council on Social Work Education. In addition to the provision of support services to professional schools of social work, the council has two important functions: it determines the necessary content of the social work curriculum, and it regularly visits, reviews, and examines each school to ensure its compliance with curriculum requirements through a re-accreditation process. The Council's overview function is in effect through all of the three levels of professional social work education: the Bachelor's, Master's and the Doctoral.

B. General Curriculum Requirements
As mandated by the Council on Social Work Education, you will be able to identify several individual components as you peruse your beginning social work education curriculum. Each will contribute an essential ingredient to your professional education.

Values and Ethics
An understanding of the value base of the profession, and of professional standards for ethical conduct, may be taught as a separate course, infused throughout the social work curriculum, or both. Grounded in the Code of Ethics of the National Association of Social Workers, the foundational values of the profession guide conduct and decision-making at all levels.

Human Behavior and Development
Taught generally within the person-in-environment framework that is foundational to social work, courses in human behavior provide theories of human development, personal relationship formation and patterns, and group and community relations. These will give you a language and a tool with which to begin to understand and assess your clients.

Multicultural Studies
Multicultural counseling, diversity, oppression, ethnicity, or other similarly titled courses are designed to provide you with insight and understanding about difference,

whether related to race, religion, ethnicity, culture, sexual orientation, socioeconomic class, ability level, or age. They explore the impact of an individual's difference upon his or her development, self-concept, interpretation of events and relationships, and worldview. "Difference" generally involves minority status in some manner, and these courses will explore the effect of such status upon the individual. Minorities have a group as well as an individual history, and coursework will also include an understanding of the experiences of the minority culture as a whole in the United States and in the country of origin where relevant.

Our profession has traditionally recognized a special obligation to the disadvantaged in our society, and thus to the achievement of social justice for all members of society. Often, perceptions of difference and minority status accompany disadvantage, and are an important factor in the life experiences of many of the clients with whom you will be working. Understanding the life experiences of minorities in the United States will assist you in establishing and maintaining good rapport. You will also be asked to explore your personal self-awareness in regard to any biases or beliefs you may hold about other groups.

Policy and Programs

Courses in policy and programs help to place the client, and the problems for which the client is seeking assistance, within a broader societal context. Policies and programs sanction, define, fund, and license the agency with whom you will be working, and are an essential part of understanding how goods and services are arranged and distributed in our society. It is only through a thorough knowledge of policy and programs that you will be able to utilize these on behalf of your client's best interests.

Research

Research courses will enable you to assess and evaluate programs and projects, and to utilize extant research in the field to deepen your knowledge and understanding of the populations, processes, and techniques and skills of the profession. Research informs and guides practice, and the ability to analyze and develop valid, relevant research is an integral piece of professional knowledge.

Social Work Practice

Foundation, methods, or practice courses will provide you with the "hows" of generalist social work practice: how to interview, how to establish rapport, how to assess, how to provide interventions, how to refer, how to consult, and how to terminate service. Here you will develop the skills you will need in direct work with your clients. You will explore different ways of understanding and working with different ages, conditions, and abilities, and develop a theoretical framework from which to consider both your clients and your own work with them. If you are a Bachelor's program student, foundation courses will provide you with the important social work skills you will need in working with clients, groups, and communities. If you are a student in a Master's program, foundation practice will provide generic practice skills, while later courses will focus on the population, context, and/or problem upon which you wish to concentrate.

Field Work

Classroom learning, as we discussed earlier, is taught in conjunction with direct practical experience. Practicum, internship, and field placement are three terms you might hear used to describe the time that you spend working directly with clients within the context of an agency practice. It is in field work that you will have an opportunity to use the skills from your foundation practice class, apply the theories learned in human development, and explore the effects and possibilities of policies and programs.

Conversely, it is from the field that you will take experiences, events, and problems back into the classroom for discussion, review, and consideration. In particular, your will find that the field experience and your practice class support and supplement each other; neither, alone, could provide the education needed for professional functioning.

Field Work Seminar

Many social work programs include an integrative field work seminar prior to and/or concurrent with student field work placements. Seminar prepares students for the field work experience, provides an ongoing forum for discussion of learning and problems, and enables the academic faculty to assist students through the practicum.

C. A Model for Establishing Field Work Education Goals

Anne Fortune's chapter in Reamer's *The Foundations of Social Work Knowledge*[1] presents the basic elements that form the cornerstones of field education. These include, firstly, the development of the student's ability to act in a responsible manner toward clients, colleagues, and the agency, to work non-judgmentally, and to know the foundational values of the profession (p. 168-169). Upon this base, Fortune defines a number of "core areas" within which the goals of the field education experience may be defined.

Goals in the area of professional development include the development of a deep commitment to social work values and ethics, to diversity and the ability to work with diverse populations, to social and economic justice, self-awareness, a commitment to professional growth, and the ability to evaluate professional effectiveness (p. 169-173).

Field education also should provide a basic knowledge and understanding of the organizational context of service — the agency's mission and structure, and develop the student's ability to function within it (p. 173-174). Familiarity with the social service delivery system, especially in terms of policy issues, and community resources and characteristics is also an important educational goal (p. 175-177).

Another "core area" of learning focuses on basic interpersonal skills, such as good communication, the ability to establish and maintain professional collegial relationships within the agency. Another set of goals involves the development of skills for working with client systems using the basic social work processes, such as the application of knowledge about human behavior and diversity, the refinement of interviewing skills and assessment, treatment planning and implementation, evaluation, termination, working with groups, using referral and resource networks, and developing advocacy skills (p. 178-183).

As you can see, the goals of field education are comprehensive and broadly based. Within this general framework, you and your field instructor will assess your needs and develop an individualized education plan to meet them. In Chapter 9, we will explore the design and development of a learning contract to best ensure your achievement of your personal professional goals.

D. Field Work Hours and Credits

The Council on Social Work Education determines the hours and conditions for the field work component in social work eduction. Separate sections address Bachelor's (B), and Master's (M) curriculum requirements. The Curriculum Policy Statement[2] for both the Bachelor's and the Master's level education considers the field practicum "an integral component of the curriculum in social work education" (B6.14 & M6.14), and stipulates that Master's level students spend a minimum of 900 hours in field work practice (M6. 15). Bachelor's level students spend a minimum of 400 hours in field work (B6.14).

In concurrent class-and-field programs, BSW students generally spend one day a week (eight hours) in the field, first year MSW students generally spend two days (sixteen hours), and second year students two and a half days (twenty hours). Block programs provide a similar number of field work hours.

Within these very broad parameters, programs vary in providing choices and conditions for meeting the requirements. Some programs have specific days, weeks, or months set aside for field work. Others allow flexibility in how the time requirement is met, such as permitting the splitting up of days, or ten-hour days. Still others provide arrangements for part-timers such as evening or weekend field work placements. It is important for you to know how your program structures its field work requirement hours, as these will have a strong impact upon your day-to-day planning and functioning while you are in school.

Field work is considered a course and is given a number of credits, as are all the other courses in your program, even though the number of contact hours per credit is much greater than with classroom courses.

E. Kinds and Choices of Placements

Generally, Bachelor's program and first year Master's program students have little choice of specific placements. The Office of Field Instruction tries to accommodate special needs, such as transportation problems or strong setting preferences, but often can make no guarantees regarding specific settings or populations. Matching students and field placements is a highly complex and difficult process, and you may find yourself working with a population or kinds of problems that you did not plan for, desire, or expect.

This can, however, be an exhilarating experience. You will learn about a kind of problem that was unknown or unfamiliar to you. You will work in a setting that will offer you new and different kinds of experiences. You may never return to that setting or population again, but your experiences with them will serve to enhance your practice throughout your professional career. After all, education is about learning and broadening your knowledge base, and field work is often just such a unique opportunity.

Generally, students are placed in social agencies, in community centers, in state or federal programs, in the judicial system, in schools, or in hospitals. Social agencies are the traditional milieu in which social work services are rendered directly to clients. The latter three kinds of settings are called "host" settings: those where social work services are not the primary reason for the existence of the agency or institutions. Justice systems exist to maintain and administer justice, schools to educate, and hospitals to treat illness. Social work services support these primary functions. Your field placement may also be with an organization which writes or implements policies and programs, or in the administrative department of a social welfare organization. Your program may offer additional kinds of field work placements as well.

Your school will have assessed all of the field work placements it offers, ensuring that each can provide a good education experience, congenial and comfortable surroundings, and personal safety for each student. Field work placements are assessed and re-assessed on a regular basis and your input, along with that of your fellow students, will form an important part of that assessment. When a field placement and a school agree to work together, a contract is signed between the two, stipulating the obligations and responsibilities of each party.

A part of the assessment and agreement stipulates the number of students that an agency will accept from a school. Some agencies will accept one student, some two or three or even more. Some will accept students from one school of social work only, while others may have students from two or three schools placed with them. Some agencies accept interns from several related disciplines, such as social work, psychology, and counseling.

Each kind of arrangement, of course, offers a different kind of experience. If you are the only student in your placement, you will quickly form relationships with professional colleagues and have an excellent opportunity for learning. If you are with other students, you will be able to share experiences and learn from each other. If you are with students from other schools of social work, you will be able to explore some of the differences in programs and orientation between them. Agencies with large numbers of students often have special education programs for them as well.

F. The Matching Process

Some time prior to the beginning of your first semester of field work, or in the first several weeks of the semester, the Office of Field Instruction will provide information regarding field placement. In most cases, you will then visit the placement and have an interview with a potential field instructor, with a director of student placements, or with the agency's director. You will have an opportunity to visit the agency and to explore its setting. You will also be able to explore the community in which your agency is located.

You may be asked to provide various kinds of information to a potential agency, such as your prior experiences with helping others, your educational majors, and your career interests. You should also feel free to ask questions and to explore the kinds of problems and clients the agency serves.

After your interview, the agency will contact the Field Work Office at your school, and let them know that they will accept you as a student. You may then be asked to provide additional paperwork. If the agency determines that they would not be a good "match" for you, you will be sent on to another interview and the process will be repeated. Should this happen to you, don't be discouraged. Agencies have many reasons for refusing a student, few of which have anything to do with your own personal qualities and achievements. Remember, they don't even know you!

It is important to clarify insurance issues during this early process. Agencies often require students to carry malpractice liability insurance of some kind, which thereby absolves them of liability through any errors students might make. Most schools carry this liability insurance for you as a student. Still, it's best to check this before beginning your placement.

You have been matched with a placement, done the necessary paperwork, and checked insurance coverage. The initial phase is completed, and you can sit back, relax, and enjoy the beginning of your classes, for in most cases, field work placements do not begin until several weeks into the academic semester.

---

[1] Reamer, F. (1994) *The Foundation of Social Work Knowledge.* NY: Columbia University Press.
[2] Council on Social Work Education (1994) *Handbook of Accreditation Standards and Procedures.* Alexandria, VA: Author.

CHAPTER TWO

YOUR FIELD WORK EDUCATION TEAM

Your field work education is, as we have seen, an essential ingredient in your professional education. Careful and deliberate planning by the school and the agency has prepared your placement to receive and to assist you toward your professional goals. Both school and agency provide a structure to ensure good communication and cooperation in support of your learning experience. However, your personal involvement is vital to planning and structuring a placement that addresses your unique needs and interests.[1] This chapter will assist you to become a knowledgeable consumer of field work education by providing information about the structure of school and field for practicum instruction, and the manner in which they interface to address your personal educational goals.

Imagine an equilateral triangle with you at the apex. You are placed in this position because you are central to this project: it is because of you that the triangle exists at all. The other two corners form the foundation. One is your field placement, the other your field office.

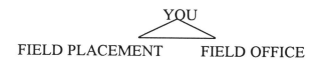

A. <u>Your Field Placement</u>

Your field work placement, generally a social agency, is designed to facilitate services to its client population. It may exist as an independent structure, be located in a building with other social agencies, or be a part of a "host" setting, such as a hospital, school, justice department, or other setting. To ensure privacy and confidentiality, social agencies generally contain multiple offices, and some common areas such as waiting rooms, lounges, and work stations. Some agencies provide each social worker with a private office, while others utilize "interviewing rooms." Still others provide all interviewing in the field, and therefore may have several workers sharing office space. In addition to professional social workers, agencies employ support personnel, and may also utilize paraprofessionals and professionals in other disciplines, such as psychologists and educators.

In the course of your field work experience, you will work with many different professionals and other staff members, and have an opportunity to observe many facets of your agency's functioning. However, the two agency professionals most directly involved with your placement are your Field Instructor and the agency's Director.

The Field Instructor

Within your field placement, your Field Instructor is primarily responsible for your learning, providing supervision, support, instruction, and advocacy if needed in your behalf. The role of your Field Instructor will be presented in greater detail below, and also is addressed in Chapter 6. In addition to your Field Instructor, an agency with a large number of students may also have a Training Supervisor, Coordinator of Student Education, or In-Service Instructor. This person will ensure that you are learning and progressing as well. In addition, he or she may provide educational programs for all of the agency's students as a group, arrange for field trips to appropriate agencies, resources, or conferences, and have planned regular meetings with all the students as a group. (If your agency does not have a Training Supervisor, your Field Instructor will arrange these kinds of experiences for you.)

If you are in an agency that has several field instructors, they may all meet together to plan special activities for you, and to discuss the agency's field work program. Showers and Cuzzi have found that field instructors benefit from sharing experiences and receiving support from each other and from the agency.[2]

New field instructors are often prepared for their special role of supervision and training through training programs run by schools of social work or placement agencies. Field instructors will be familiar with the requirements of your school's program, and with its other education components.

The Agency Director

Every field placement also has a director, a department head, or other executive who is ultimately responsible for the agency's overall functioning. You may have met your agency's director during your interview and agency tour, or you may meet her or him later in the course of your placement. It is generally your agency's director who approves of the agency's serving as a field placement, signs a contract with your school program, determines who will provide field instruction, oversees and approves arrangements for your office space, and arranges for the adjustment of your field instructor's schedule and caseload to accommodate field instruction.

The director must also address any issues where a conflict of interest might arise between the needs of the agency (primarily concerned with the provision of services) and the school's educational program (primarily concerned with the provision of education).[3]

Depending upon his or her own responsibilities, the agency's director is often an excellent resource and can provide needed information and guidance. Your access to the director depends upon the policies of your agency. Some directors have an open-door policy, and will welcome you at any time. Others will ask that you arrange in advance for an appointment with them.

The agency director, program director, or other agency administrator may serve as field instructor for students who are in macro placements, or who are on an administration track. In that case, he or she will function within the guidelines for field instructors as well as in an agency administrative capacity. Patti explores several models for such placements through a series of articles which affirm the value of an agency-wide commitment to education and training to provide an optimal milieu for effective training.[4]

B. The Field Work Office

You have had your first introduction to the Field Work Office during your initial placement process. The Office is responsible for the overall coordination of all field work placements at your school, recruiting, developing, and evaluating placement, matching students and field work agencies, assigning liaisons, and addressing any field-related problems. In many schools, the Field Office retains ultimate control over the grade you will receive, following closely the recommendations and evaluation of your work provided by your field instructor.

The staff of the Field Office generally includes both professionals and administrative personnel, for a great deal of record-keeping, telephoning, and interviewing are necessary.

Field Orientation

The Office of Field Work usually holds an orientation for all students entering a field work placement prior to the first day of field work. Orientation will provide you with guidance regarding your school's policies and a variety of procedures to follow while in the field. The semester or year schedule will be reviewed in terms of assignments, forms, and other paperwork. Procedures for communicating with the various players on your field work team will be presented, along with safety information, policies regarding cars and transportation, insurance, vacations and sick days, and other essentials. You may be asked to purchase a special textbook such as this one or other written material to use for general information and for reference. At the Field Orientation, you may meet your field consultant/liaison, or have another opportunity to talk with your field instructor.

Your school may also, or alternatively, provide a course of several weeks' duration to assist you to prepare for field, or may hold a series of ongoing seminars during the course of your field work placement to enable you to address concerns, ask questions, and assess your progress, as well as share experiences with other students. It is important for you to participate actively in field work preparation and training, so that you will be comfortable as you approach the agency on that first, all-important day!

The Director of Field

The Field Office is headed by a Director, Coordinator, or Chairperson, who is a member of your program's faculty. The Director may be responsible to the Dean, the Program Chair, the Department Head, and, at times, to an Advisory Board. The Director of Field has ultimate responsibility for your overall field experience, and oversees your field instructor as well as your liaison, both of whom are a part of the Field Office.

The Liaison or Field Consultant

Liaisons or Field Consultants are a part of the Field Office. You will have a Consultant or Liaison assigned to you who serves as the representative of your program to your field placement agency. Your Liaison or Field Consultant is available to you both by telephone and in-person to answer your questions, solve problems, and offer support and guidance. The role of this key person in your field work education team will be addressed in greater detail below.

C. The Academic Faculty

Although all of the courses and faculty members that you will be experiencing during the course of your educational process will impact upon, and be impacted by, your experiences in your field work placement, there are two members of the academic faculty whose roles place them in close proximity to your field work experience: your Theory and

Practice and/or Practicum instructor(s), and your Adviser. If your school has a course to prepare you for field, or ongoing field work seminars, these instructors are primarily involved in your field work experience as well.

The Foundation, Practice, or Methods Instructor

Your Foundation Practice or Methods instructor, as well as the members of your class, will be closely involved in your field work educational process. You will be bringing experiences from the field into the classroom, and sharing them with students and instructors there. These experiences will contribute to the learning of your classmates, and their input will enable you to think about your client, case, or agency setting from viewpoints other than your own. Practice instructors are therefore indirectly also members of your field work education team. Their role is addressed in greater detail below and is also discussed in Chapter 10.

The Adviser

Although not directly involved with field work, and thus not a primary member of your field work education team, your adviser is aware of your field work placement and is available as a resource regarding field in the event that questions and/or problems arise which affect your overall education and experience. Advisers are also discussed below in terms of their role in your field work experience.

The Field Work Seminar Instructor

Your school's program structure will determine the extent and time frame of your experience with your field work preparation or seminar instructor. Field work preparation may terminate once field placement begins; however, the instructor is a good resource for you should you have any questions or concerns. Ongoing field seminars offer regular opportunities for sharing, learning, and question-asking throughout the course of your field work placement. If your school provides these instructional experiences, please read the material which applies to your practice instructor as including these instructors as well.

D. Communication

Ultimately, all of your instructors and advisers are responsible to the director of your program, Dean, or Program Chair.

The agency/school hierarchy may look something like this:

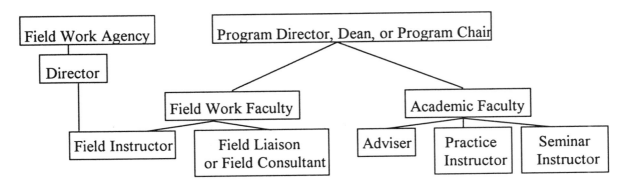

It is important to recognize that, although roles have been diagrammed separately here for clarification of functions, members of your field education team may serve in more than one capacity in working with you. For example, your seminar instructor may also be your field consultant; your liaison may also be your adviser or your practice instructor; and the agency director may also be your field instructor.

Each of the team members may communicate with you, and with each other, regarding your field experience. In other words, your liaison may speak with your field instructor, or vice versa. Your practice instructor may speak with your field consultant, or with your adviser, or with the coordinator of field. The coordinator of field may speak with your adviser, your practice instructor, or with the Dean. The number of people involved, and the level of their involvement, will depend upon the reason for the communication.

Generally, there are two circumstances when communication regarding your field work experience occurs: those which are a planned part of the program, such as liaison field visits and field instructor evaluations, and those which occur primarily when a problem or concern arises regarding your work or your placement.

Structured Communication

Opportunities for communication occur regularly during your placement, and serve to provide information to the school and to the field placement regarding your progress. Some of these are verbal, some are in writing, through the use of forms and reports. Structured verbal opportunities for communication occur primarily during your liaison or field work coordinator's visits to your field work placement, and through planned telephone contacts between your field instructor and liaison.

Written communication includes the various kinds of written material that will pass back and forth between placement and school during the course of the year, such as periodic evaluation forms, grading sheets, your learning contract, a report of your field liaison's visit to you at your agency, and others. You will always have an opportunity to read, review, and comment upon any reports which pass between school and agency in your regard.

Communication Around a Problem or Concern

Problems or concerns may come to the attention of any member of your field work education team, or to you yourself. In this case, the level of involvement, and who gets involved, is determined by the kind of problem or concern and by considerations of the best and most effective way of resolving it. If you are expressing the problem or concern yourself, you can choose the team member whom you feel will address it best, depending on your relationship with the team members, the kind of problem, and the accessibility of those who are able to address it.

Whether it is you or another team member who first brings attention to an issue or a problem, you will always be informed, and will have an active part to play in its resolution. Problems in the field are addressed in greater depth in Unit Five.

E. Your Personal Field Work Team

Field work educational and advisory professionals are generally assigned by the program director and director or coordinator of field, and reflect school policies and priorities, as well as the school's experience with what seems to work best for their students. Each is a member of your educational team and each can be utilized by you as needed to ensure an optimal experience.

The roles of each member as described below help to further clarify each member's function in your educational process.

Your Field Instructor

Your field instructor has two major responsibilities in relation to your placement: to you and to your education, and to the clients with whom you will be working. While classes are designed to teach basic social work knowledge and skills, your field instructor's work with you will be very strongly practice oriented, focusing on the problems and clients in your own caseload. She or he will be familiar with each of your cases, and have a good understanding of the needs and problems of each client. At times, your clients may actually be cases transferred from your field instructor's own caseload.

Your field instructor selects cases for you based on his or her assessment of your learning needs, your level of experience and comfort, and the availability of appropriate clients. He or she will offer suggestions and guidance in your work in terms of the basic social work processes: relationship-building and interviewing skills, assessment, coordination, interventions, and evaluation.

Your Liaison or Field Work Consultant

Liaisons and Consultants generally work with a number of students and placements. There are various arrangements possible for the assignment of liaisons, and programs differ in the ways that these are selected to work with you. Some programs assign your foundation practice instructor to serve in this capacity, as this can be a helpful and very productive way to encourage and support coordination between field and classroom. Some assign your adviser as your liaison or field consultant, believing that this is the best system for ensuring that your field experience is fully integrated into your total professional program. Others feel that students are best served by having a number of professionals working with them.

Still others assign liaisons or field work consultants primarily based on the geographical proximity of the field work placements or context of practice (a liaison with expertise in medical social work, for example, may be assigned students placed in medical settings). Some schools assign only faculty members to this position, while others feel that experienced social workers in practice in the community bring a valuable perspective to the field education experience.

Conroy's study of field liaison arrangements has found that there is no significant difference in satisfaction with part- or full-time field liaisons, but did reveal a lack of clarity on the part of students regarding the role of the field liaison. To assist you in clarifying this important role, Chapter 11 will explore your relationship with your liaison.[5]

Your liaison or consultant is the bridge between school and field placement, and will visit you in your field placement. If any problems or special issues are brought up by you or your field instructor during the visit, they will be addressed and a plan for resolving them developed. Liaisons should be especially sensitive to your experiences with diversity and ethnicity while in your field placement, and may be able to offer assistance with any personal special needs.[6]

Your liaison or field consultant will report back to the Director of Field or Field Coordinator regarding your progress in your field placement and the nature of your experiences. These reports will become a part of your field work placement file.

Director of Field or Field Work Coordinator

You will probably have little contact with the Director of Field, unless you experience difficulties which require his or her intervention. However, you do have access to the Director or Coordinator should the need arise. Though you may have minimal contact, your progress will be closely monitored by the Coordinator through his or her reading and reviewing all of the material and evaluations provided by your field instructor and liaison or consultant.

Your Foundation Practice or Methods Instructor

Your Foundation Practice Instructor is crucial to your learning the skills that you need to become a competent professional. In his or her class, you will learn the theory, knowledge base, and skills that are essential to social work practice. Reading, class discussion, and case examples, often supplemented by appropriate videos or other material, will be utilized in your learning process.

This class often serves as a forum for discussion of client problems, difficulties with assessments, and other experiences encountered in the field. In essence, your classmates and your instructor become a kind of advisory body to assist you to understand and develop strategies for addressing needs and problems. Each class member will contribute case experiences, and each will learn in the process of listening and advising. Suggestions for successfully integrating your classroom and practicum learning are included in Chapter 10.

The instructor guides student case discussions, and often provides guidance and input directly as well. Because this course is so closely interrelated with your field experience, you will find the greatest amount of crossover between Field and Foundation Practice classes. Your instructor is also a resource for you should you experience questions or problems in your field work placement. He or she can contact your liaison or coordinator, or your field instructor to discuss concerns if necessary. However, your instructor will not do without your explicit consent, and all clients and problems discussed in class should always remain confidential within the class.

Your Adviser

Your adviser is responsible for coordinating your overall learning and experience with professional education. Field work is a part of that experience, and thus your adviser is a resource for you as well. You will probably meet with your advisor several times during the semester. At minimum, you will work with your adviser in planning your overall program.

Advisers are often the persons on the faculty that students turn to when faced with important decisions such as what to specialize in, what kind of field placement to seek for the following year, or what kinds of populations to work with. A good understanding of your field experience, from you personally as well as from the field office, will assist your adviser to develop a plan with you that best meets your interests and desires.

Your Field Work Seminar Instructor

Field Work Seminars are often taught by members of your field education team. Your liaison or adviser may also be your seminar instructor. This double responsibility helps to ensure that a member of the faculty is closely involved with your field work placement on a regular basis.

All of the members of your field work education team are committed to the professional as a whole, and in particular to social work education. All of them recognize that they, as well as you, share the responsibility in ensuring that you attain the highest possible level of competence in professional practice.

Now that you are familiar with the members of your field work education team, we can begin to focus on your own work as a student social worker. The next chapter will explore professional demeanor and comportment, and suggest some general guidelines to assist you to begin work in your field placement. Of course, each agency is unique: you will always need to consider your agency's practices and the behavior norms expected there, and ensure that you will function comfortably within them.

---

[1] Welsh, B.L. (1979) The initial phase of field work placement: an educational process. *School Social Work Quarterly* 1(2): 117-127.

[2] Showers, N., & Cuzzi, L. (1991) What field instructors of social work students need from hospital field work programs. *Social Work in Health Care* 16(1): 39-52.

[3] Marshack, E.F. (1988) Ethics in field work. *The Jewish Social Work Forum* 24:41-44, Spring.

[4] Patti, R.J. (1980) Field education at the crossroads: exploring alternatives for administrative practice. *Administration in Social Work* 4(2): 61-104.

[5] Conroy, K. (1993) Field advising by full and part-time faculty in social work education. Doctoral Dissertation, City University of New York.

[6] Gladstein, M., & Mailick, M. (1986) An affirmative approach to ethnic diversity in field work. *Journal of Social Work Education* 22(1): 41-49.

CHAPTER THREE

PROFESSIONAL DEMEANOR AND COMPORTMENT

Field work placement is your introduction to the professional practice of social work. It is also your introduction to the world around you <u>as a social worker</u>, a representative of a profession. The things that you say and do, the way you dress and speak, and the manner of your interaction with others reflect upon the profession as a whole, and therefore should be representative of the way in which competent professionals present themselves.

This does <u>not</u> mean that you must change yourself into another person, and abandon your own personal style or way of doing things. It <u>does</u> mean that you need to develop an awareness of yourself as a professional, and comport yourself in a manner that reflects core professional values and behavior within your own personal style <u>while you are functioning professionally</u>.

When you are away from work, and are a private individual, you are generally accountable only to yourself. You need make no changes in this private individual, with only the exceptions mentioned below. However, when you are at work, and functioning as a professional social worker and representative of your field work agency, it is important to recognize that all that you say and do reflects both upon the profession as a whole and upon your field work agency. You <u>represent</u> the profession of social work to you clients. You *represent* your agency to clients, other professionals and organizations, and the community.

A. <u>You, The Private Individual</u>

As noted above, when you are away from work, you are a private individual with full liberty and freedom to act as you desire. Your life is your own to live as you choose. However, there are several circumstances that may come up while you are a "private individual" that you may want to consider beforehand, so that you may be prepared should they occur.

Possibility: You may run into a client.

It's a small world, and there are many clients. Some may be your own, others may be clients of the agency with whom you are familiar. What will you do when a client gets on line behind you at the supermarket? Or passes you in the street while walking with a friend?

Have you ever met your teacher, your therapist, your physician or the nurse in her office in similar circumstances? How did you feel?

Your choice of action depends upon your personal style, the client's need and problem, your relationship with the client, and your agency's custom. It is wise to discuss this potential situation with your field instructor, who may be able to provide guidance. Some possible choices: (1) a glance of acknowledgment, no spoken words; (2) a brief greeting; (3) pretend you don't see the client; or (4) leave it up to the client to initiate contact. As a private individual, it is not appropriate to suggest coffee, or accept if it is suggested by your client. You are now in the public domain, so to speak. This in and of itself makes your relationship different, and can potentially harm the professional rapport that you worked so hard to build.

It is best never to accept a client's invitation to socialize outside of the office. Rather, explore with the client in the professional milieu some of the reasons he or she wishes to socialize. You may gain many insights in this manner!

Possibility: Someone you know may say something about your client, while unaware of your relationship.

This problem is much easier to resolve. Your obligation to client confidentiality and privacy dictates absolutely that you not let anyone know that you have a professional relationship with the client. No matter what is said, you cannot breach confidentiality in this instance.

Possibility: While out with friends, or at a party, someone asks your "professional" advice about a problem.

You want to help! After all, your desire to help others is the reason that you chose to become a social worker. However, there are hazards to helping or offering advice. You are now no longer "just" you. You are a professional social worker, presumed to have a body of knowledge which others do not have. The things that you say will carry more weight, and can be considered as absolute truths!

It is not helpful to others, nor professional, to offer "professional advice" under such casual circumstances. Because you know the person who is asking for advice or help, it is not advisable to become involved professionally with them. In fact, such "dual relationships" are proscribed by the NASW Code of Ethics, to which you are bound. However, it is appropriate and professional to offer a referral, or suggestions for sources of help for the problem.

Possibility: You meet another professional or staff member of your agency at an event, meeting, or on the street.

You might want to be guided by the degree of formality that exists between you and that person while in the agency. If your agency director is "Mrs. Turner" at work, it's not "Elsie" outside of the office. If your field instructor is "John" at work, it's "John" outside of work as well.

B. You, the Professional Social Worker

While you are functioning as a professional social worker, you need to be aware, as noted above, that you reflect upon the profession as a whole, and upon your agency. You also are an important role model for your clients and therefore should model the kinds of values, goals, and behavior that best support your own personal beliefs and your client's goals.

It would be impossible to present and discuss all of the situations which might arise in your professional life which require that you reflect upon the appropriate course of action. As you become more experienced in your professional role, you will respond automatically as a professional, and have internalized the response and demeanor that is expected of you. It will have become, essentially, a part of who you are, of your identity as a person. However, in these first early days, it is important to learn and reflect upon some of these professional expectations.

The examples and situations presented here do not presume to be an exhaustive list, but merely suggest the <u>kinds</u> of questions and issues you may encounter. An attempt has been made to provide some suggestions or guidance. As in other areas of your learning, your instructors, adviser, and field instructor should always be consulted for advice and guidance.

The material that follows has been rather arbitrarily divided into three sections. The first section, entitled <u>General Guidelines</u>, draws primarily from the Code of Ethics of the National Association of Social Workers which addresses professional comportment. The second section, entitled <u>Agency Guidelines</u>, offers suggestions for professional conduct in relation to your field placement agency. The third, <u>Personal Guidelines</u>, includes suggestions for personal comportment while you are in a professional role.

C. <u>General Guidelines</u>

General guidelines for professional comportment may be drawn specifically from Ethical Standards Section 4 in the Code of Ethics. Please refer to the Code, included in the appendix of this book, for specific references.

<u>Competence</u> (Section 4.01)

As a social worker, you should always base your practice on the recognized body of knowledge which supports the profession. This means using the recognized methods and theories that are generally accepted by social workers. You will be learning these methods and theories during the course of your professional education.

<u>Non-Discrimination</u> (Section 4.02)

During the course of your professional work, you should provide services equally and without distinction to all, without discriminating in terms of race, religion, ethnic or national origin, sex or sexual orientation, marital status, political belief, or disability whether mental or physical. You also should not collaborate with persons or with policies that are discriminatory, nor facilitate circumstances which promote discrimination.

<u>Fulfillment of Professional Responsibilities</u> (Section 4.03)

As a professional social worker, it is important that you not allow your private conduct or behavior to interfere in any way with the fulfillment of your professional responsibilities. Some examples of private conduct which could interfere in this way are presented below, in the section entitled Personal Guidelines.

<u>Dishonesty, Fraud, Deception</u> (Section 4.04)

Social workers have a professional obligation to be honest, and not to be associated with, not collaborate with, dishonesty, fraud, and deception in their relationships with clients, other professionals, and agencies and community resources. Social workers hold both a public trust and the trust of their individual clients, and both must have confidence in your honesty as a professional.

While you may personally fulfill this obligation well, you may find it more difficult not to be "associated" with fraud and dishonesty. As in most other fields and workplaces, dishonesty, fraud, and deception in some form may be present at your field work agency. There may be instances where you become aware of such problems, either in your work with a client (you learn that she is misrepresenting her earnings to an income maintenance program, or she tells you she is allowing her husband to care for the children when this was limited by the court), with a colleague (you learn that she is misrepresenting hours in the field, or is using an agency vehicle for personal business) or with your agency as a whole (you learn that they are altering statistics in order to receive additional funding, or that they are counting telephone contacts as in-person visits). Addressing these issues is difficult, and suggestions will be offered in future chapters to assist you in fulfilling your professional obligation to honesty.

Personal Impairment (Section 4.05)
Because your work intimately affects the lives and well-being of others, it is vital that you function at your best. Therefore, current or unresolved issues and problems in your own personal life, such as substance abuse, mental health difficulties, personal problems, and legal problems that may keep you from working optimally with clients must be addressed and adjustments made to protect your clients from any adverse effects. Personal problems which carry over into practice can have a strong negative impact upon the functioning of clients, who are themselves vulnerable and in distress.

Misrepresentation (Section 4.06)
It is important that you do not misrepresent yourself to the clients with whom you are working. A frequent issue for beginning students is whether all clients should be informed of the fact that they are students. The Code of Ethics specifies this kind of disclosure, and non-disclosure may be considered a violation of your client's right to know (informed consent). You may wish to tell them that you are an "intern," or a "student," or a "graduate student." If you realize that there is an assumption on the part of clients that you are a licensed professional, you must assist them to understand your present status. It is usually best to provide this information to clients upon first meeting with them, rather than to go back and change their assumptions about your qualifications at a later date. In this way, clients will have an opportunity to ask questions and resolve any concerns they might have early on, and your status as an intern will be an accepted part of the relationship that you build together.

Students sometimes feel that letting clients know of their status as students or interns will undermine the work that is done, and their ability to gain their clients' trust and respect. On the contrary, most clients readily accept interns and enjoy the extra time, attention, and effort that interns give to them. Adolescents who are in school themselves will often feel a special bond, enabling you to quickly and easily establish an excellent relationship with them.

As a social worker, you should be careful to distinguish between statements and actions made as a professional, and those made as a private individual. In the earlier discussion of advice-giving, we noted that many people will assume that all that you say and do is done in your professional role. When you express a personal belief or political position or opinion, you must clarify that this is, indeed, your personal statement, and that it does not necessarily represent the position or belief of the profession if you feel that there might be some confusion on the part of the listener in this regard.

Sexual Relationships, Physical Contact, Sexual Harassment

Sexual relationships are proscribed in several sections of the Code of Ethics. The power and knowledge imbalance between workers and clients, workers and supervisors, and students and field instructors renders such relationships potentially very harmful. This proscription extends not only to current clients, bu also to their relatives and others with whom the clients maintain a close personal relationship, and to former clients. Services to individuals with whom workers have had a previous sexual relationship is also proscribed (Sect. 1.09).

Workers must also refrain from physical contact with clients when there is a potential for psychological harm to such clients (Sect. 1.10). Sexual harassment, which includes advances, solicitation, requests for sexual favors, and other sexually oriented behavior, is not permitted (Sect. 1.11).

Because of the potential for harm, similar rules regarding relationships, physical contact, and sexual harassment apply to the relationship between field instructor and students, and between supervisors and supervisees as well.

Dignity and Worth of Persons

It is a foundational principle of social work that all persons be treated with dignity and respect and with consideration for their feelings, concerns and circumstances. This applies not only to clients, but also to colleagues, staff, outside resources, and all persons with whom you will be interacting in the course of your professional training.

D. Agency Guidelines

Your professional comportment reflects both on your agency and on yourself as an individual. Most of the suggestions and guidelines offered in this section are common sense, and would apply in any employment setting. The difference here is that, as an unpaid intern, your status is a bit more complex: you are not an employee, but you have many of the same obligations that regular employees have. You have made a commitment to your field placement agency, as they have to you, and there are mutual obligations inherent in these commitments.

Loyalty and Trustworthiness

During the course of your field placement, you will develop a feeling of respect and pride in your agency, and in its ability to provide the services it offers in a caring, careful, and efficient manner. It is rare that a student will find that an agency's policies or functioning is not of high quality; if it were not, it would not have successfully undergone the schools' scrutiny to become a field placement. However, occasionally a student may object to a policy or procedure, and wish to draw attention to the problem so that it may be addressed.

Although you are not an employee of your placement agency, professional values ask that you treat the agency and its reputation in the public domain with loyalty and trust.

This means addressing agency problems within the agency, except in the most extreme circumstances. Undermining your agency's reputation may injure clients, and compromise its ability to provide services in the community.

Agencies have specific mechanisms that foster such discussions, such as staff meetings, team meetings, and grievance committees. Follow your agency's guidelines for effecting change or questioning a policy, procedure, or service. Suggestions for addressing these kinds of problems are offered in Chapters 17, 18, and 20.

Agency Resources

Workers are also the stewards of the agency's resources. These include money, services, equipment, and personnel. You must exercise care and responsibility in distributing these resources in a way that supports your agency's mission and intent. This means ensuring that they are used fairly and equitably, and that the maximum benefit is obtained by clients.

You (and other social workers and staff) are also an agency resource! Your time and your services, are the best resources your agency has available. Therefore, it is important to allocate your time in a way that benefits clients and provides the kinds of services the agency supports.

Work Times and Schedules

You and your field placement agency, through the director or your field instructor, have established a schedule which sets the hours that you are committed to the agency in fulfillment of school requirements. It is your responsibility to be prompt, and to remain at your placement during the hours that have been scheduled for you. Should it become necessary to make permanent or temporary changes in this schedule, you must obtain your agency's consent.

Work Space

An appropriate work space has been assigned to you. Generally, this includes a desk and chair, a telephone, and a client's chair if you will be interviewing in your office. It is important that you keep your work area clean and neat, attractive and welcoming to clients, and in a style that is in harmony with the rest of the office. This is especially vital if you are sharing your work space with others.

In the Field

When you are out in the field during the course of your professional responsibilities, you represent your agency to the public. The way that you speak, the way that you dress and act — all of your behavior represents your agency as a whole. Some suggestions regarding your comportment as a representative of your agency are presented here.

E. Personal Guidelines

Demeanor and comportment during the course of your professional work is an area where the "personal you" and the "professional you" must come together. Each of us has a personal style that includes our way of dressing, moving, speaking, and acting. We have developed this style over the years, and it is comfortable for us.

Professional development includes a meaningful and comfortable integration of your personal tastes, likes, and dislikes with an expected professional code of comportment. This does not mean that all social workers dress, speak, and act alike, or that you must become an automaton representing a profession with no personal style remaining. It means that there are some rather broad boundaries that define professional comportment, and that while you are functioning as a professional you will need to adhere to these boundaries.

Formality and Informality

Many agencies require a certain degree of formality in relationships and address, while others prefer a casual and informal atmosphere. You should take the cues for your behavior from observation of those around you. When you begin your field placement, it is best to assume a more formal approach. Address co-workers and staff as Dr., Mrs., Ms., and Mr. until and unless told to do otherwise. Because formality helps to support a professional atmosphere for client service, many agencies tend to keep to this kind of stance.

Clients are always addressed formally unless it is a policy or the practice in your agency to use first names or nicknames. The reason for this formality with clients is that many people consider the use of first names demeaning. Older people and people from other cultures and ethnic groups are particularly sensitive to the use of first names. Often, clients are already feeling vulnerable and powerless. Addressing them informally by their first names only tends to reinforce this feeling. Using last names and titles also helps you and your client to maintain an appropriate professional distance — it makes it clear that you are not a friend or a buddy, confidant or sibling, but a professional rendering a professional service.

There are specific settings and agencies where such formality is inappropriate, and where the use of first names is encouraged. In certain kinds of mental health settings, and in working with children and adolescents, a casual informality can serve as an important tool for developing trust, and establishing a good pattern of communication.

Take your cue from your agency — they have had years of experience and know what will work best in their setting and with their population.

Dress

Similar considerations apply when considering appropriate dress for field placement. Generally dresses, suits, jackets and ties, or dress pants are worn. It is important to appear neat and clean, and attention to dress communicates a professional image as well. It is especially important not to dress in a manner that is sexually provocative, overly casual, or very extreme.

Again, as with matters of address, take your cues from your agency, and follow the style and "dress code" that are appropriate for your placement. If you are working in a setting where informality has therapeutic value, such as those described above, jeans, sport shirts, and other more casual dress are appropriate.

Language

As a professional, it is never acceptable to use profane or derogatory language.

Alcohol and Drugs

Social workers should never drink alcoholic substances nor use non-medicinal drugs in the course of professional functioning.

Demeanor

Your behavior while in your field placement should always inspire confidence and trust in your clients and co-workers, and in others with whom you will come in contact, and should not call undue or inappropriate attention to you. Loud, abrasive, silly, or aggressive speech or actions are generally not considered professional.

Within these broad guidelines, you will find that you are able to express yourself, your taste, and your personality in a way that is uniquely yours.

CHAPTER FOUR

PROFESSIONAL RESPONSIBILITIES

From the day that you enter a professional social work program, it is your responsibility to practice according to the standards delineated in the Code of Ethics of the National Association of Social Workers. In Chapter 3, we explored professional comportment, and found that the Code of Ethics includes some general guidelines to help us understand professional behavior. In this chapter, we will explore some of the ethical responsibilities social workers assume in relation to clients, clients' families and close relationships, agencies and organizations, society as a whole, and colleagues. Portions of the Code of Ethics deal specifically with issues you will encounter as a student in a field placement, while others are applicable throughout the course of your professional career.

It is important to place our discussion within the framework of social work's core values, which provide the ethical parameters for professional functioning. These are defined as:

- service
- social justice
- dignity and worth of person
- integrity
- competence
  (NASW Code of Ethics, Preamble)

Thus, while in your field placement, you should consider your obligation to service to your agency's clients, whether individuals, groups, or entire communities, and treat both them and your colleagues with the dignity and respect that underlies a belief in the value of people. This supports honesty and integrity in your dealings with others, and reflects your efforts to gain competence in practice. Your responsibilities also include a commitment to social justice — to the prevention of discrimination, oppression, and abuse wherever they may be found — within the world of your client and placement, or within the community and the society as a whole.

The major ethical obligations you will encounter in your field placement include your responsibilities to you client, to your client's family and close relationships, to your colleagues, to your field placement agency, and to society as a whole.

A. <u>Responsibilities to Clients</u>

Your ethical responsibility to enhance and support your clients' well-being is primary, and you should always act with their best interests as your first responsibility (1.01). This means placing your clients' interests above your own, those of your agency, or of your colleagues, <u>while you are functioning as a social worker at your field placement</u>. You owe your clients loyalty, respect, honesty, and careful and competent practice.

This holds true in most circumstances. However, there may be times when your obligations to the society as a whole, or to specific others, may limit your consideration of your client as primary (1.01). Examples of these circumstances might include instances where your client threatens to harm a third party, where there is child abuse, and/or where certain laws are violated.

This primary responsibility gives rise to several more specific ethical obligations, each of which supports the client's best interests in most circumstances. These include:

Self-Determination

The core value of dignity and respect of persons asks that we consider our clients as self-determined human beings, with the right to make decisions about matters which affect their lives. It is always our responsibility to assist our clients to explore their own goals and values, and to determine a plan for change that is consonant with these values and goals. This means assisting them toward their goals, rather than developing goals for them. It also means ensuring that their goals are carefully reasoned and reflective and consonant with their life plan, rather than spur-of-the-moment wishes or whims.

There are several considerations you must remember when working with clients toward goals setting:

- The client must be able to reflect, reason, and arrive at a plan. This requires a measure of competence, of maturity, of comprehension, and of an ability to communicate.
- The plan that the client makes must be capable of achievement. Clients may at times develop plans based on their desires which do not consider the specific circumstances within which these must be put into effect.
- The client must himself or herself be able to put the plan into effect. A plan whose success is dependent upon actions of others may fail through the lack of cooperation of those necessary to its achievement.

Limitations in any of these areas compromises goal-setting and may engender negative, rather than positive, results.

There are also circumstances where self-determination may not be possible for your client. A client who is unable to communicate, who is not mentally competent through reason of age or mental functioning, or who is incarcerated may be unable to be self-determined in all things. Remember that even with young children, the mentally challenged, and the senile elderly, it may be possible to offer some limited choices. It is important to such clients that you expand and utilize the realms of available choices, and that you honor them. When barriers to communication exist due to lack of facility with the English language, your responsibility to your client asks that you obtain the services of interpreters as needed to support self-determination.

Your client's cultural values and beliefs may be quite different from your own. The obligation to self-determination asks that you honor and respect these values and beliefs, educate yourself about cultural, religious, and ethnic differences, and assist your client to develop goals that are consistent with his or her own worldview. Your classes in multicultural counseling, diversity, or ethnicity should assist you to become knowledgeable and comfortable working with clients whose values and beliefs differ from your own.

Self-determination may be limited when the actions of a client "pose a serious, foreseeable, and imminent risk" to themselves or others (1.02).

Informed Consent

The obligation to informed consent is drawn from self-determination. Some of the more common areas where you will encounter informed consent issues include:

- limits of confidentiality, including information provided to third party payers
- agency policies and practices
- programs and agency resources available
- length of service, including limits imposed by third party payers
- reimbursement arrangements, costs of service
- risks related to receiving services
- alternatives to service to be provided by your agency
- your status as an intern or student
- rights to refuse service, including consequences (especially important for non-voluntary or mandated clients)

Informed consent may be divided into two separate issues for clarification:

Information Issues

You must provide your client with all the information necessary to make a careful decision. This may involve information about your qualifications, agency services, and/or community resources. It may involve sharing information about your client's type of problem, possible effects of change, and theoretical information about methodology or approaches.

It is sometimes difficult to decide how much a client needs to know. Too much information may be overwhelming; too little may lead to a decision which is not truly in the client's interests. Remember that you are responsible for sharing information. Information is a form of power: without it, oppression and abuse may more readily occur. Limiting information limits self-determination.

There are three common standards used to help determine how much information should be given to clients.

The Professional Practice Standard

This standard asks that you provide the amount of information that members of the social work profession have determined is adequate and helpful in making a specific kind of decision, or for people with a specific kind of problem.[1]

The Reasonable Person Standard

Often the standard accepted by the court system, the reasonable person standard asks that you provide the amount and kind of information that "any reasonable person" (the person on the street) would want to know in order to arrive at a decision and a plan.[2]

The Subjective Standard

The individual is central to this standard, which specifies the provision of the information that your specific client would want to have in making a decision. This takes into account the client's personal issues and tailors the information to specific needs. With this standard, two different clients might be offered different levels and types of information for making similar decisions, based upon the information-giver's perceptions of the client's needs in this regard.[3]

Because it is commonly acceptable, the reasonable person standard may be the standard of choice. You should discuss these standards with your field instructor to elicit guidance about agency policy and practice in this regard.

As noted above, it is important that information be provided in language the client can easily understand, and that you attempt to determine that your client has, indeed, comprehended the information you have provided (1.03b). When your client is unable to provide informed consent, you must locate a third party who is able to give consent for the client, and who will respect the client's interests and wishes (1.03c).

Consent Issues

You must also ensure that your client's consent is free of coercion and force. This is often difficult because of the power imbalance inherent in the professional relationship. However, to the extent possible, you need to determine that your client freely agrees to the plans for service that are developed and to any limitations upon these.

Consent often <u>appears</u> to be absent with non-voluntary or mandated clients who are "required" to receive services from you. Remember that these services are never absolutely obligatory: your client's choices may be limited such that refusal of services may be unfeasible, but, in fact, there is such a choice, though the alternative may be incarceration, loss of employment, loss of visiting privileges, or even removal of children. Children, as well as adults, always have the option to refuse to participate, withdraw, or miss or cancel appointments.

Best Interests

As noted earlier, your primary obligation is to your client's best interests. When you agree with the plan that your client self-determinately develops, you and your client's perceptions of best interests coincide, and there is generally little difficulty.

However, there may be times when you do not feel that the plan that he or she has developed is truly in his or her best interests. A teenager may decide to drop out of school, a depressed, suicidal client may decide to refuse medication, a physically challenged client may decide to refuse shelter and nutrition services and remain homeless, an alcoholic may decide to refuse treatment. How, then, can you reconcile your obligation to your client's best interest, and your obligation to support your client's self-determination?

You will encounter these kinds of ethical problems frequently in practice. Clients tend not to want to do what we think is best for them quite frequently, leaving us frustrated, challenged, and sometimes more than a little worried about their welfare.

There are several ways to address these differences in perception of "best interest." Remember, always, that your client is acting a way that he or she <u>believes</u> supports his or her best interests. It is natural to want what you believe to be in your best interest. The differences may result from several causes:

- client's lack of adequate information upon which to make a decision
- client's lack of competence due to the condition for which the client has need of the service, such as mental illness, childhood, compromised reasoning capacity, or substance abuse
- client's limited or compromised worldview based on life experiences, educational level, or mental status

So far, we may think we just need to "change" the client. We feel justified in supporting our plans for our clients. Careful thought will assist us to see that we, too, have limitations that affect these differences in goals and best interest plans:

- lack of awareness of client's life experiences and need to integrate these into best interest plan
- lack of knowledge of, or consideration for, client's ethnicity, culture, worldview, religion, and race as determinants of choices
- lack of understanding of the impact of these two upon the client's planning and goal development
- lack of understanding of client's milieu and need to develop a plan consonant with client's daily experiences, relationships, and functioning

Most often, it is a combination of several of these that create differences between you and your client in terms of understanding "best interest." When such differences occur, we must step back and explore the potential reasons, first within ourselves and with our field instructor, and then with our clients. The client(s) will sense your concern and interest in his, her, or their well-being when you initiate such a discussion of differences in understanding and goals. Often, such differences are resolvable with effort, thoughtfulness, and consideration of each others' viewpoints.

Confidentiality

It is an essential cornerstone to the social work profession that we keep private and confidential the information shared with us by clients. Confidentiality generally enables and supports the development of the trust that is an essential ingredient in a professional relationship (1.07).

However, your obligation to support confidentiality is usually not absolute. An early discussion of the possible limits of confidentiality helps clients to develop trust and to make decisions about what they wish to reveal. Waiting until something is said which requires disclosure on your part can create a painful confrontation between you and your clients, and a justified feeling of betrayal and violation of trust.

"But you (said/implied) that everything I told you was a secret. How can you now decide to tell? I never would have told you if I had known."

This is the sentence you do <u>not</u> want to hear! Protect yourself and your clients by clarifying confidentiality limits from the very beginning, and remind your clients of them periodically. Contrary to popular belief, studies have shown that limiting confidentiality does not hamper the development of a meaningful helping relationship if such limits are carefully and clearly presented at the beginning.

Some of the conditions which may limit confidentiality obligation include: harm to self or others, illegal acts, requirements of supervision and the educational process, and the "rules" of third party payers, referring agencies, courts, or other outside sources.

You must obtain your client's informed consent to any limitations of confidentiality. It is best to obtain such consent in writing, and your agency may have forms for this purpose. If not, you can develop your own form. If you and your field instructor believe that written consent is not feasible, you should carefully document your discussion of limitations of confidentiality in the client's record to serve as a formal record of your discussion. You may also ask clients to initial your documentation.

As with other informed consent issues, a third party may accept limitations of confidentiality on behalf of a client who is unable to give consent.

B. Responsibility to Clients' Relationship Networks

While your work is focused on your clients, family members, friends, and associates are often strongly impacted by client problems, and by treatments and interventions. You may have direct contact with your client's network during the course of services. Often, you will be aware of the concerns and problems of others involved with your client and his or her problem.

Although your primary obligation is to your client, this primacy may be superseded when your client's actions or statements indicate that others in the client's relationship network may be at risk of "serious, foreseeable, and imminent" harm. If your client threatens to set a bomb in his boss's car for firing him, to beat his children next time they refuse to eat supper, murder his wife if she leaves him, or asphyxiate his mother if she throws out his beer supply, you have a clear duty to warn them and/or the police of danger. (You also have this obligation if your client threatens to harm him or herself.)

Threats should always be taken seriously and carefully explored. You should also consult with your field instructor, who will assist you to assess the potential danger and closely monitor the situation with you. It is important to familiarize yourself with your agency's policy on the conditions which require a duty to warn.

While the examples used above offer clear and convincing threats of harm, there are others which may be less unambiguous. A potential for infection with the AIDS virus often provides an ethical duty to warn a third party, creating a dilemma for the social worker with a client who states that he will commit suicide should anyone learn of his condition. Agency policies differ in this regard: some agencies feel that complete confidentiality is necessary for the protection of clients from prejudice, abuse, and ostracism, while others believe that their obligation to society as a whole must take precedence.

You and your agency may disagree about this or any other duty to warn or protect responsibilities. It is very important for you to be aware of any value differences between you and your agency's policy. These issues will be discussed in Chapter 5 and Chapter 22.

There are times where the "best interests" of your client, your primary obligation, may run against the "best interests" of another person or persons in your client's system.

You should try to minimize negative effects of interventions upon others as much as possible, and seek advice and guidance from your field instructor.

You may become closely involved with your client's system if decisional capacity is limited in some way, and a family member or other person must provide informed consent on the client's behalf. In such instances, it is best where possible to have the client present as well; even if he or she is unable to give consent, participation increases your client's feelings of empowerment and self-determination, and supports dignity and self-respect.

Remember that your client is primary, so share information with a family member or friend only as necessary in the client's best interest. Care should be exercised to respect client confidentiality no matter how frequently you have contact with others in your client's network, or how genuinely interested and concerned they are with your client's well-being.

C. Responsibility to Field Placement Agency:

You have both an ethical and a legal responsibility to your field placement agency. Your legal responsibility is defined by your field placement's contract with you and with your school. Some of the terms of your relationship with your field agency may be spelled out in writing. Some are tacitly understood, or grounded in a verbal agreement. These generally define your commitment in terms of time to be spent, use of agency resources, supervision provisions, and other practical matters.

Your ethical responsibility to your field placement involves respect for the agency's mission and policies, support for its goals and programs, honesty in dealing with administration and other agency personnel, loyalty, and fair and accurate representation of your agency in the public domain. Undermining your agency's policies and programs affects not only the agency but also all clients, and should be avoided. You are also responsible for the reasonable and appropriate use of your agency's resources, in time, money, and material goods. This means that, while your client's interests are primary, you must exercise care in avoiding disproportionate or inappropriate use of agency resources on her or his behalf. With limited resources, overuse by your client will deprive another agency client of needed services.

While you may feel that, as a student, your more limited knowledge and skills can contribute little to your agency as a whole, this is not true in practice. You are, after all, learning new and up-to-date information: you are on the "cutting edge" of all new developments in the field, many of which are not known to others in your agency. Sharing knowledge of theory and practice, ethics, research, and policy can make a major contribution to your agency's policy and program development.

Agencies often ask students to present a case using knowledge learned in school, to present views on a professional article, or to discuss the impact of a new government policy. In doing this, you contribute your knowledge to the whole of your agency, broadening perspectives and suggesting alternative ways of thinking or addressing problems. This is not just an assignment: it is an opportunity to influence the professional practice of social work!

Standards for ethical responsibilities to practice settings are presented in the third section of the NASW Code of Ethics.[4]

D. Responsibility to Colleagues

Colleagues and other agency staff, like clients, should be treated with dignity, consideration, and respect. Colleagues can be an excellent source of support, information, and advice during the course of your field placement. However, it is important for you to recognize that your primary learning relationship is with your field instructor. Chapter 6 will focus on this vital relationship.

General guidelines for social interaction apply to your relationship with your colleagues: you should respect and hold in confidence any personal information (and client information inadvertently shared) which your colleagues share with you; you should be careful to maintain a helpful and positive relationship with colleagues; you should not speak negatively about colleagues to other colleagues or, most especially, to clients.

You may be placed in a field agency with other students from your program, and/or with students from other programs. Students often develop close and enduring friendships with fellow students at their placement. Be careful, however, about comparing field instructors, caseloads, and kinds of clients and problems. Remember that students' needs differ, field instructors' and students' personalities and relationships differ, and students' interactions with clients differ. Often, there are valid reasons for the differences in treatment that you observe between yourself and another student at your field placement agency. If you become concerned about differences, discuss them with your field instructor. Never share them with clients: this will undermine the field agency's ability to serve them appropriately. Your relationship with professional colleagues is discussed in Chapter 7, and potential problems are included in Chapter 21.

E. Responsibility to Society

Helping professionals are not simply members of society: they are representatives of society, charged with the responsibility of supporting and promoting the values in which the profession is embedded. Social workers, in particular, often have an important role as the administrators of public monies — the funds provided by the society as a whole for the programs social workers administer and utilize in working with clients. Social workers are responsible, therefore, to the society for the work that they do.

During the course of your placement, you will have the opportunity to use general societal resources, such as social welfare programs, to assist your clients in need. It is important always to remember that these are public funds, and that the public has determined how they are to be spent (the parameters of the program). If the general guidelines are not followed, or if clients violate the program's policies, you need to be aware that, as a custodian of public funds and resources, you have an obligation to see that these are wisely used.

In addition, society holds certain general values, such as freedom, justice, equality of access to goods and services, etc. As a social worker, you will be working toward maximizing these values for all members of the society. Thus, it is important to understand that your professional world is broader than your work with your clients — in a sense, all of society is your client, and you are in service to all.

[1] Beauchamp, T.L., & Childress, J. F. (1994) *Principles of Biomedical Ethics.* NY: Oxford University Press, Chapter Three, The Respect for Autonomy.

[2] Ibid., p. 148-149.

[3] Ibid., p. 149-150.

[4] National Association of Social Workers (1996) *Code of Ethics.* Washington, D.C.: Author.

UNIT SUMMARY

The first four chapters have presented a general orientation to field work in preparation for beginning your placement at your field work agency. The first chapter presented the rationale for a direct practice experience as a vital and integral part of professional education for the service professions, presenting social work field work in the context of practice teaching in education, and hospital and clinical experience in medical and nursing education.

Chapter 2 introduced the principal players in your field work education — your field work education "team." Members of your personal team are associated primarily with either your school's program or your practicum agency, though there is overlap possible between them. The school's primary field instruction team members are a part of the Office of Field Instruction. Your field liaison serves as the link between field and school and visits you in your field placement. The liaison consults with you and your field instructor regarding your progress, and assesses your field placement, field instructor, and your learning experience. The Director of Field is responsible for the overall coordination of your field work experiences.

Your Foundation Practice instructor is also an important member of your field work team, providing the theory base and skills necessary to competent practice: the tools that you will use in your field work placement with clients. There is a close interface between the material taught in your Foundation Practice class and your work in the field. Your adviser is also aware of your placement and experiences, and is a resource for you in planning. If your program has a field work seminar, the instructor, who may also be your liaison or your adviser, is also an important member of your field work education team.

In the field, the primary person responsible for your learning is your field instructor. The agency's Director has signed a contract with your school to serve as a field placement agency, and has arranged for your field instruction and your work space.

Because professional practice is a major commitment, it is important to understand the differences between your personal and professional selves, and the expectations of the profession in terms of professional comportment. Chapter 3 addressed professional conduct, as well as exploring several common problems you may encounter in the interface between your personal and professional worlds. Chapter 4 addressed the primary professional ethical responsibilities: toward clients, client systems, agency, and colleagues, and explored several basic tenets of the Code of Ethics to which you are bound as a student professional.

In the next Unit, we will suggest some important guidelines for working as a student professional in your field work agency. Chapter 5 will introduce the work you must do to familiarize yourself with the mission, policies and practices, customs, and functioning of your field placement agency, the necessary first step in your work in the field. Chapter 6 will discuss the most vital relationship you will have in your agency: your relationship with your field instructor, who is primarily responsible for all of your learning and experiences in the field. Chapter 7 will present some of the other relationships you will encounter in your field placement: with other students, with professional social workers, with paraprofessionals, with professionals of other disciplines, and with support staff. Chapter 8 will (finally!) introduce you to your clients, their families, and the community in which they live as we explore relationships with clients and client systems, and with communities.

CHAPTER FIVE

GETTING TO KNOW YOUR AGENCY

You have visited your agency at least once during the interview and placement process. Now, your first day is here, and you arrive at your agency that very first morning, perhaps a bit apprehensive about this new experience which is about to begin.

Apprehension is normal and natural. After all, you are not only encountering a new and unfamiliar experience; you are also taking what might feel like the first "real" step toward your chosen career. You might believe that you will be expected to <u>be</u> a social worker at the agency — to know what to do as soon as you begin. You may worry that you will be asked to see clients that first day, and not know what to say or do. You could also worry about your field instructor and whether you will like working with him or her and be able to learn what you need to learn.

Your field instructor has also experienced that first day once — often not so very long ago. She or he will be very understanding and will, in most cases, have a structured day prepared for you. You may be asked to read your agency's policy manual, be taken on a tour and introduced to all of the staff, or be invited to attend a special orientation meeting. Your field instructor may ask you to "shadow" him or her to get a feel for how your agency operates. Some agencies plan special events to welcome students, such as lunches or coffees.

All of these experiences are a part of the vital first step in your field placement experience: they will help you to orient and familiarize yourself with your field placement agency. This is necessary for several reasons:

- you will represent your agency to your clients, and you must know it well in order to represent it fairly and accurately
- knowledge of the agency's procedures, policies, programs, and resources will enable you to maximize your ability to help your clients with their problems
- familiarity and ease with your surroundings will enable you to focus fully on your client
- you will be better able to provide services that are consistent with those provided by other agency professionals
- knowledge of your agency's outside resource network will enable you to reach into the community on behalf of your clients as needed

There are several steps that you can take to familiarize yourself with your field placement. Your field instructor may suggest some of those outlined below or others to assist you. However, you can follow these guidelines independently as well. Don't hesitate to ask your field instructor for help. He or she will want you to become as comfortable with your practice setting as possible in order to enhance your learning and provide the best possible service to clients.

A. Getting "the Lay of the Land"

Inside Your Agency

One of the first things you might want to do is learn the physical layout of your agency. Your agency tour may have led you past a confusing array of offices, support staff areas, lounges, and meeting rooms, and finally either back to your own office or to that of your field instructor.

When you have a moment, with or without your field instructor, walk around again. You may find it helpful to make a little map of your agency, locating yourself and your field instructor, the director, and others. You probably won't need this map after the first few days of placement, but it may be useful at first.

A great way to get to know the way things work in your agency is to spend some time in the reception room or lobby. There you will be able to observe many things, such as the way clients are greeted by staff upon arrival, and the process of getting client and worker together. You'll see clients interacting with each other, and with staff, and get a wonderful feel for the atmosphere at your agency. Are staff welcoming and polite, or abrupt and harassed? Do they address clients in a casual, friendly fashion, or more formally? Can you sense tension in the air of the room, or calmness and support? Look at the decor, and at the condition of the furniture. These kinds of things can tell you a great deal about your field placement!

Outside Your Agency

Your agency's "field" is the community in which it is located. Use lunch hours or time before or after work to learn about the community. Who lives around the agency? Are there many old people? Young families? Is it a poor neighborhood? Are there diverse ethnic groups, or only one? Look at the buildings around you. Is the community run down? Has it been newly rehabilitated? Are the streets clean and free of debris? As you walk around, notice what shops are nearby, and what other social service agencies are operating within the community. Where are the schools, hospitals, grocery stores, police, and other essential services?

There are two reasons for this walk: (1) to become familiar with the route you will take, whether walking, riding, or driving on your way to and from your field placement; and (2) to get to know the world your clients live in, and to understand its problems and its resources.

B. Understanding Why Your Agency Is Here

Agency History

Your agency has a history that began well before service was provided to the very first client. Knowing your agency's history will assist you in understanding the policies and programs that it supports. Agencies come into being in four principal ways:

- a group of people see a need, and develop a plan and a program to meet it (private agencies)
- the government passes a law that mandates certain kinds of services (public agencies)

- either the government or a group of individuals developed a program or institution to meet a need (not social service related), and then recognized that social workers could assist them in meeting the need efficiently and effectively (host agencies, such as hospitals, schools, or court systems)
- a group of individuals recognize an unmet need for a service, and form an organization to provide it (for-profit organizations)

Although this appears to draw clear lines between public and private agencies, they are generally not as separate as they might appear. Private agencies are often dependent upon public agencies for funding of services and programs, and public agencies often purchase certain kinds of services from private agencies.

Host agencies have added social services to the primary service they provide, usually at a later date, and have the same private/public interplay as the "host" service. (A hospital, for example, may accept medical assistance or Medicare, and their social service department policies and procedures are then affected by overall medical assistance and Medicare policies, as well as any policies these programs might have directly related to the provision of social services.)

Increasingly, schools are also utilizing for-profit settings, such as private mental health services, nursing homes, outpatient health care agencies, hospitals, or health maintenance organizations, as field placements. Because of the field placement's for-profit orientation, students may find a lessening in the traditional social work values and ethics which demand a high level of commitment to the poor, underprivileged, and oppressed. If you are placed in a for-profit setting, it is important that you utilize classroom material to integrate the traditional core social work values into your personal professional development.[1] Some of the special issues around for-profit placements are explored further in Chapter 17, Section C.

Your agency may have gone through several phases in its history. A child-welfare agency may have begun as an orphanage for abandoned children. With time, it may have developed foster homes, and closed the orphanage. Later, it could have added adoption services to provide permanent planning for children. When abortion became legal, and fewer children were following the traditional relinquishment-adoption path, the agency may have chosen to shift its focus toward at-risk adolescents. Specialized foster homes and small residential centers may have been added to meet all of the needs of this new population.

Agency histories are fascinating in themselves, and can also provide you with insights into how your particular agency developed the programs and services you will be providing. You will be able to see that, as the community and its needs changed, your agency also changed, developing new programs and closing old ones to meet current societal needs. To remain viable and relevant to community needs, agencies must be able to change and grow, adapting and shifting focus and services to address the surrounding community's unmet needs.

Mission Statement

Your agency will also have a mission statement, often connected closely to its history. These statements are generally quite broad, such as "to safeguard the lives of children," "to enable general health and well-being," or "to enhance the mental health of the community." They may not give you clear operative guidelines, but they will help you to understand what the agency views as its overall purpose.

You may find that the mission statement is a part of the agency's policy manual. Or, you may find that you encounter blank stares when you ask to see the mission statement: sometimes it is quite inaccessible, rarely referred to, and no one remembers where it is or what it says. You may be providing a new impetus to self-examination and self-assessment to your agency when you ask to see the mission statement!

Sometimes, despite the best efforts, agency staff are not able to locate the mission statement. Don't worry too much if this happens to you — just move ahead to the policy manual!

C. Understanding How Your Agency Works

Policy Manual

Your agency's policy manual will define its programs and the policies that govern their administration, employee policies, supervision, resources and funding, and other necessary material. You may be asked to read and review your agency's policy manual early in your field placement. You will probably want to focus most closely on the material that is relevant to the program in which you will be working, but understanding how all of the agency's programs work together will be very helpful to you.

Reading policy manuals is one of everybody's least favorite things to do: after all, you are in field placement to work with clients, not to read boring pages of what appears to be irrelevant material. Being aware of your agency's policies is important to your work with clients — they tell you <u>what</u> can be done, <u>for whom</u>, and <u>under what circumstances</u>.

Procedures and Practices

Some agencies' policy manuals also contain procedures. The policies tell you <u>what</u> can be done; the procedures tell you <u>how</u>. For example, your agency, a hospital, may have a <u>policy</u> that social services will assist patients in planning discharges in a timely manner. It will then have <u>procedures</u> that will define how this is to be done, such as meeting with the patient, contacting the family, referring to outside resources (and often, to which ones), and the time frames to be used in specific circumstances.

A foster care agency may have a <u>policy</u> that states that all prospective foster parents must successfully complete a home study to determine their qualifications to care for children. The <u>procedures</u> might include two home visits, three interviews, and obtaining references from employers, followed by a staff meeting to discuss the prospective parents and arrive at a determination of suitability. Often, you will be following similarly specific agency procedures during the process of providing services to clients.

Agency <u>practices</u> are the unwritten, but commonly understood and accepted, ways that an agency addresses certain issues. For example, few agencies have a written policy on terms of address with colleagues and clients, or accepted dress for client contact. When we discussed these issues in Chapter 3, however, it was suggested that you observe, consult, and follow your agency's accepted pattern in this regard. This is an agency practice. Your agency may have a common practice for setting up interviews, for visiting clients in the field, or for sharing the cost of the coffee pot. Practices are best learned by observation, or by asking your field instructor or colleagues. It may take a while to learn your agency's practices, just as it would in any other kind of employment.

Agency Structure

All agencies are structured in some manner. Often, there is a formal and an informal agency structure, and you will want to become familiar with both.

The Formal Structure

You can learn your agency's hierarchy and formal structure from the policy manual, from the director or your field instructor, or from diagrams. All agencies have a formal structure which defines power and responsibilities. It will be very helpful to you to draw your own diagram of your agency's structure. Look carefully at where your program fits into the overall agency pattern. How does it connect with other programs within the agency? Look at where you and your field instructor fit into the diagram. To whom is your field instructor accountable? How many people stand between your field instructor and your agency's director? In some large agencies, there may be many supervisors in between. In others, your field instructor will be accountable directly to the agency's director, or may even *be* the director.

If you are placed in a host agency, look at how social services fits into the overall structure of the institution. To whom is social services accountable?

The Informal Structure

You will have access to your field placement's formal structure early in your experience. It may take some time and observation, possibly several months, to understand the informal structure. Yet, as in all employment, it is important to understand how the informal structure works if you want to have the best possible experience for you and for your clients. Two examples may help to illustrate this point:

You want to obtain a supplemental check for clothing for your client, because you have been working with her to prepare for job interviews, and she is ready but has nothing to wear. There are forms for such requests, and a long chain they must follow in order to gain approval. Your client has a job interview scheduled for next week, however. Where do you go to cut through the process and enable your client to get funds to purchase an appropriate interview outfit? Your agency's informal structure can assist you to determine who can expedite this request for you on behalf of your client.

You have been working with an adolescent on behavior control, and see some improvement, but sense that he feels isolated from others and does not have a good support network. You know that there is a boys' group that meets once a week at your agency, but it is a group program, and therefore is in a different department. Upon inquiry, you learn that there are several boys on a waiting list, and you think there might be enough to begin a second group. You yourself would love to have some group experience, but you are placed in a program that serves only individuals. Who would you ask about starting a second group?

The answer to these and other similar questions may generally be "ask your field instructor," and this is a good first resource, for your field instructor will advocate on behalf of you and your clients, and will also be very familiar with the informal structure of your agency. However, there may be times when this is not possible, or when your supervisor may be unable to resolve your problem. Knowing to whom you should go for the specific thing you are seeking means knowing the informal structure.

D. Understanding Your Agency's Network

Your agency functions within a community of service agencies. Other agencies may have programs that supplement, or complement, the programs of your agency, overlap with your agency's programs, or offer alternative programs.

For example, if you are working with substance-abusing clients in an outreach program, you may find that housing resources, medical clinics, employment support, and other services can complement and supplement the specific services that your agency can offer. Knowledge of such services can help you to provide a more comprehensive service to your client than your agency alone can offer.

On the other hand, there may be services in the community which overlap with your own. They may be more narrowly focused on a portion of your agency's population, such as services to substance abusers who are elderly, on parole, or dually diagnosed. You must then determine if your client is best served by your outreach program, or by one of these more focused programs. Your assessment of your client will help you to arrive at a determination. If you feel that your client is hard to reach, not in trouble with the law, and not elderly, for example, you may determine that your agency's services best meet her or his needs. If you find that your client is dually diagnosed, and your agency does not provide services for your client's other diagnosis, referral may be most appropriate for meeting needs.

You may find that there are several potential services that might assist your client. They provide alternative settings and treatment methods. Your outreach agency provides community-based services to substance abusers. Alternatives available to your client might include residential services or day treatment programs. You and your client together may want to consider these other programs.

Determining the appropriate services for your client is a complex matter: you will need to know all of the resources available to him or her, whether there are waiting lists, their ambiance and population, your client's desires and prior experiences with other services, and the success of these alternative resources in working with your client's kind of problem.

It is important for you to be familiar with other resources within the community, and to know the agencies with which your agency maintains both formal and informal relationships. When you are comfortable with your agency, you may want to visit other agencies in your community to familiarize yourself with the different settings and treatments available.

With knowledge of your agency and its place in the community, you will be better prepared to begin direct field work experience. To optimize your learning, it is important to develop and maintain a good working relationship with your field instructor. Our next chapter will present some guidelines for working successfully in supervision.

> ** In the event that your field placement is with an agency where you are also an employee, it is essential that you follow the preceding steps, taking a fresh look at your agency's history, mission, policies, and practices. You may find some misconceptions, such as generally taken for granted policies which indeed are not policies, but rather agency practices, or a broader mission than the one actually followed. Starr and Haffey explore the importance of engaging students in such "work-study" arrangements fully in the learning process.[2]*

> ** If you are entering a program as a part-time student, and are juggling school, field, full- or part-time employment in another setting, and family obligations, the work of getting to know your agency as described above may be much more difficult. For all students, however, this is an essential part of your graduate education, for it will provide you with experience in utilizing a method and an approach to beginning professional employment which will be very useful throughout your career, and actually reduce future stress!*

---

[1] Hancock, T.U. (1992) Field placements in for-profit organizations: policies and practices of graduate programs. *Journal of Social Work Education* 28(3): 330–340, Fall.

[2] Starr, R., & Haffey, M. (1987) Teaching work-study students: curriculum delivery and design issues. *Journal of Teaching in Social Work* 1(2): 141–153, Fall/Winter.

CHAPTER SIX

WORKING WITH YOUR FIELD INSTRUCTOR

In many ways, your relationship with your field instructor parallels your relationship with your clients. Both are professional, and not social, relationships. Both require time, effort, and hard work. Both have goals and objectives, and both are centered within the relationship process. Both need trust, privacy, fidelity, and confidentiality to enable the best growth and development. In both, each party to the relationship is affected by the other. There is a power imbalance in both, and often differences in values, personalities, and ways of understanding. Thus, there is an important task in both which consists of developing a mutual understanding, a common language, and a way of working together effectively. The person with the greater knowledge, skill, and power takes a leadership role in both relationships, but, also in both, is guided by the other person?s perception of needs, events, and experiences.

Although your field instructor will provide guidance and opportunities for learning, you must let him or her know how you learn best, and what you need to learn. Your field instructor will provide opportunities tailored to meet your unique, personal, and individual needs.

A. Field Instruction Is a Supervisor's Choice

Becoming a field instructor is a personal, voluntary choice, and not an assignment given by the agency's director or the instructor's supervisor. Your field instructor has chosen to take on this role, with all of its attendant rewards and responsibilities.

There are many reasons that people chose to become field instructors. Most field instructors genuinely love to teach, and see field instruction as an opportunity to teach within their agency setting. Many field instructors also have a strong desire to make a contribution to the field as a whole, and to its future. Field instructors generally love social work, enjoy what they do, and want to communicate their love and enthusiasm for the field to those newly entering the profession. There is also status within the agency associated with being a field instructor. Field instructors enjoy being a part of an academic institution, and field instruction is a faculty position in many schools. They also enjoy relating to others in a supervisory role, and are comfortable with the additional responsibilities that field instruction engenders.

Rohrer et al. found that there are some specific benefits through the university affiliation that accompanies the field instructor position. Use of university library facilities and equipment, continuing education program offerings, and the official status of an adjunct faculty member were found to be some of the more common benefits.[1]

Schools generally have certain requirements for field instructors. A minimum of a Masters degree in social work is necessary, and schools may require a certain amount of experience in the field (such as one or two years or more), employment at the field placement agency for a certain period of time (six months, a year, or more), or board certification in the state in which the field placement agency is located. Your school will have reviewed your field instructor's qualifications and determined that they meet the school's criteria.

Field instructors make an important commitment to the academic institution as well. Your school may require that your field instructor attend orientation for field instructors, and/or attend your field work orientation. It may require regular, on-going meetings to discuss policies, review the program's goals and objectives, and to provide a forum for discussion of problems field instructors may encounter in their work. Both your school and your field instructor make a commitment to work to establish and maintain a positive working relationship, with you as the central focus.

B. Your Student-Field Instructor Relationship

Your relationship with your field instructor is the most important one you will have at your practicum. Your field instructor teaches, guides, evaluates, advocates on your behalf, and provides the opportunities you need to become professionally competent. A relationship with a field instructor which is positive and satisfactory is one of the most important measures of overall student satisfaction with field work.[2]

Defining the Professional Supervisory Relationship

This field instructor-student relationship is your first introduction to one of the basic characteristics of our profession: on going, regular supervision. All professionals, throughout the entire course of their social work careers, have supervision and consultation in their work. Supervision serves many functions, but is especially important in providing a resource for discussion, consultation, and reflection for workers. Social workers encounter clients and client systems under stress and in crisis. They must often make painful and difficult decisions on behalf of clients which affect their lives in a major way. This can create a measure of tension and anxiety in the worker, and feeling "all alone" with the problem can be difficult. Supervision assists workers by providing a way to "share the load," in a sense, with another responsible professional.

It is easy to over-identify with a client, to be manipulated, or to become over-involved in the client's network. Sometimes, workers may find themselves actually disliking clients, or becoming overly angry with client behavior. This endangers the professional relationship and may negatively affect outcomes. Supervision provides a safe place to explore and examine your own professional functioning, and to distance yourself emotionally if needed.

Supervisors are generally presumed to have more expertise than supervisees. Therefore, they are a good resource for exploring alternative approaches or interpretations of a client problem. In addition, Reamer, who has studied liability cases in social work, found that supervisors may be held legally responsible for:

(1) actions of supervisees who ordinarily are under their supervision;
(2) actions of supervisees who ordinarily are not under the social worker's supervision;
(3) the delegation of responsibility by the social worker to a paraprofessional or unlicensed assistant.[3]

Field instructors may be held legally liable for actions of students. Your school and your field placement agency have both acknowledged and addressed this issue in their joint formal "field training agreement," accepting joint responsibility for actions of students.[4] It is important for you and your field instructor to clarify legal issues as you begin to work together.[5]

Supervision comes in many forms. The classical relationship is that of a worker with a supervisor in the same agency. However, social workers may arrange for supervision by a professional at another agency. Workers who are in private practice often arrange for supervision from a more experienced worker in private practice, or from someone at an agency. "Peer supervision" involves several workers of approximately the same level of experience who provide group supervision to each other. No matter which arrangement is chosen by a worker or defined by a practice setting, the essence of the work done in supervision remains the same.

Defining Your Personal Supervisory Relationship

The supervisory relationship is not a social relationship. Your supervisor is not a friend, and the relationship between you is not equal. The supervisor always has a certain measure of power and control over the supervisee, and has responsibilities to the supervisee and his or her clients. In a sense, this relationship shares many characteristics with supervisory relationships in any employment situation.

You and your field instructor will build a professional relationship. You will come together to discuss clients, your schedule, your learning, and your experiences in the field. Because this is primarily a teacher-student relationship, your field instructor cannot provide therapy, or assistance with your personal concerns. Brief interventions may be offered if your problems impact your professional functioning, but extensive help, should it be needed, must be obtained outside of this relationship. While there is great variation among field instructors in this area, field instruction is generally not the place to discuss marital problems, spiritual crises, relationship issues, or other personal matters.

This does not mean your field instructor does not care about you as a person. It means only that this relationship has a clear purpose, and that purpose should not be compromised in any manner if you are to reach your full professional potential. Of course, this does not mean you can't mention your child's illness, or your friend's spousal abuse; it means that these cannot be central to your field instructor-student relationship. You will surely share many personal experiences during the course of your field placement — outside of the formal supervisory relationship!

When you begin your field placement, you and your field instructor immediately begin to build your relationship, a process which will be on going during your entire field placement. You learn each other's preferences in manner of address, degree of formality or informality, and style of interaction. As you begin to learn and process your learning with your field instructor, you will develop the foundations of good professional interaction: openness, trust, loyalty, and confidentiality. You will feel safe in sharing problems and concerns with your field instructor, knowing that these will be carefully and seriously addressed. You will see that your field instructor will "look out for you," and will advocate for you should this be needed.

It is within the student-field instructor relationship that you will begin to assume the role of a professional social worker, practice skills and techniques, become more self-aware, and learn aspects of assessment.[6] You will learn and experience the impact of the value base of the profession upon practice, including your ethical responsibility to social justice, by observing and listening to your field instructor.[7] Your field instructor's positive feedback will empower you and increase your professional confidence and, through your own empowerment, you will be able to empower your clients.[8]

C. Preparing for Supervision

Effective supervision requires planning and effort from both you and your field instructor. Neither of you can make a success of supervision without the goodwill and cooperation of the other. Some suggestions are offered below which may be useful to you in considering how to make the best possible supervision arrangements.

Amount of Supervision

The amount of time that you receive supervision is often determined by your school. An hour a week is most common, but an hour and a half is also used. The amount of scheduled supervisory time can also vary by the number of hours per week spent in field placement, your program level, and your setting. This time should be one-on-one, not group supervision, which can supplement but not replace personal supervision.

Timing of Supervision

You and your field instructor will set a regular time for supervision. This should remain as constant as possible during your placement, so that both of you can plan your schedules efficiently. If a supervision time must be changed, arrangements should be made in advance, and a new time set immediately. Agency work can be hectic, and crises abound, often interfering with planned meeting times. This is a natural part of social work practice, and need not be disruptive as long as alternate plans are made and carefully honored by both you and your field instructor.

Conditions of Supervision

Supervision should be provided in privacy, so that you and your field instructor can feel free in expressing ideas, concerns, or questions. Privacy is also important because you are sharing information about your client which has been told to you in confidence. While it is both necessary and appropriate that you share information about your client with your field instructor, you should safeguard your client's personal matters from those not directly involved.

During your supervision times, interruptions and phone calls should be held to a minimum. These disrupt the flow of your discussions and fragment your learning. In many settings, it will be impossible for your field instructor to hold all calls, but non-emergencies should be able to wait until your time of supervision is completed.

Function of Agendas

You have one hour, approximately, to discuss with your field instructor what has gone on in the other seven or fifteen or twenty or forty that you were at your placement, plus a few things you may have learned in school that are relevant. You can't cover it all! Therefore, you must select, order, and prioritize the cases, problems, issues, and concerns that you bring to supervision each week.

You do this by making an agenda of the subjects you want to cover, in order of their relative importance. After you have prepared your list, give a copy of it to your field instructor. It is important to do this a day or two before your supervision time, so that your field instructor has time to think about the issues you will be raising, and to prepare him- or herself for the meeting with you.

Preparing an agenda is, in and of itself, a very useful and helpful exercise: you will be evaluating the events of the week and determining which are the most urgent, important, or needing of help and advice from supervision. With a busy caseload, you may find yourself doing this kind of prioritizing in several different contexts!

Planning for Emergencies

Emergencies occur routinely in social work. Clients lose their jobs or their homes, are abused, become catastrophically ill, threaten suicide, are institutionalized, or any of hundreds of other crises frequently. Crises like these tend not to occur conveniently ten minutes before supervision, when advice and assistance are readily at hand. Whenever emergencies occur in your caseload, you may find yourself needing help and direction from your field instructor. It may be very helpful to make arrangements ahead of time with your field instructor regarding procedures to follow when you need immediate consultation, and also for what to do if he or she is not available to assist you. There may be another worker that your field instructor prefers you to contact in his or her absence.

Having a good plan for getting supervisory help in emergencies will help both you and your field instructor feel comfortable and secure with your work.

D. Learning Tools

You field instructor will probably use several tools for teaching you the practical skills that you need in your work. These may include reading, observing, direct practice, taping/videotaping, and process recording.

Reading

You may be working with a problem, or a population, that is unfamiliar to you, or with whom you have had little experience. Your field instructor may suggest appropriate reading material to help you to become knowledgeable about the particular kinds of problems, populations, or issues your agency services. While your class assignments prepare you for generalist practice, readings suggested by your field instructor are directed specifically to your field work experience and to your individual needs.

Observation

Field instructors differ in their ideas of the role of observation in your learning. Some field instructors ask you to "shadow" them for the first few days that you are in the field. Others may assign a worker to take you with him or her to interviews and field visits. Still other placements use one way mirrors which enable you to observe both clients and workers. All of these offer you the opportunity to actually observe what social workers do with clients in your agency setting.

Direct Practice

No matter how much you read and observe, there is no substitute for direct experience, and this is the "nuts and bolts" of your field work placement. During your placement, you will also carry a caseload of clients, groups, or community programs of your own. You will interview, establish relationships, assess problems, and develop and implement interventions.

Your experiences help you to see what works and what does not work for you with clients: each of us is different, and we each have a different style of relating to others, within the professional parameters. While observation can teach you much, you need to develop your personal way of interacting with clients, and this you can do only through direct contact.

Tape Recording

Your field instructor may ask you to tape record an interview with a client. He or she will listen to the tape, and together you will review what you did, and why you did it, during the taped encounter. Listening to yourself on tape can be extremely instructive for you as well, and can provide you with many insights about what you say, how you say it, and what you mean to communicate to your clients. Tape recording requires written consent from your client, who should always be aware of the taping.

Video Recording

Video recording may be used in the same way as tape recording, except that it enables you to review an additional dimension — position and body language — which is extremely important in learning professional use of your self. As with tape recording, video recording requires the written consent of your client. Be careful with videos — unlike tapes, videos identify clients completely and thus can easily violate confidentiality!

Process Recording

"Long a fixture of social work education, the process recording is a means through which students examine and analyze their work with clients." [9]

A process recording is simply a written record of the interaction between you and your client — the "he said and I said and then he said" with complete content. In addition to the verbal content, process recordings allow you to write your thought process during the interview, as well as your intuitive reactions to what is occurring. Process recordings help you to make conscious every sentence, gesture, or intuition you experience during your client contact so that you can analyze why and how you did and said things during the interview. Process recording has been used in all kinds of practice settings and with all kinds of clients.

In addition, your field instructor may develop and tailor specific learning tools that are useful for your particular setting, populations, or kinds of problems.

E. Maintaining a Good Working Relationship

Both you and your field instructor have made a strong commitment of time, effort, and energy to this partnership for your professional development. Both of you desire your success, and bring to your work together goodwill, respect, and consideration of the other partner. Like any relationship, your relationship with your field instructor is not fully realized the day that you begin your field placement. The relationship is there in potential only, and it will take time, openness and confidence, loyalty and fidelity, and careful nurturing for it to blossom to its fullest potential.

The beginning tasks of learning each other's working style, personal characteristics, and approach to professional functioning will assist you in laying a strong foundation upon which you can build over the course of your placement. It is helpful to work to develop and clarify the relationship during these early stages, for clear guidelines and procedures will be very helpful in avoiding misunderstandings over the course of time.

You and your field instructor will have moments that may be less than idyllic: either one or both of you may be stressed, anxious, upset, absent-minded or forgetful, or inconsiderate of the other at moments. Your field instructor's position of authority will magnify any problem you may feel that you are experiencing. It is generally best to discuss your concerns directly with your field instructor: the good will and desire for your success that both of you share will help to ease any temporary problem you might experience, and talking it over will help you to resolve it quickly and easily. Some of the problems and situations you may encounter during the course of your relationship with your field instructor are addressed in Chapter 20.

Remember, your primary goal is to become a competent professional social worker! While your field instructor is primarily responsible for your learning at your placement, colleagues will provide other kinds of helpful learning experiences for you, as well as contacts with professionals on a more equal basis. In the following chapter, we shall explore some of these other kinds of relationships within your field placement settings.

---

[1] Rohrer, G.E., Smith, W.C., & Peterson, V.J. (1992) Field instructor benefits in education: a national survey. *Journal of Social Work Education* 28(3): 363-369, Fall.

[2] Cimino, D., Cimino, F., & Neuhring, E., Raybin, L., & Wisler-Waldock, B. (1982) Student Satisfaction with field work. *Contemporary Social Work Education* 5(1): 68-75.

[3] Reamer, F.G. (1989) Liability issues in social work supervision. Social Work 34(5): 445-448, September.

[4] Gelman, S.R. (1988) Who's responsibile? The field liability dilemma. *Journal of Social Work Education* 24(1): 70-78, Winter.

[5] Swain, P.A. (1994) But what happens if . . . ? Quasi-legal considerations for social work student placements. *Australian Social Work* 47(2): 13-23, June.

[6] Glassman, U., & Kates, L. (1988) Strategies for group work field instruction. *Social Work with Groups* 11(1/2): 111-124.

[7] Conrad, A.P. (1988) The role of field instructors in the transmission of social justice values. *Journal of Teaching in Social Work* 2(2): 63-82.

[8] Richan, W.C. (1989) Empowering students to empower others: a community-based field practicum. *Journal of Social Work Education* 25(3): 276-283, Fall.

[9] Bisman, C. (1994) *Social Work Practice: Cases and Principles.* Pacific Grove, CA: Brooks/Cole Chapter 6, Communication in social work defined, process recording.

CHAPTER SEVEN

COLLEGIAL RELATIONSHIPS

In addition to your field instructor and the director of your placement agency, you will be working with other social work professionals, with consultants, with professionals in other agencies, and with support staff. You may also be working with other students from your own program or from other nearby programs.

Relationships with colleagues in a field placement are often the same as, or similar to, relationships with colleagues you have experienced while employed in other settings: let the overall tone and atmosphere in your field placement be your guide. Some agencies encourage socialization and friendship among all employees, while others separate employees into categories, most commonly professional and non-professional. Host agencies may additionally tend to separate people by discipline.

A good place to get a feel for relationships among people at your agency is to observe the lunchtime ritual. Who sits with whom? Who goes out to lunch and who uses the lunchroom? Who eats in a personal office, and with whom? This kind of observation can also tell you a great deal about the informal power structure and lines of communication within your agency, and help you to begin to find your own niche within the informal structure.

A. Social Work Professionals

Generally, social workers are gregarious and very friendly as a group, and you will find that other social workers at your agency are eager to get to know you, and happy to share information or to assist you if you need help. Your relationship with other social workers at your agency will probably be much more casual than your relationship with your field instructor — after all, they won't be grading you!

As we discussed earlier, you are in the process of developing a new professional "you," in addition to the more familiar personal "you." Relationships with colleagues challenge you to find the balance between these two roles during the course of your workday at your field placement.

Some Things Are Social

Lunchtime, break time, time spent outside of your agency are times to relax and get to know your colleagues on a friendly social basis. As in any other place of employment, you'll find people you like more than others. You can, of course, enjoy their company comfortably as long as you don?t create an atmosphere of exclusion of others.

Some Things Are Professional

Friendship with a colleague does not include sharing any information about clients, nor anything told to you in confidence. It is best not to discuss clients or problems with colleagues — that's what your field instructor is there for!

In certain settings, such as special schools or court settings, you will share clients or members of a client family with colleagues. Each of you will have a direct, though different, role to play with the same individuals. In such cases, the temptation to discuss problems and get someone else's take on the situation is always there, especially while you are a student. It is generally best, however, that you set up special times and conditions for this kind of discussion and sharing, such as case conferences, staffings, care plans, or consultations. Within the formal structure, sharing information is helpful, useful, and expected, and planning can be implemented in a professional manner.

You may also want to consider very carefully before sharing with a colleague discussions that have occurred during the course of your formal field instruction. Like client information, details of your experience with supervision are best kept in confidence to preserve the trust necessary for optimal learning.

> ** Remember, once you have shared something with someone — whether about a client, a field instructor, or yourself — you have effectively relinquished any control over it. The person with whom you have shared it may then decide how the information can be used. And there are no assurances that it would be used in the manner than you would wish!*

The NASW Code of Ethics addresses relationships to colleagues specifically in Ethical Standard Two: Social Workers' Ethical Responsibilities to Colleagues. Colleagues should be treated with respect, and unwarranted criticism of colleagues should be avoided (2.01). When appropriate, social workers should seek consultation from colleagues (2.05) with the understanding that information shared during the process of consultation should be kept confidential (2.02). You will find suggestions for addressing concerns about colleagues or ethical issues involving colleagues in Chapters 22 and 23.

B. Treatment Teams and Multidisciplinary Teams

Most host settings and many social agencies also utilize a team approach in working with client systems or organizations. These team settings call for another kind of relationship between yourself and your colleagues — collaboration. Members of a team generally have distinct responsibilities and roles. Ideally, these are complementary; however, sometimes there are "conflicting demands and loyalties" on the part of different members of the team or group.[1]

Team members may or may not all be social workers. If members are trained in other disciplines, their approach and theoretical framework may be quite different than yours. For example, in a long-term care multidisciplinary team, the nurse may be primarily concerned with the prevention of injury, while you may be primarily concerned with self-determination and personal rights. In a school setting, a teacher might be concerned with maintaining a classroom atmosphere which maximizes learning for everyone, while you are concerned with your client's right to equality of treatment and education. In planning a new community program, you may be more concerned with the specific services offered, while other members of your team may be more concerned with the program's impact upon the schools, the transportation system, or the ethnic and cultural mix of the community. It is easy to see that such divergences in viewpoints can lead to problems in team functioning. In addition to client advocacy, social workers also must present the unique person-in-environment view of the problem and strategies for intervention that come from within the social work professional perspective.

There may be conflicts of interest between professionals who are social workers as well, for each team member may have a particular client, group, or organization whose interests are primary for that worker. If the team is working with a family, for example, different social workers might represent the parents and the children, or even each parent and each child. While all are interested in optimizing the best possible resolution to the problem under consideration, each member has the specific concerns of her or his own client as a primary obligation.

Thus, collaborating as a member of a team often involves a <u>process:</u> building a common purpose and setting common goals and objectives, and giving equal consideration to each team member. Participating in a team, whether composed completely of social workers or of members of other disciplines as well, will be a highly educational experience for you, enabling you to develop skills in communication, collaboration, and leadership.[2]

C. Professionals in Other Settings

You will probably also have experience with relating to professionals — social workers, teachers, psychologists, community planners, physicians — outside of your agency on behalf of a client or an agency program. Because there is less opportunity to socialize, these kinds of relationships are generally only professional.

Remember, you must have your client's consent to share information with an outside source, most preferably in writing. Even with consent, you should share only what is absolutely necessary for the outside professional to know. It is best to maintain your client's confidentiality and privacy as carefully as possible.

Except in very extreme and unusual circumstances, outside professionals should not be told of problems you might be experiencing, difficult areas in your agency's functioning, or any other information that would reflect negatively on your field placement agency. Sharing problems freely with outsiders might compromise your agency's function in the community, as well as the clients it serves.

D. Other Agency Personnel

Agencies also employ non-professional staff, such as receptionists, administrative assistants, and paraprofessionals. If you've observed the lunchtime pattern, you will have many clues about what is considered the proper relationship with other staff in your agency. At first, it's usually best to follow the agency's pattern. As you get to know other staff members, you can create the same kind of delineation between personal life and professional life that you developed with other social workers.

Paraprofessionals and other agency staff may also be involved directly with the agency's clients and programs, and have a specific responsibility in the overall helping process. They may be members of treatment teams, and also may consult with you regarding a problem in the client system. All agency staff has a particular area of expertise that is necessary to the overall professional functioning of the agency. They may be an excellent resource for information based on their specific areas of involvement, and their input is often essential in gaining a complete understanding of a client or a problem.

E. Other Students

Good relationships are common between students placed at the same agency, and you may find your closest relationships are with your fellow students. Often, students share office space or other work arrangements, such as telephones or cars.

Although it's often hard to maintain, you must be careful of client confidentiality among your fellow students as well. It's also a good idea to keep details of your supervisory experience private, although in practice students share experiences frequently.

There are a few things you may want to think about, though, to create and maintain the best possible rapport.

- Different field instructors have different ways of working: for example, one might believe that students are best off "jumping right in," and assign cases immediately, while another might believe that a period of observation and familiarization is needed before a case is assigned. Both systems will enable excellent learning experiences!
- Different students have different needs: your caseloads may vary in quantity, kind of problem, and type of intervention needed. Comparisons are difficult for everyone!
- Different programs have different requirements: you may have to prepare a process recording every week, while your fellow student from a different program may have to prepare one a semester, or none at all. One way is not necessarily better — they are just different!
- Field instructors have different personalities, ways of working, and kinds of relationships with students. One field instructor may be very formal, another casual. One may be organized in terms of supervision and expectations, while another may "go with the flow." You can learn well from many different styles of teaching and relating!
- Even if you share the same field instructor as a fellow student, your experiences in supervision might be quite different. Your own personalities will produce different relationships with your field instructors!
- While compatibility may make supervision more pleasant, you can learn just as much, if not more, from the experience of working with someone quite different from yourself.
- Different schools have different schedules, vacations, and assignments. Each will provide students with good professional educations.

If you are in a placement with other students, your field agency may have instructional seminars, field trips, or shared supervision times for you in addition to your personal supervision time. You may also be meeting regularly with your fellow students to share with and lend support to each other. Other students are often easiest for you to relate with, for you are sharing a common process of learning and professional development.

All of your colleagues will add tremendously to your overall experience with placement. They can teach you a great deal, and also offer support and caring. Social work colleagues, you will find, are particularly supportive and tend to relate easily and well.

---

1 Bisman, C. (1994) *Direct Social Work Practice.* Pacific Grove, CA: Brooks/Cole, Chapter 2, Becoming a Social Worker.

2 Ibid., p. 38.

CHAPTER EIGHT

CLIENT-WORKER RELATIONSHIPS

Becoming familiar with your field work agency, working with your field instructor, developing good working relationships with colleagues — all these have been a vital preparation for the primary purpose of your placement: to begin to work with clients in a professional capacity. You will, of course, be reading many texts devoted entirely to the subject of working professionally with clients, and this subject as a whole is highly complex. In this chapter, we will explore some areas which relate directly to your functioning as a student in your field placement agency.

Relating professionally as a social worker means establishing a relationship on terms that are quite different from most of the relationships you have had until now. As we have discussed earlier, the role of social worker and the role of client are quite different than the roles of friend or confidant — different from these, and different from each other.

There is an ease, a casualness, and a sharing back and forth in personal relationships. While professional relationships also may involve these same ingredients, they are communicated differently. Professional relationships are not equal. You will learn much about your client's life, problems, and relationships. Your own, however, do not have an important part to play in these professional encounters. Introducing details of your personal life may shift the focus from your client, may add additional stress to your client, and may appear to reverse the helper roles.

You and your client are each presumed to have expertise vital to your work together, but the areas of expertise are quite different. You are presumed to have theoretical knowledge of your client's problems, and skills for working with it. You are presumed to be aware of resources which can be called upon to better your client's condition. Your client, on the other hand, is the expert about him- or herself. He or she knows how the problems started, how they feel, what the effects are upon him- or herself, or upon others. He or she knows what has been tried in resolving the problem, what has helped, and what hasn't. These very different areas of expertise come together in the professional relationship to create the possibility for hope, change, and growth in your client.

While of course you, too, will learn, change, and grow through your work with your client, your own growth is not the focus and purpose of the relationship. Your client, his or her problems, and the potential for ameliorating or resolving them is the central focus of the professional relationship.

The greatest potential for growth, change, and/or resolution of problems for your client will occur when you create a general atmosphere and tone in your work which is conducive to mutual trust and respect, and where your client feels valued as a person. It is important to consider your client's ethnic, cultural, and socioeconomic background in planning your interaction and communication.

A. Preparing for an Interview

You will be able to work best with your client if you spend some time preparing for your interview. There are some simple physical and mechanical things you can do to help both you and your client, and some mental things you can do to prepare yourself for your work.

Physical Preparations

1. Space: You will need to arrange a place for you and your client to meet. While it may not always be possible, it is helpful to use and arrange your space such that it is comfortable, pleasant, and harmonious rather than formal and stiff, overly cluttered, too hot or too cold. Soft lighting and comfortable armchairs are ideal. However, not all settings will provide these conditions. It is still possible to create an ambiance of ease, warmth, and trust through positioning of seats, furniture and other items.

2. Privacy: Ensuring privacy will assist your client to feel comfortable in sharing information with you.

3. Uninterrupted Time: An uninterrupted block of time will enable good focusing and communication to occur, and also help your client to feel valued: after all, she or he was important enough to you that you had your phone calls held! Of course, there may be an occasional interruption for an emergency — such things cannot be helped and your client will understand this.

Mental Preparations

1. Quiet Time: If at all possible, allow yourself a little quiet time before an interview. Go somewhere where you can be alone, and begin to try to prepare yourself for your work. Quiet time is not only for student social workers: seasoned workers also need quiet time before an interview with a client to prepare themselves to give their best.

2. Clear Your Mind: This is the time to put aside any personal issues you are involved with: a worry about a child, a fight with a significant other, a concern about bills or budget, a car that needs repair all need to be placed on "pause" in your mind. You can't resolve these in the next hour — you will be with your client! An important part of professional relationships is the ability of the professional to suspend his or her own life issues and concerns and allow those of the client to assume the central position.

3. Focus on the Client: Review, in your mind or in the client's chart, the client's problem, history, and life experience. Focus completely on your client. If you like, this is a good time to re-read the client's chart, especially notes of the last interview.

While focusing on your client, be aware of cultural differences between yourself and your client, and the potential impact of these upon your interaction and communication. Think about your client and the problem within the broader context of the client's ethnic, social, cultural, and economic background.

4. <u>Plan Your Interview</u>: Of course, you can't plan your interview exactly, for you do not know what your client will say or do, or what experiences and problems he or she will bring to the interview. But you can plan some of what you hope to cover. For example, you know that in a first interview you must address informed consent issues, and agency policies and procedures. You must begin to establish a relationship of trust. In a later interview, you may plan to discuss a child's behavior, preparation for employment interviews, applying for a certain program, an issue about a relationship that was raised in a previous interview, discharge plans from a hospital.

Whatever plans you make may need to be completely set aside because of some concern, problem, or issue your client brings to you. However, thinking through the interview in your mind will help you to maintain a goal-oriented framework during the process.

Generally, you should think about the purpose of your interview. Why are you meeting with this client at this time? What plans did you make during your last contact for this next one? Where are you in the overall process of working with this client? You may want to say a sentence or two about this as you begin — depending upon where your client is!

B. In the Office

Where you hold interviews will depend very much upon your field practice setting. Some agencies do all interviewing within the agency's premises; others do all of their interviewing in the field; still others have a varying mixture of agency and field interviews. If your field placement agency interviews at the agency at all, it is likely that your first interviews will be there, to provide support and a secure agency structure. You will have discussed with your field instructor arrangements for privacy, space, and uninterrupted time. You will have reviewed the client's record, and be comfortable and familiar with the contents. You will probably also have discussed with your field instructor your plans and goals for this interview. You are having your quiet time, waiting for your client to appear. Finally, your phone rings. Your client has arrived!

Bring the Client to Your Office

Your agency may have a particular way in which clients get to you. If possible, it's a good idea to go out to the waiting room and get your client. This more casual and personal moment enables the client to feel that you are interested, enough to come out to receive him or her.

The waiting room is not a place to chat, for there's usually no privacy there. Show your client to your office and indicate that this is the place for your work together.

Settle Yourself and Your Client Comfortably

Make sure that you and your client are both seated comfortably before you begin. You can position the chairs so that eye contact is possible. There should be some personal space around each of your seats, so that the client does not feel trapped or cornered. Some workers like to sit behind their desks, while others find that the desk is a barrier to the kind of relationship that they feel is most beneficial. Arrange your space in the way that works best for you. Make sure that your door is closed, or ajar, and make whatever arrangements are necessary for privacy and confidentiality.

If You Take Notes

Some students, and workers, prefer to take notes while they are interviewing, in order to ensure accuracy of documentation and good recall of the sequence of events. If you are planning to take notes, a simple acknowledgment and explanation are helpful. Try to make your note-taking as unobtrusive as possible, and get used to using a minimal amount of words. You will remember well anyway — all you may need are a few words to jog your memory!

Interview Structure

You will be working on structuring your interviews in your Foundation Practice course, and reviewing this material with your field instructor. Structuring is referred to here to assist you in overall planning. You may want to begin by introducing yourself, your agency, or your program, if this is a first interview, and by discussing any informed consent issues. If this is a later interview, you may usually begin by reviewing what happened in the last interview in a sentence or two, and then discussing with your client the purpose of this interview. This focuses the interview and prepares you both for the work ahead.

As you reach the end of your time with the client, be sure to briefly review and summarize the main points of your work together, lay the foundations for your next meeting, set a time and date, and agree on what is to occur in the intervening time. This will help you and your client to maintain a sense of the continuity of your relationship.

Escort Your Client Back to the Waiting Room

Escorting your client back to the waiting room again affirms your interest and concern, and your respect for the client as an individual. Agencies are often large and confusing places, clients have often experienced powerful emotions during interviews, and accompanying them back to a familiar spot will help them to prepare to leave your office.

C. In the Field

Home visits give workers the opportunity to experience and understand the client in his or her natural setting.[1] Visiting a client's home will give you an understanding of his or her daily life experiences, tastes and interests, and patterns of relating which will be very helpful to your work together. A home visit literally "opens a door" into the client's personal life in a way that cannot be replicated through office contacts. If your field placement provides this opportunity, you will find that it is very beneficial to your learning. You can optimize the experience for yourself with careful planning and preparation.

When going out in the field to interview clients, you will still need arrangements for space, privacy (much harder to achieve, sometimes!), uninterrupted time, a chance to clear your mind and focus and prepare. You will also need to use all but the "escorting" guidelines in the Office section, above. However, there are a few additional steps you will need to take to facilitate your field visit.

If you know that you will be making many field visits in the course of your placement, by all means get a good map of your own and carry it with you when you are out in the field.

Set a Convenient Time

You will need to consider your own schedule in planning field visits. What else are you planning that day? Where are you coming from? Where will you be going? Try to plan things in a logical sequence for maximum efficiency and ease. Avoid rush hour, and nighttime visits to areas where you may feel uncomfortable.

Get Good Directions

A must!! All of us, no matter how much we know we need directions, have gotten lost at times, especially when we are going for the first time to a new place. Good directions are essential. Often, your client will be able to provide these. The previous worker will be able to provide good directions, too. You may get directions from the police department. After you get the directions, plan your route using your map of the area. Write the directions down and carry them with you.

Allow Extra Time

No matter how well we plan, we may encounter stopped, bumper-to-bumper traffic, be unable to find a parking place within miles of the field visit, or wait for long periods of time for public transportation. It is best to allow some extra time so that you will not become anxious, or your client worried. If you are going to be late, stop and make the necessary phone calls!

Let People Know Where You Are

Your field instructor and other people at your agency should know where you are at all times. You should inform them of when and where you are going, your expected time of arrival there, and your expected time of return back to the agency. This is important for your own security, and also so that you can be reached should emergencies occur. This is addressed more fully in Chapter 24, Personal Safety and Security.

If Necessary, Take Someone with You

Because of the difficult situations in which many of our clients find themselves, social workers often visit in neighborhoods or in situations with a higher than average potential for crime or violence. You should never feel that you must make such visits alone, or at unsafe hours. You can discuss your feelings with your field instructor, and arrangements will be made for someone to accompany you on your visit. This is also discussed more fully in Chapter 24.

A Guest in Your Client's Home

When you visit a client, you are, in a sense, a guest in your client's home. You should follow whatever guidelines custom or common sense dictate for being a guest. Wait to sit down until asked to do so, or until your client sits down. Do not wander into other rooms of the house without your client's express consent. You may want to ask your client to show you around — this is very appropriate in many situations. Your client may also introduce you to other members of the household that are at home during your visit.

If you notice that there are other people around, and that your conversation can easily be overheard, you may wish to point that out to your client, and ask if there is a way to ensure privacy during your visit. On the other hand, this may also be your opportunity to include other household members in your interview. Always check with the client before asking another member of the client's household or a visitor to join you.

Your client may offer you food and drink during your visit. Accepting coffee or a cold drink is fine, if you wish, but you may politely refuse food. Your agency may have guidelines on this for you as well.

If you are visiting a home where there are unsanitary conditions, such as insects or rodents or unclean areas, you may prefer to remain standing or to sit in a hard chair, such as a dining room chair. You may also suggest sitting outside or on the front steps if this is appropriate to the home and the weather conditions. In all cases, it is important to be courteous and calm — remember, this is the home of your client!

Setting the Client at Ease

You may also sense that your client is uncomfortable with your presence in his or her home. Embarrassment, shame, reticence, and unease are frequent feelings clients experience when a new person, any new person, enters their home, and you may become aware of some or several of these feelings in your client. There may be many reasons for this in addition to the physical condition of the home. There may be a feeling of violation of privacy, of embarrassment at needing the help of an outsider in a way that may be visible to neighbors, shyness about "hosting" a professional, and many other reasons for your client to feel uncomfortable.

You can help your client feel at ease by complimenting something in the home, by expressing interest in something, or by including someone else who is obviously present (a child, a parent, a friend) in your beginning conversation. You can also share your experiences in getting to the home (there was so much traffic, the road was really interesting). A few moments of a more casual kind of conversation will enable your client to feel comfortable with you. You can then re-focus on the reason for your visit to his or her home.

Visiting a client at home is an interesting and very helpful experience in your work. You can often learn more about your client and his or her world in one home visit than you can in many, many hours of office interviews. After all, "a picture is worth a thousand words!"

D. **Visiting in Another Setting**

You also may go out into the field to visit a client who is living or working in a setting other than his or her home. Your client may be hospitalized, in prison, or living in a rehabilitation clinic. You may visit a client at a residential school, in a long-term care facility, in a shelter, or on the street. No matter what the setting, the place where your client is living — whether temporary or permanent, is "home," and there is a "space" — sometimes large, sometime painfully small, that is personally the client's in any setting. It is important that you honor and respect that space, no matter what the circumstances, while also recognizing the effect of living in that space and in that condition.

Your client's sleeping, eating, and personal hygiene arrangements and leisure and recreational spaces will have a strong impact upon your planning and your work with him or her. In setting goals and objectives, and in designing interventions and activities, it is important to consider the overall milieu in which the client is living.

You may also be visiting your client in a setting in which he or she spends only part of a day: a school, a day treatment setting, or a workplace. Unless there are clear, easily supported reasons for not alerting administrators and personnel that you will be visiting, the guidelines for such visits are similar to those for settings where your client is living on a full-time basis.

Guidelines for visits to clients in alternative settings are similar to those for home visits, with a few additional considerations:

- You will need to let the setting's representative — an administrator, other social worker, nurse, or other responsible party, know in advance that you are planning to visit. Depending upon the circumstances, you may need to make arrangements for a space which ensures privacy and an uninterrupted visit. If a client is confined to a hospital bed, it may be possible to arrange for a roommate's absence; if a client is in a residential school, there may be an office or unused classroom that could be available to you.
- You should check in upon arrival, and let personnel know that you are present in the facility.
- You may want to consider allowing a time and space for a visit with the shelter director, charge nurse, prison warden, or other professional who is working with your client on a day-to-day basis. This will enable you to gain another helpful perspective upon your client's problems and functioning. However, there are many circumstances in which this is not advisable, and when keeping the relationship strictly between you and your client will enable more effective service. You may consult with your field instructor regarding the appropriateness of a "consultation" with others involved in rendering care to your client.
- Developing a professional working relationship with others who are working with your client will generally enable you to coordinate your efforts and work toward commonly held goals.

Be sure to let others know when you have completed your visit and are leaving the facility, and to thank them for their hospitality.

E. Gifts and Offers of Services

It is helpful to think ahead about the possibility of a client offering you food, gifts, or services, so that you can plan an appropriate response. Your agency may have guidelines about accepting gifts from clients as a part of policy, or there may just be acceptable practices that workers generally follow. The best source of information is your field instructor, and he or she can also provide good guidance for you. You want to support and maintain your good relationship with your client without compromising your professional comportment or your objectivity.

One of the first things you may want to think about is whether you want to take a motivation-oriented approach or a policy-based one. If you use a motivation-based approach, you may need to think through the entire relationship between you and your client should a gift be offered. It is very important with this approach to think about what this offer means to the client. Is it normally a part of the client's cultural milieu? Is the client trying to make you more comfortable? Express appreciation? Be manipulative? With this approach, the reason may affect your acceptance or non-acceptance. If you are unsure, this offers a wonderful opportunity for exploring with your client!

However, it is important to recognize that using a motivation-oriented approach may create an inconsistency between what you do with one client and what you will do with another. If you accept one client's gift, because it is an important cultural element to that client, and refuse another's, because it is manipulative, you may create difficulties for yourself. What if your clients know each other, or somehow learn about the difference? For example, they may see a box of candy with an appreciative client note on your desk, and have their gift of a home-baked cake refused? Just imagine all the possible implications of that, and the effects on your client-worker relationship!

If you use a policy-oriented approach, you can either adopt the policy of your agency or, if they don't have one, develop one of your own and use it in all cases. Thus, all gifts would be refused, or accepted, or accepted with certain conditions.

One possible way of dealing with this issue that minimizes the potential for manipulation by the client is to say that you can accept only things that can be shared (flowers, a box of candy, a cake), and that you will share this with everyone on the staff of the agency. You then place the flowers, fruit, candy, or other gift on a counter, or at a table, in the public area of your office, for the enjoyment of all. This allows your client the opportunity to give a gift, yet does not make it a personal one.

F. Documentation

You will keep many forms of documentation during the course of your field work placement. Reports, forms, team meeting notes, records of consultation, reports from other sources (such as schools, hospitals, or courts), and record summaries. The most basic documentation, and the most frequent in most cases, is the documentation of the contacts you have had with your client and client system. These include the notes that you will prepare for the client's record after each contact. "Proficient recording enhances the quality of services provided to clients. Records identify, describe, and assess clients' situations; define the purpose of service; document service goals, plans, activities, and progress; and evaluate the effect of service. . . . recording enhances continuity of care."[2]

An important factor to bear in mind while thinking about or preparing documentation is the purpose for which the record or report is being prepared. Is it to serve as an ongoing record of contact and progress? Is it to recommend a course of action? Is it to assess and evaluate? Will your documentation be used in-house, or will it be sent to referring agencies, courts, or other agencies who are involved with your client? The purpose of your documentation should tell you what needs to be included, in what detail, and from what framework.

Another factor involves access to records. Who will be reading what you write? Are you writing for yourself and your field instructor alone? Will other social workers be reading your record? Will professionals of other disciplines? It is important to remember that, under certain circumstances (which may vary by state and type of client system), your entire record, or excerpts from it, may be subpoenaed in court. You should also be aware that your client, or your client's representative if there is one, has the right to request access to the record at any time.

You will also need to consider your agency's guidelines regarding documentation. Is the general expectation detailed and comprehensive recording? Or is a brief, narrative style preferred? If your placement is in a host setting, you may be asked to keep two sets of records: a brief summary of contacts in your client's multidisciplinary record, and a more detailed record in social service files.

Your field instructor is your best resource in determining where, when, and in how much detail documentation should occur. The general guidelines below may be used to supplement your field instructor's suggestions and your agency's requirements.

- Write in a clear professional manner, using appropriate professional terminology. At first, you may want to practice on a separate sheet of paper, and ask your field instructor to review your notes for professionalism.
- Be careful, accurate, and objective in documenting what you have observed, or the events that have transpired.
- Avoid using value terms, such as "destructive," "bad," "helpless," "abusive," etc. Instead, describe what you see and hear. Remember that being non-judgmental is an important attribute of a competent professional.
- Document concisely without sacrificing the "flavor" of the person or event you are describing. Social workers tend to be a wordy group, but overly long and detailed descriptive recording often sacrifices immediacy and energy. Also, others who may be reading your documentation will tend to lose interest and skim over your record if it is unusually lengthy and descriptive. They may therefore miss the most vital and important material you wanted to present!
- Always remain aware that you may not be working with your client(s) until services are completed and goals are met. As a student, you will be transferring many of your clients to another worker at the end of your field placement. The documentation that you keep should assist the new worker in providing continuity of services to your client(s).
- Careful, accurate, and complete documentation is your best protection against malpractice and liability.[3] Be sure to include documentation of any consultation and referrals in your case record. Although the possibility for a lawsuit is minimal, especially as a student, good documentation habits will be helpful to you throughout your professional career. Reamer suggests that all records contain: informed consent procedures and signed forms for release of information; a description of all contacts with third parties, whether by telephone or in-person consultation; a complete social history, treatment, and assessment plan; a description of your reasoning for decisions you make; and instructions, recommendations, and advice you give clients.[4] Your client(s) may have been transferred to you, and their records might contain all of the

above information. However, it is your responsibility to review it, and to ensure that it is accurate and up-to-date. Record all necessary information carefully. Remember, "If it isn't recorded, it didn't happen."[5]

G. When "the Client" Is a Group

Your field placement's program may focus on rendering service to clients within a group context, or may have groups to render additional special kinds of services to clients. Working with groups is an exciting and fascinating enterprise, one that calls upon a high degree of focus and concentration from you as the group's leader. Leaders must be aware of what each member in the group is experiencing, and also of the group process itself in order to maximize the group's potential in assisting each member.

You may be asked to work with a variety of groups. Task-oriented groups address specific problems or needs, such as the development of a new set of procedures, the revision of policy, or the definition of problems in an organization. It is the task, not the people involved, which is the focus of attention. Therapeutic groups are oriented toward the needs and problems of individual members and may provide support, a medium for exploration and change, or an experience in socialization. Therapeutic groups are often structured around a particular age group, problem, or circumstance, such as teens who have been convicted of a crime, women experiencing identity crises or problems, or people with low self-esteem who seek self-confidence. Support groups assist members to feel that they are not alone with the kinds of problems and situations they face, and offer the opportunity to gain insight as well as support from the experiences of others in similar circumstances. Support groups may focus on areas as divergent as widowhood, overeating, infant death, or alcoholism. They are generally led by members of the group who are also experiencing the problem, but may have professional consultants as well.

Hartford defines the purposes of groups as: (1) corrective; (2) preventive); (3) normal social growth; (4) personal enhancement; and (5) citizenship responsibility and participation.[6]

It is important for you to be very clear about the kind of group with whom you will be working, the group's purpose, and your role within it. All groups require that you work simultaneously on three different levels: with individual group members, with the group as a whole, and with the group's environment.[7] It is especially important for you to consider the group's cultural milieu; ethnic, racial, religious composition; age; gender; sexual orientation and any other factors which might both impact on the group and assist you to better understand the group dynamics.

You may inherit a group that is already functioning, or you may be asked to begin a group yourself. If you are asked to form a group:

Prior to the First Meeting:
1. Determine the purpose and focus.
2. Define a potential membership pool.
3. Interview individual members, and explore their interest in participating in a group experience.
4. Formulate individual goals with each member.
5. Arrange a space and a time for the first meeting.

During Early Group Meetings:
1. Assist the group to formulate rules that will govern group interaction.
2. Assist the group to develop goals.
3. Assist members to relate and begin to develop a shared value system and language.

Your field instructor will be able to assist you to develop your group and lead it effectively. You are much more experienced with groups than you may realize at first: all of us have been members and sometimes leaders in groups from early childhood. Scouts, church groups, play groups, study groups, and social groups have been a part of our lives and continue to be. We have knowledge about how groups run, effective and ineffective leadership, and what makes a positive group experience. We have also seen group members assume typical roles within groups, such as the scapegoat, the gatekeeper, and the leader.

If you are inheriting a group from a previous worker, you will be entering a group where relationships and structure have already been formed. As you yourself are new, however, it will be very helpful and necessary to review the group rules and to ask each member to introduce him- or herself. Reviewing the rules helps the members to recognize that the expectations of behavior and group functioning will continue, and introductions will provide insight into each member's perception of the group and his or her membership in it.

Groups require special kinds of documentation: a documentation of group process, as well as documentation of the functioning of each individual within the group. At first, this may appear to be a daunting task. However, brief forms or outlines, either used by your agency or developed by you, will help routinize your documentation and assure that nothing essential is omitted.

Group leadership provides an exciting opportunity for learning new skills, observation of interactions and behavior patterns, and the development another method for providing service to others. No matter whether your interest is in individuals, organizations, or communities, group experience will provide a valuable professional tool.

H. When "the Client" Is an Organization

As budget cuts, managed care, strict accountability, for-profit agencies, and the shift from "client" to "consumer" become everyday realities in the world of social welfare, private agencies, government agencies, and social welfare organizations are finding it necessary to restructure, redesign, and revise programs, policies, procedures, and practices which had been used for decades. These changes have posed difficult challenges for administrators and planners, calling for professional competencies and skills vital to the very survival of the organizations themselves. It is an exciting time to enter this special field.

Social work students who are interested in administration and program planning may be placed in field work settings where the organization itself is the focus of assessment and change. Students may be asked to develop a new program, assess an existing program, explore and design new methods of effective communication within an agency, review, revise, or rewrite an agency policy, or restructure an existing program. They may work with assessment of political groups and revenue sources, client populations and referral sources, other organizations, or with policies, procedures, and practices to set goals and objectives and to develop an intervention strategy. They may also work in implementing a strategy that has already been developed.

If you are placed in a large organization, you will generally find yourself assigned as a part of a team that is addressing a particular project or program. Team meetings are an essential ingredient of the process of change, and team members work together to effect the desired outcomes. Your field instructor may be the agency's director, or one of the leaders of the team. Because effecting change or developing programs involves a complex series of steps and strategies, students might at first find themselves doing a great deal of listening, and very little direct acting, upon the problems being addressed.

It is vital for you to have a good grasp of the work that is to be done, and the means through which change is to occur. It is also vital that you understand the organization as a whole, and the place and effect of the change effort within that whole. You need to take the time to understand all of the players in this effort, and to observe their interaction.

It is easy to slide along in this manner for an extended period of time; you are, after all, learning and observing the process of organizational development and change. However, it is essential for you to "carve out" that perhaps very small piece of the overall pie which will become your particular sphere of action and service. If this does not seem to be occurring on its own, you can take the initiative asking the field instructor what, specifically, will be your own responsibility in the overall scheme of the work to be done. When this has been determined, you can then diagram or draw the place that your particular assignment has in the overall effort that is to take place. Who can enable the success of your work? Who will be most affected by it? Is your work dependent upon the completion or implementation of the work of other people or groups? How should others be brought into your particular task, and at what stage?

Planning for organizational change is an exciting and dynamic enterprise which offers many challenges and calls for strong professional skills in interviewing, assessing, and interpersonal relationships. It is extremely rewarding to effect a new program of policy which will touch all of the agency's staff as well as all of the client populations the agency serves.

I. When "the Client" Is a Community

If the uniqueness of the social work perspective lies, at least in part, in its "person-in-environment" orientation, then it is essential to address the "environment" in a competent professional manner.

"Being a social worker," Netting, Kettner, and McMurtry state, "requires seeing the client as part of multiple, overlapping systems that comprise the person's social and physical enviornment."[8] Whether you prefer to work with individuals, with groups, or with organizations, the impact of the community upon each of these must always be considered.

Agencies whose focus is the improvement of conditions in communities to better meet the needs of members of the community have the community itself as the locus of the change effort. Rather than focusing on changing the individual or the group, such agencies find that community change offers the opportunity to affect large numbers of people in a positive manner. If your field placement is in this type of setting, your client may be the community as a whole, and your focus may be the assessment of community needs, and/or the development of programs and strategies to meet these needs.

If you are placed in a community-focused agency, you may want to take extra time during the process of getting to know your agency to familiarize yourself thoroughly with its milieu, for this is your "client population." A map is essential. Walk around the community and note shopping areas, schools, hospitals, recreation facilities and parks, social and government agencies, the police and fire department, public transportation, and any other details of the community. Observe the ethnic, racial, and cultural mix. If different areas are home to different groups, note their location and proximity on your map. Note the socioeconomic level, the condition of the buildings, the cleanliness of the streets.

Study your map and reflect upon what you have noted. What are the strengths that you have observed? Do the shops and services support the ethnic and cultural mix? Is there a strong community network? Are there good recreational facilities available? Did you see a number of posters advertising community events? What have you noted that might be problems for this community? Is there a pile-up of trash in alleyways? Are the buildings in need of repair? Are there groups of unemployed young people on the street corners? Does the school have bars on the windows?

Working with communities requires strong powers of observation, as well as good people skills and ability to negotiate complex systems. You can strengthen your powers of observation easily by spending time walking your community and getting the feel of it.

As a community social worker, or change agent, you will be working with three overlapping circles, or focus points, in effecting change within a community. These are:

Arena: the community as a whole. Your agency is a part of that community, as are all other organizations within it. All of the people who live within the community are a part of the arena, as are all the services and systems available to them.

Population: the group of people within the community upon whom the change effort will be focused. This may be the elderly, retirees, the unemployed, pregnant teenagers, schoolchildren, and the homeless.

Problem: change efforts will be focused on a particular problem that exists within the community, such as alcoholism, chronic mental illness, school dropout rates, or violence.[9]

You may find, as you begin your placement, that your agency has already identified a problem, and is in the process of developing a strategy for intervention. You will then be responsible for specific tasks in this process. On the other hand, your agency may be at an earlier or later stage in the process: workers may be doing outreach into the community to assist community members themselves to determine what issues in the community need to be addressed; or they might have completed a part or all of the change, and be in the process of assessment and evaluation.

Any of these stages will allow ample opportunity for direct involvement and for learning. You will be working and interacting with other professionals, but also with community leaders, local organizations such as church and civic groups, and community members.

As with other areas of practice, it is vital that you become familiar with the cultural, racial, and ethnic characteristics of your community. You may also want to know about the history of the community. Are there many new immigrants? Who lived in the community 50 years ago? When was it first settled, and by whom? Were there any major natural or man-made disasters (such as major fires) that affected the growth and makeup of the community? What kinds of programs, activities, or approaches have been successful? To what is the success attributed? Interviewing community leaders and members will draw you closer to the community itself, help you to understand its history and problems, and assist you in developing invaluable personal relationship networks to help you in your change effort.

Familiarity with your client community can assist you in your work, but also will provide you with wonderful opportunities for personal as well as professional growth.

There are an unlimited number of possible situations in which you may find yourself with clients. A good general guide is to use your common sense, and to relate to your clients always in a professional, rather than a personal, manner. There is almost nothing you can do with or for clients that can't be amended, changed, or rectified if you find that it is not comfortable for you. Your field instructor will be able to help you to plan for most eventualities. The unplanned ones — they are the surprises that are an integral part of the social work profession — and you will never, ever be bored!

---

[1] Kadushin, A. (1990) *The Social Work Interview*, Third Ed. NY: Columbia University Press.

[2] Reamer, F.G. (1994) *Social Work Malpractice and Liability*. NY: Columbia University Press, p. 177.

[3] Ibid., P. 176-178.

[4] Ibid., p. 178.

[5] Ibid., p. 176.

[6] Hartford, M. (1964) Frame of reference for social group work. In *Papers toward a Frame of Reference for Social Group Work*. NY: NASW Press.

[7] Toseland, R.W., & Rivas, R.F. (1995) *An Introduction to Group Work Practice*. Boston: Allyn & Bacon.

[8] Netting, F.E., Kettner, P.M., & McMurtry, S.L. (1998) *Social Work Macro Practice*. NY: Longman Publishing.

[9] Ibid., p. 8

UNIT SUMMARY

This Unit has offered information, suggestions, and guidelines for familiarizing yourself with the most important components of your field work placement. Chapter 5 addressed your agency as an entity that transcends, in many ways, the separate identities of all of the individuals of whom it is composed. It is important for you to understand your agency in the context of its historical roots and mission, and the way in which it both affects and is affected by the milieu which surrounds it and the population that it serves. Suggestions have been offered which will assist you to view your agency in this broader context by additionally exploring policies, procedures, and the resource network in which it is embedded.

Chapter 6 addressed that all-important relationship within which much of your formal learning in the field placement agency occurs. Your field instructor will be your mentor as you encounter your first clients, formulate your first assessments, design your first intervention strategies, and evaluate your work. He or she will provide guidance, support, and a place to turn for useful advice and comfort when things seem to go wrong, as they sometimes will. There is a rhythm to your relationship with your field instructor that sets the pace and tone for the weeks to come — the formal structure of agendas and supervisory conferences, consultation and evaluation will be supplemented by the informal luncheon meetings, the advice-given-on-the-run, and the emergency calls which will be returned quickly and helpfully. Together with your field instructor, you will plan your learning in your practicum, and together you will assess the progress that you have made. Your field instructor is the person at your agency who best understands your learning needs and school program.

In addition to your field instructor, there are many other people with whom you will interact in your agency. Relationship with colleagues — both professional and non-professional, both within your field placement agency and in other settings, have been addressed in Chapter 7.

The final chapter in this Unit addressed your relationship with clients. This, in and of itself, will be the focus of many courses and readings during your professional education. In this chapter, we addressed some of the mechanics that will help you to prepare for contacts with your clients, as well as suggested specific techniques and skills that will assist you to feel at ease and able to focus on the client's problems and concerns. Sections on groups, organizations, and communities have presented some of the unique challenges of those "special" kinds of clients.

Unit Two has helped you to plan for beginning your placement. If you have followed the guidelines which have been included here, you will have created the beginnings of an excellent field work experience. The third Unit, entitled Maintaining an Optimal Field Work Experience, will offer some ideas and suggestions for keeping it that way throughout the course of your practicum.

One of the early tasks you will encounter in field work placement is that of developing a learning contract. A sample form is included with the discussion of learning contracts in Chapter 9, and reviewing and revising your learning contract, an ongoing process throughout your field work placement, is addressed in Chapter 13.

You will learn best if your field work experience and your classroom learning complement and supplement each other well, and, as the primary link between field and school, you are the best person to ensure that this occurs. Chapter 10 suggests some guidelines to assist you in this regard. Another link between school and field is your liaison, or field consultant, whose role in your field work education is presented in depth in Chapter 11.

While each student's experience is unique, your school needs some way to assess your work and determine a grade for field. Schools use written reports, which are always shared with you beforehand during a field work evaluation by your field instructor. This complex but necessary process will be explored in Chapter 12.

UNIT THREE

MAINTAINING AN OPTIMAL FIELD WORK EXPERIENCE

The first two Units focused on preparing you to begin your field placement with an understanding of the purpose, roles, and people who are basic to your field work experience. This third Unit focuses on several areas which will help you to make it, and keep it, a productive, interesting, and meaningful learning experience thoughout the entire time of your placement.

Sometime during the first weeks of placement, you and your field instructor will be developing a learning contract. This is required by your program, and provides the school with an understanding of the principal objectives of your field placement learning experience. Your learning contract provides an opportunity for you and your field instructor to plan and prioritize your learning tasks; reviewing it enables you both to evaluate progress, and revising it will assist you to change your goals as you progress in your learning over the course of your placement. Learning contracts will be presented in Chapter 9.

Throughout this book, we have alluded to the importance of integrating school and field learning throughout the course of your practicum experience. Chapter 10 will suggest some of the ways you can facilitate this process. You are the pivotal person in this endeavor, for you are both in class and in your field placement, and you alone can work to ensure that both support and enable optimal learning.

Chapter 11 will assist you to prepare your liaison's visit to your field placement. Visits are always special occasions: they are opportunities to show a representative of your school's program your agency, to present the specifics of your caseload and your learning experiences, to discuss areas of congruence and difference between school and field learning, to ask questions, to plan for future learning, and to explore the school-placement-student triangle to ensure its optimal functioning.

Your learning in the field is assessed by your field instructor during your regularly scheduled supervision times, and plans are also then made for future experiences and projects. There are specific times during the course of your placement, however, when more formal assessments are made of your field learning. Written, formal field work evaluations become a part of your academic record. They are used by the Field Office in assigning a grade for your practicum learning. Chapter 12 will address preparing for field work evaluations, and present the evaluation process.

Often, a part of field work evaluation includes a review of your learning contract, presented in Chapter 9. You and your field instructor will review objectives and tasks, and revise the contract as needed to meet your new learning needs. Revision of the learning contract may occur at other times during your practicum experience as well. Chapter Thirteen will present some suggestions for planning your learning contract reviews, assessing your achievements, and determining further learning goals.

CHAPTER NINE

DEVELOPING YOUR LEARNING CONTRACT

Your learning contract, generally written after several weeks of practicum, may be one of the first written assignments you will encounter in your field work placement. It is important for you to have some understanding of your agency, your clients, and your learning tasks prior to undertaking the writing of a learning contract.

A learning contract, as noted earlier, can be helpful in several distinct but interrelated ways: it will help you to formulate clearly the concepts, skills, and knowledge you wish to focus on during your placement; it will help you and your field instructor to evaluate your progress over the course of time; and it will provide a mechanism for revising and reframing your objectives as you progress through the weeks and months of your placement.

The Field Office and/or your liaison should be provided with a copy of your learning contract, signed by both you and your field instructor, according to your program's requirements. The learning contract provides a written record for the Field Office to use in understanding where and how you will be focusing your learning during your placement. Some field offices may request copies of learning contract evaluations and revisions as well. During the course of your field liaison's visit to your field placement, your learning contract may be used to focus the discussion of your field work experience.

Contracts are used with clients in a similar manner: they define goals and objectives, specify the ways in which these will be met, and serve as a tool for evaluating progress and change. Managed care providers generally require some form of written therapeutic contract between a worker or agency and a client, and familiarity with the process of contract formulation will be very helpful to you in your work. The actual process of contracting with clients can be therapeutic in the same way that the actual process of contracting with your field instructor can be a learning experience.

You will also see parallels between the structure of your learning contract and your agency's mission, policy, and procedure manual. The broadest statement, the agency's mission statement, is similar to your goal or "mission" in developing your field work experience. The policies of your agency define programs and clarify purpose. These may be compared to your learning contract objectives, which specify what you are working to achieve. The most specific, the approaches and methods you will use to achieve your learning contract goals is similar to your agency's procedures. Both address how objectives or policies will be met and put into effect, and both can be used to assess and evaluate functioning.

Thus, you will see an underlying commonality of structure, though not of content, between your learning contract, your agency's written structure, and the contracts that you will develop with your clients. Some field placement agencies specify particular learning goals and objectives for all students, consonant with the agency's goals and purposes related to its educational mission. Some schools may require that all students include certain items in their learning contracts, such as familiarization with agency policies and procedures, or the development of a safety plan for field visits.

A. Sample Form

Generally, schools have developed forms which they distribute to students for learning contract development. The form included here will be used as an example for this chapter's discussion. You may also use it in working with your personal learning contract if your school and field agency agree.

LEARNING CONTRACT

Name _____   Program & Level _____

Learning Goal _____

Objective	Approaches/Tasks/ Methods/Interventions	Date	Evaluation: Comments
1.	1.		
	2.		
	3		
2.	1.		
	2.		
	3.		
	4.		
	5.		

B. Exploring the Specifics of Your Contract

The learning contract is divided into several sections, each of which has a specific function. The form generally goes from most general (goals), to more specific (objectives), to most specific (methods) during the development process, and from specific to most general during the evaluation process.

We will assume here that you are beginning to develop your first learning contract, and will discuss the sections moving from most general to most specific.

Learning Goals

Your learning goals are stated in the broadest terms, and may remain the same during the entire course of your field work placement. Learning goals attempt to address the question:

"Now I am at this point in my professional learning. Where is it that I want to be at the end of this field work experience, or semester, or academic year?"

State your learning goal in ordinary language, and in general terms:

"I would like to be able to establish a good rapport with a client, and assist the client toward growth and change."

"I would like to be able to function as a professional."

"I would like to be able to use myself in a professional manner."

"I would like to understand all of the social work processes and be able to use them to help clients."

"I would like to be able to use the person-in-environment perspective competently to assist my clients."

It is important that you spend some time thinking about how you will answer this question. Each of us might answer it in a slightly different way, using slightly different words. The way that you state it should be meaningful to you personally. You will find that though you may state your goal differently than a fellow student, your objectives will probably be quite similar!

Your learning goal attempts to describe in general terms what you wish to achieve in your field work experience.

Objectives

Now that you know <u>what you are trying to achieve</u> in a broad sense, you will begin to focus a little more specifically. You can begin to think about <u>what will enable you to achieve</u> your goal. The specific knowledge or skill that will enable you to achieve your goal can be stated as an objective. When you state an objective, you must <u>always</u> include the manner in which you will evaluate whether you have achieved it, and a time frame.

Though you don't need to use these exact words, what you are trying to state should include something that might describe:

(The thing you wish to learn or achieve),
as demonstrated by
(the thing that will enable you to judge whether you have achieved it)
within
(the amount of time you will allow yourself to achieve your objective).

Some of your objectives will be "knowledge objectives" — the achievement of a particular body of information. Others might be "skill objectives," such as the ability to establish a helping relationship. Still others might combine the two — assessment according to systems theory, for example, or development of a plan for change using cognitive-behavioral interventions. Several examples might assist you in formulating objectives.

One of the first knowledge objectives you might have is to familiarize yourself with your agency, its programs, and its structure. You might state it this way:

"Familiarity with Field Placement Agency, as evidenced by ability to describe specific agency programs and diagram agency departmental structure and hierarchy in one month."

If your agency's population is unfamiliar to you, one of your early objectives might be to learn about that population. You could develop an objective such as:

"Cultural competence with Mexican-Americans as demonstrated by ability to discuss Mexican-American life cycle events and family relationship patterns in supervision in one month."

A skill objective might be to establish a relationship with a client:

"Ability to set up an appointment and to meet with a client to discuss a problem as evidenced by (charting)(documentation in client's chart)(process recording) in one month."

An objective that utilizes both knowledge and skill:

"Ability to utilize the strengths perspective to develop an intervention plan with a client as evidenced by a written plan in one client's record in three months."

Or:

"Ability to engage client in the process of developing an eco-map that reflects interpersonal relationships, as evidenced by its inclusion in the client's chart in three months."

The way in which you will develop and state your objectives will depend very much on your agency's programs and population, your learning needs and interests, and your place within the agency's structure.

As your goal defined the WHO (you wish to become), so your objectives will specify the WHAT (will enable this) and the WHEN (it can reasonably be expected to occur).

While you want to include enough objectives to allow yourself optimal room for experiences and for growth, it is important not to overwhelm yourself with a great number of objectives, and to be sure to allow a reasonable time to meet them. It is better to set fewer objectives, and add others as these are completed, than to write a comprehensive learning plan so complex you will become discouraged in trying to fulfill it.

Methods and Approaches

The methods and approaches that you use to fulfill your objectives are the most specific "nuts and bolts" items in your learning contract. Generally, each of the objectives that you define will suggest several approaches that will enable you to achieve them. Methods will add the final two pieces to your learning contract development process: the WHERE (you will learn or do or experience) and the HOW (through reading, acting, observing or other).

You should state your methods in order of priority and time. For example, you must first call a client to set up and interview, and then hold the interview, so that the former should precede the latter on your methods list. You must first learn the strengths perspective, and then discuss strengths with your client; first read about your agency's population, and then discuss life cycle events.

Each of the objectives in your learning contract should be attainable through the use of the specific methods you select and define.

For example, the objective: "Ability to engage client in the process of developing an eco-map that reflects interpersonal relationships, as evidenced by its inclusion in the client's chart in three months," might be achieved through such approaches as:

- Read and learn how eco-maps are formulated, and the mechanics of their design.
- Practice by doing an eco-map of yourself.
- Draw or obtain a form for eco-maps you can use with a client.
- Develop an eco-map with a client.
- Retain eco-map as an integral part of client's chart.

To achieve the objective: "Cultural competence with Mexican-Americans as demonstrated by ability to discuss Mexican-American life cycle events and family relationship patterns in supervision in one month" you might design a methodology which could include:

- Discuss this objective with multicultural or diversity class instructor, and with field instructor, eliciting information about learning resources.
- Develop a list of resources (books, videos, organizations) providing cultural information about Mexican-Americans.
- Read a book or view a film which illustrates Mexican-American social issues, customs, and traditions.
- Plan a presentation at school, in the field, or to the field instructor about Mexican-American life cycle events and traditions.

Your choice of methods or approaches is a combination of your personal preferences and available resources and experiences, with the suggestions and direction of your field instructor.

Utilizing Your Contract

After the completion of your learning contract, both you and your field instructor will sign it, and each will retain a copy. Another copy will be sent to the appropriate person(s) in your school program. Your agency's Director may also wish to review a copy of your learning contract.

Your copy can be used as a guide to direct your specific learning projects. Explore the approaches and methods you defined for attaining your objectives. When you complete an objective, check it off or mark it in some manner to indicate completion.

You should arrange with your field instructor the specific procedure to be followed when the specified time frame has passed for an objective. Suggestions for valuating your learning, and for revising and reviewing your contract are presented in Chapter 13.

C. Putting It All Together

We have discussed all of the pieces that, together, make up the learning contract that will define your specific goals and objectives, and provided a sample form to illustrate the manner in which the several parts go together.

You and your field instructor together will decide how you will develop your own contract. Some field instructors prefer students to write their own learning contract, and then bring it to the field instructor for review. Others prefer to set up some objectives with you, and then ask you to develop approaches and methods that are meaningful to you to meet the objectives. Still others will prefer to go through the process with you step by step. These are a reflection of your field instructor's teaching style only: any of them can be used successfully!

When you write your learning contract, always begin with your goal. Then, define a series of objectives. Five or six is a good number — more than that will diffuse your learning effort too greatly. Write your objectives out, decide what "evidence" you will use to demonstrate achievement, and a time frame that you believe is reasonable. If you wish, order your objectives either by time needed for their achievement (one month objectives come before three month objectives) or by their natural order (setting up an interview comes before developing a therapeutic alliance) or by their importance to you (learning about your clients may be more important to you than learning your agency's hierarchy). Try to be consistent in whichever method you select. Leave space between objectives to allow room for approaches and methods, which often take up more room!

After you have ordered each of your objectives, examine them one at a time. Determine what methods or approaches would enable you to achieve the objective as you have stated it. List these in order of time, sequence (one must be completed before another can be started), and priority. You should always have several different approaches or methods for achieving your objective. When you are satisfied that you have addressed an objective thoroughly, move on to the next one.

When you have completed your learning contract, review it carefully. Does it all seem to hang together? Does it plan the kind of educational experience that you feel will best meet your individual needs and goals? If you see some problems, revise the contract as needed, and explain your reasoning to your field instructor.

CHAPTER TEN

INTEGRATING FIELD WORK AND CLASSROOM LEARNING

You will realize early in your field work experience that the times when you feel that you are truly learning the most are the times when your field work experience and your classroom learning come together, complementing and supplementing each other. The greater the "fit" between school and field, the greater the potential for the achievement of true professional competence.

Your field instructor will, in all likelihood, have been provided a copy of the syllabus and/or course outline for at least your foundation practice course, if not for all of your courses. This will enable him or her to know what material is being covered, in what order, and using which readings. She or he will also be aware of any written assignments, examinations, or class presentations required for school. This is very important, because you will need your field instructor's assistance and cooperation in some of the work you will be doing in class.

The field office and your liaison will be aware of your learning contract's goals and objectives, and have an understanding of what you are working to accomplish in the field. Generally, however, your instructors' knowledge of your field experience will depend upon what you yourself will be sharing, either on an individual basis or in class, or both.

Because you are the only person who is both experiencing your field work placement and attending your specific classes, you are instrumental in assuring that the two come together in a way that is meaningful for you. You will be bringing some of your field experiences into the classroom, and taking some of your classroom learning back into the field. This chapter will offer some suggestions for careful and responsible sharing of information and experiences.

A. <u>Bringing the Field Into the Classroom</u>

Your field experiences will impact upon your learning in all of your courses. An agency policy will inform your perception of the government programs your will learn in Policy. Your work with Chinese immigrants will provide an authentic experience in Diversity or Multicultural Studies. Working with adolescents will illuminate your understanding of life transitions in Human Development. Your field work experiences will provide you with varied interesting and informative experiences to share with your classmates.

In this section, we will be focusing primarily on your Foundation Methods course, for this is most closely related to your work in the field. You will find that your caseload and your experiences with supervision, colleagues, community resources, and your agency will be an integral part of your own and your classmates' learning during your classroom instruction. You may be asked to present a case, describe your agency setting, or discuss a field visit experience as a part of your assigned work. Process recordings are often used to target specific skills and explore theory applications. You may also share an experience during classroom discussion.

Each of these offers you a valuable opportunity: a viewpoint of another, or others, who are not directly connected to your agency, field instructor, or clients. This permits a measure of objectivity which can be very helpful in considering problems or special issues. Class offers a safe and secure place for reconsideration of questions of special problems you may be encountering.

The suggestions offered here are also applicable to your Field Work Seminar, if this is an on-going class in your school's program.

Create a "Safe Space"

While creating a sense of safety and security within your practice classroom is primarily the responsibility of your instructor to initiate, the understanding and cooperation of each member of the class are necessary for the effective development of trust. Certain kinds of sensitive material frequently discussed in a practice class, such as a fellow student's case, a student's personal feelings or reactions to a problem encountered in the field, an agency problem, or a difficult situation with a field instructor or colleague, must remain within the class and not be discussed with other students, friends, colleagues, or family members.

Respecting your classmates' privacy will ensure the security of your own. This is a joint enterprise!

Respect and Honor Confidentiality

Information shared with you by your client, or available to you through your agency's records, must always be kept in strict confidence. Your client has entrusted you with personal material, even with his or her very identity. Extreme care should be taken when discussing clients in the classroom, or using client material for written assignments.

You should <u>always</u> disguise your client's identity by:

<u>Changing Your Client's Name:</u> This is more difficult than it seems at first. With the best of intentions, during a discussion, your client's real identity may accidentally slip out. While writing, and using an assumed name for seven pages, you may accidentally write the real name on the eighth. You should of course exercise extreme care in this regard; however, it is helpful to remember that, if you make a mistake, your fellow students and your instructor are professionals who will honor your client's privacy at all times, and respect the personal client material that you share.

> ** Some students find it easier to chose an "alias" that sounds like the real name, such as Mary for Molly. Some find that it works better to have a set of names you will <u>always</u> use for clients. Others prefer to use Ms. Y. or Mr. P., the "real" initial of a first or last name. This protects your client but avoids the extra mental step of changing something each time you mention a client. Choose any of these, or develop a system that works for you!*

<u>Changing Your Client's Description:</u> The change that you make should not be so extreme as to render your account of your client's problem or experience meaningless. You can

make clients a bit older or younger; locate them in a different neighborhood; or change their physical appearance, ethnic origin, family constellation, place or type of employment, interests, or skills. Just be sure that the changes that you make still preserve the uniqueness of the client in terms of what you are trying to present or communicate to your classmates!

Avoiding de Facto Identification: Keep in confidence any information which would de facto identify your client, even with a disguised name or description. This is particularly important if your client is a public figure.

Avoiding Specific References: Use generic descriptions of problems, situations, or experiences. "I have a client who . . ." can work well in many instances!

Share Experiences Only if They Contribute to the Class's Learning

You may desire to share with your class an experience which has involved your client, your field instructor, another student, or another professional. This is appropriate if you believe that this will be a worthwhile learning experience for the class as a whole. If your problem is unique to you, or if it contains material that you are uncertain you should share in the classroom forum, make an appointment with your instructor, and share it one-on-one first. Your instructor may be able to assist you in determining whether your experience would be instructive to the class.

> ** Be very cautious and respectful when presenting material involving your field instructor, your colleagues, fellow students, or your agency. This is the kind of material you might want to check with your instructor prior to presenting it to the class as a whole.*

It is important that material which relates to other professionals or to your agency be presented with care, respect, and consideration for the person or entity. Derogatory language or expressions, destructive criticism, and direct anger should have no part in your presentation, which should always be as professional as possible. Remember that there is often a rationale for the manner in which a colleague has acted, a policy is written, or an incident handled!

Respect the Iinput of Your Classmates — Even if You Don't Agree With It!

By sharing your experience, you are providing a learning experience for your classmates. Their reactions, ideas, and thoughts can give you a fresh insight into your problem or client which you may find very helpful. You will find, however, that you do not always agree with their suggestions or interpretation of events. Accept their ideas, discuss them to be sure you truly understand them, and consider them carefully at a later time.

Bringing a case or a problem situation to class, sharing it with your fellow students, eliciting and respecting their responses, views, and ideas, and processing them yourself for applicability and validity to you and your personal situation are beginning experiences in one of the kinds of supervision available to professional social workers:

peer supervision. Peer supervision in practice involves a group of social workers, usually three to six people, sharing client problems and issues together. This form of supervision provides an objective forum, a sharing of knowledge, theory, and experience, and also the support that workers often need to address difficult, stressful, and emotionally laden client issues.

Take Care Not to Dominate Classroom Discussions

You may have many interesting experiences, or difficult problems and situations in your field work placement that you would like to share. You truly believe that each of them will contribute to classroom learning and engender productive discussion and consideration. We each learn differently, however, in discussing another's experience, and in presenting our own. Your classmates need both kinds of experiences! In like manner, although you may feel that you have a useful contribution to a quantity of things being presented, be sure that you allow room for discussion by all members of your class.

Count the number of students in your class. Make sure that the number of times that you speak is approximately in proportion to the number of members of your class.

Written Assignments

When preparing a process recording or any other written assignment, care should always be taken to maintain your client's confidentiality. This is easier to do in writing than verbally, for you have an opportunity to review what you have written and fix any undisguised references.

If you are writing about colleagues, it is preferable to respect their privacy by not mentioning their name. Agencies are more difficult to disguise, and there is less concern over privacy and confidentiality, for they are public entities. Present information regarding your agency as accurately, fairly, and objectively as you can, and always include the agency's rationale for a policy, program, or procedure.

B. Bringing the Classroom Into the Field

You will have the opportunity to apply much of the material you learn in class during the process of your field work placement. You will best be able to utilize classroom learning if you make sure that you keep your field instructor up-to-date on what is happening in your Practice class. Field instructors generally are quite interested in what you are learning in class: they enjoy teaching, welcome your sharing of information, and want to share in your academic educational experience. Sharing what you have learned is essential if you are to maximize your educational opportunities, for your field instructor can adjust and tailor your field experience to "fit" with your classroom learning.

Your field instructor will be able to assist you by providing you with appropriate opportunities for practicing your classroom learning. He or she can select cases, provide problems, suggest issues to explore, and otherwise utilize all of the resources of your agency on behalf of your learning.

You will also have many opportunities to share your learning with colleagues and other professionals. Remember, you are in school: your learning is freshest, and most up-to-date. You can make a meaningful contribution to your field instructor and your agency by sharing some of your learning with them.

Applying Theories

You will be gaining much theoretical knowledge in your Foundation Practice class. Your caseload will provide an excellent place to explore the application of theory to actual cases and problems. For example, you have learned in school that a change anywhere in the client system will affect every part of the system. You can work with one of your clients to assess whether this really occurs, and how the change manifests itself throughout. You can chart, observe, and review changes in your client over the process of your interventions.

Practicing Skills

In school, you will learn some of the basic interview skills, such as using empathy, focusing, mirroring, and being authentic. Your learning will be intellectual: you will know how to do these things, but you lack any experience in actually doing them. Your caseload will offer you the opportunity to practice and sharpen your interviewing skills by allowing you to use them with a variety of clients and situations so that you develop the ability to adapt and be flexible while still utilizing professional techniques and skills.

Experiencing Social Work Processes

Your classroom learning will provide you with an understanding of the process of social work, which includes establishing a relationship, assessing a problem and potential avenues for resolving it, developing a plan for intervention and contracting, putting the plan in action and evaluating change and growth. Your contacts with clients will provide you with the experience of actually moving through the various processes, linking them together, and planning future work.

Contributing to In-Service Education

Many agencies will offer you the possibility of presenting at a staff meeting, case conference, or training session. The material that you prepare and present will contribute to the ongoing education process of your colleagues and other agency staff. You may present an article which addresses a new technique or special research related to your agency's focus, a policy that impacts your agency's clients or programs, or a new interpretation of a condition or problem. A popular subject for such presentations is the NASW Code of Ethics, an ethical dilemma, or a societal issue with ethical implications.

Sharing Learning with Your Field Instructor

Your field instructor may be eager to share some of your learning experiences as well. New research, new systems of delivery, the details of new government policies or programs will all be of interest to your field instructor. Managed care will affect each social work professional, and is affecting most already. Yet, many professionals struggling to function within the confines and limitations of managed care programs often do not have the opportunity to understand and reflect upon some of the wider social issues contained within the heated managed care debates. As you learn about these and other current issues in the classroom, you will be able to share information with your field instructor.

Evaluating, Defining, Describing Policy

You may well wonder how you can begin to assess and consider your agency's policies from your position as a student. However, many students are able to make meaningful contributions to their field work agencies in the area of policy. You will be exploring your agency's policies with a fresh perspective. You will be unimpeded by tradition, custom, or personal habit. You will, through classroom learning and discussions, be aware of alternative ways of addressing particular problems, concerns, or social issues. You will find that, over the course of your placement, you will have many opportunities to assist your agency to review and reconsider "the way things are done," possibly benefitting clients and colleagues alike.

This chapter has suggested ways to integrate classroom and field learning experiences to ensure that you obtain the best possible comprehensive educational experience. As you can see, in this process of integration, many other people will benefit as well: your classmates and instructor, your field instructor and agency colleagues, and, of course, your clients. Chapter 11 will explore another link between school and field: the role of your liaison.

CHAPTER ELEVEN

LIAISON VISITATION AND RELATIONSHIPS

In order to provide a system of linkage and feedback between the school's program and the field placement agency, the Field Work office assigns specially trained professionals to establish and maintain a close relationship between them. Difference programs use different terms to describe this function: liaisons, field consultants, and field work advisers. We will use the word "liaison" here as this appears to be the most common usage; though the name used at your school may be different, the function is the same.

Your field liaison is a vital link between your field work placement and your school's program. As was noted in Chapter 2, schools may use different methods and criteria for assigning field liaisons to students. Your liaison may be a faculty member who carries a number of students and placements in addition to teaching some classes, or a faculty member whose responsibility is exclusively to serve as field work liaison. Liaisons also often serve as instructors of field work seminars and/or field work orientations. He or she may be your Foundation Methods or Practice instructor, or your adviser. Liaisons may be professionals in the community who are interested in social work education and have chosen to serve in this capacity with your school.

Whatever system your school uses to assign liaisons, your liaison's function is clear from the name — "liaison" is French for link, or relationship. Liaisons are knowledgeable about school requirements in terms of field work learning, and they are also experienced in assessing and developing field placements to serve the needs of students.

Your liaison will be assigned to you around the time that you begin your field work placement, if not before. Liaisons often attend field instructor orientation programs and special training sessions to prepare them for the needs and problems they might encounter during their visits in the field. They are accountable generally to the Director of Field, although this too may vary somewhat according to the school's program.

Six roles and four functions have been identified as the liaison's responsibility.[1] The roles include:

1. Adviser: assisting students to plan for the field work experience
2. Monitor: assessing agencies, field instructors, and student learning
3. Consultant: assisting field instructors to develop skills and to understand the school's programs and policies
4. Teacher: serving as a role model and assisting the student to develop ways of integrating school and field learning
5. Mediator: assisting in the resolution of problems between field instructors and students, or between agencies and students
6. Advocate: advocating for students and presenting information to academic review committees

The four functions:

1. Field placement development: developing field placements, selecting field instructors
2. Linkage: providing and interpreting school policies and procedures to field placement agencies, and strengthening the tie between field and classroom learning
3. Evaluation: evaluating students, field instructors, and field placement agencies
4. Administration: oversees the completion and adequacy of forms related to field placement

A. Establishing a Relationship with Your Liaison

You may receive a note or a telephone call from your field liaison as your practicum begins, or your program may plan an opportunity for you to meet your liaison directly. If you have not heard from your liaison, it is important that you contact him or her so that you may begin to establish a relationship. If your liaison is at your school, you may wish to stop by during office hours as well.

During the early days and weeks of your placement, you may have questions regarding your role, supervision, caseloads, or other issues about which you feel unsure. Your liaison is available to assist you with any concerns you might have, either through individual consultation or through your field seminar. Your liaison may also "check in" several times with you and with your field instructor to make sure that everything is progressing as planned in your field placement.

B. Preparing for Your Liaison's Visit

Your liaison will visit your field placement according to your school's program schedule. Generally liaisons visit once a semester, around the middle of the semester. If there is a need or a problem, liaisons may visit earlier or more frequently. Some liaisons prefer to visit more frequently — you should not interpret frequency of visits as the sign of a problem, unless you have been told that one exists!

Generally, liaisons will contact field instructors to set up field visits at mutually convenient times. Sometimes, liaisons prefer to make the arrangements through the student, and you will be asked to coordinate date and time. The visit should not detract from your supervisory time, and both you and your field instructor should be available. It is useful to plan on an hour for your liaison's visit.

The structure of liaison visits varies widely — there is no one accepted format. Some liaisons prefer to see both you and your field instructor together. Some see you each separately, and some choose to see each of you separately and both of your together. Some ask direct questions, and some prefer to leave the content of the visit up to you and to your field instructor. Some ask to see your work — process recordings, charts, or other records, while some might ask you to talk about your caseload. Some will ask specific information about interviews and field visits, others prefer to get a general feel for what you are doing and learning.

This variation makes it difficult for you to plan carefully for your first liaison visit. It might be helpful to prepare some material ahead of time, and have it available if requested. In this way, you will feel ready for any questions or discussions that might occur during the visit.

You may want to gather:

- your caseload list
- your learning contract
- a sample supervisory agenda
- a sample of your work, such as a process recording or record documentation
- a typical week's schedule showing how your time is spent
- some thoughtful questions
- an example of school/field crossover learning

As your liaison may ask to see your work station, you may want to be sure that it is neat and orderly. You may also want to be sure that your recording and documentation is up-to-date and timely.

You and your field instructor may plan for your visit together, for your field instructor also will need to share information about material being covered, outside learning opportunities or field visits to other agencies, the rationale for cases assigned to you, and other information. Your field instructor may also plan to introduce your liaison to the agency's director, or the student training coordinator (if your field placement has one).

C. Your Role During Liaison Visitation

In most cases, your liaison will arrive at your agency and ask the receptionist for you and/or your field instructor, taking a seat in the waiting area with your agency's clients. He or she will observe the interactions, note the ambiance, and begin to form an impression of your field placement agency in the same way that you did.

Most students come to the waiting room to meet their liaisons, and escort them back to their own or their field instructor's office. Following this procedure will give you an opportunity for a few moments alone with your liaison. If you would like some time alone with her or him for any reason, this is a good moment to suggest this. To maintain your privacy and confidentiality, your liaison will generally then ask to see you alone as though he or she had initiated the request!

Your liaison will also want to see where you are working to ensure that you have adequate space and facilities. You may wish to do this en route, or wait until this is requested or suggested by your field instructor.

Visiting with Your Liaison and Field Instructor

You will probably escort your liaison to your field instructor's office for your meeting. Often, your liaison will begin by asking about your learning contract, and the objectives that you and your field instructor have set for your professional learning. He or she may suggest including others, or note that you have achieved several. Your liaison may ask you to tell about your favorite client, or your toughest situation, or the client you know best. Discussions about caseloads are lively and interesting to all three participants — and provide your liaison with a good understanding of what you are doing. You may also want to share with your liaison any visits you have made to other agencies or resources, and any seminars or special training you have received.

At some point, your liaison will probably initiate a discussion of supervision and ask both you and your field instructor for input and evaluation of the experience. He or she may ask about agendas, supervisory times, and the conditions of supervision. This is done to ensure that you are receiving the amount and quality of supervision that the school has determined is necessary for your learning.

Often, your field instructor will suggest that you share an experience or a case with the liaison. He or she is eager for you to show off your learning and make a good impression on your liaison, for, after all, what you have learned reflects well upon his or her teaching!

While your liaison is listening to your experiences and to the details of your work, he or she is also observing carefully the relationship between you and your field instructor. Do you seem to relate on a comfortable and friendly basis? Does your field instructor encourage and include you, or is he or she stiff and formal, excluding you from the conversation? Is the field instructor anxious about what you might say, or relaxed and comfortable? Does he or she always take the initiative and control the conversation, or is he or she able to let you, or the liaison, take the lead? Does the field instructor share some information about the agency and its overall functioning, or stay strictly with your field learning?

A very important part of the work of the liaison is to ensure that you and your field instructor are sharing a mutually beneficial and productive experience. When the liaison notes tension, anxiety, or discord, he or she may try to address the problem directly, or set up follow-up visits to ensure that any issues that impede your learning have been resolved.

When your liaison feels comfortable with what she has seen and observed, he or she may terminate the visit. The liaison may also initiate a request for alone time with you and/or your field instructor as a matter of routine, or based on previous agreements.

Alone with Your Liaison

You may be alone with your liaison during a part of his or her visit to your field placement agency. If you have any special concerns or requests, this is the time to discuss them. Liaisons are used to addressing routine problems during visits, and you can be comfortable with sharing feelings or concerns. Your liaison will keep your conversation confidential unless he or she has your permission to share it.

It is not unusual for minor problems to occur at some point during your practicum. When the early "honeymoon phase" of field placement ends, you may be confronted with conditions and situations that make you uncomfortable or uncertain. Some of the more common, easily resolvable problems include problems with caseloads, with supervisory times and conditions, with supervisor's personality and relationship style, and with schedules and workload. Your liaison will be able to assist you to negotiate some of these difficulties and resolve them so that they do not impede your learning.

D. The Field Instructor-Liaison Relationship

Your field instructor and your liaison also develop a working relationship during the process of your field work placement. Liaisons often contact field instructors to check on students' progress, and field instructors may contact liaisons to discuss concerns or problems they are experiencing with a student.

During your liaison's visit to your field placement, your field instructor or the liaison may request time alone to discuss your progress. This may feel very threatening — what are they talking about, you may wonder, that I cannot hear? Is there some problem? Am I not doing well?

Though it is difficult, try not to become upset if your liaison and field instructor meet without you. Many field instructors and liaisons feel that meeting alone is a necessary part of their work with you. They may have had this expectation before becoming involved with your placement, or with you personally. They may feel that meeting alone to discuss your progress is a part of their professional role. You should not interpret this request as an indication of a problem.

It is important to your education that your liaison and your field instructor develop a good working relationship, where each feels free to seek advice, request assistance, or air a concern. Field instructors often contact liaisons when they feel unsure of a school policy or procedure, or when they feel that extra school-field placement coordination or communication would be helpful. New field instructors often have questions, worries, and concerns that require input from the field liaison. Field instructors with several students may have a question or concern which does not relate to you at all.

It is in your best interest that your field instructor and your field liaison agree regarding your learning goals and needs, and that they work together to ensure that your field experience provides good learning opportunities in a supportive environment.

E. Maintaining a Direct Relationship with Your Field Liaison

You may find that you have little contact with your field liaison regarding your internship, apart from the liaison visitation. It is important, however, that you keep the lines of communication open, and that you establish the kind of relationship with your field liaison which will allow you to contact him or her instantly if a problem arises.

You have begun to establish a relationship during the first weeks of school, and have deepened it, perhaps, during your liaison's visit, which gave you both the opportunity to get to know each other face to face. In order to keep this valuable resource available to you, you might want to call and "check in" every few weeks or months, just to let your liaison know how you are doing.

If you develop and maintain an ongoing relationship, it will be much easier for you to contact your liaison if problems develop in your field placement. Laying the groundwork early, and keeping in touch, enables you to feel confident and comfortable in turning to your liaison for help.

Liaisons assess and evaluate your field work experience directly through visitation and discussion. However, your school's Field Office will also require periodic written evaluations of your work from your field instructor. Generally these occur at midsemester and at the end of a semester. The next chapter will assist you in preparing for this important part of your learning experience.

---

[1] Faria, G., Brownstein, C., & Smith, H.Y. (1988) A survey of field instructors' perceptions of the liaison role. Journal of Social Service Education 24(2): 135-144.

CHAPTER TWELVE

FIELD WORK EVALUATIONS

One of the most difficult processes in field work education is that of evaluating learning, and, where necessary, assigning a grade. Because each student is unique, and each field instructor/student relationship is unique, and each agency is different in its goals and programs and expectations, arriving at a set of objective criteria by which to measure student growth and learning is a major task.

The NASW Code of Ethics addresses evaluation responsibilities, requiring that "Social workers who function as educators or field instructors for students should evaluate students' performance in a manner that is fair and respectful" (NASW Code of Ethics 3.02b).

A. Your Grade in Field

Recognizing the problems inherent in evaluating students' field performance, most schools have developed a system which involves written reports and evaluations using objective measures, student self-evaluation, and opportunities for field instructors to write about their students using an open format. Additional input comes from the field liaison, who carefully documents visits, discussions, and problems noted. Field work seminar instruction provides another dimension for assessing field work learning.

Some schools require that all evaluation materials be sent to the Office of Field, which assumes the responsibility for grading using all material from all of the sources noted. Other schools expect that the field instructor will assign a grade. Still others ask the liaison in conjunction with the field instructor to arrive at a grade. Some assign a letter grade for field similar to that used to evaluate performance in academic coursework. Others believe that such objectivity does not lend itself to field work placement evaluation, and use a system of pass/fail for grading.

While grading tends to be stressful for students, the objective of evaluation in field is something much more important and meaningful than a grade: it is the careful, reasoned, reflective consideration of the student's progress toward professional competence. Indeed, periodic formal evaluations are used throughout a social worker's professional career, and are often the basis for granting raises and promotions, the "grades" workers receive in formal employment.

While the evaluation and grading process is a distinct and formal one, it is very rare that a student is unaware of the quality of her or his learning and progress throughout the course of the practicum. If there have been problems or areas which have required extra work and attention, these will have come up in the course of weekly supervision. Major problems would have involved the liaison and the field office as well. The process of evaluation thus is more a time for summation and review than a time for revelation and discovery.

B. The Evaluation Form: Your School's Criteria

Evaluations occur periodically during field work placements. Generally, there will be a mid-term evaluation (which may be brief) and a final evaluation each semester or quarter that you are in field. The schedule your school uses will be included in your field work calendar, so that you and your field instructor will have ample time to prepare. The calender date is the date which the evaluation form is due at your school. Therefore, your actual evaluation conference must be held prior to that date.

Your school will ensure that your field instructor has the required forms several weeks prior to the date that evaluations are due. These may have been included in a field instructor's handbook or manual prepared by your school, or may have been mailed to your field instructor. In some cases, you may be asked to take the evaluation form to him or her yourself. You should check with your field instructor at least two weeks prior to the due date of the evaluation form to ensure that he or she has a form.

Evaluation forms vary in content. Generally, there is a space for identifying information, an area which describes your caseload and assignments, and a checklist which your field instructor fills out. Often, this provides a method of ranking your achievements in a variety of areas. Careful review of the form will demonstrate that there are several areas of your work which will be evaluated. You will be evaluated on your knowledge: agency policies, goals and missions, cultural differences in the client population, theoretical knowledge of the social work processes and of human behavior are some of the items that may be included. You will also be evaluated on your skills and abilities, with items such as ability to engage with clients, to manage a caseload, to document appropriately, to use empathy, to be sensitive to cultural issues, and to comport yourself professionally. You may also be evaluated on your affective growth, with items such as personal insight, awareness of differences between your experiences and those of your clients, awareness of use of self, and responsibility to your agency.

Some programs will supplement these "checklist forms" with a section where the field instructor can write a description of your work, and any comments on your progress and ability which might not be covered sufficiently in the checklist. Field instructors may use these pages to elaborate on students' achievements and to suggest areas where future learning might be focused.

Your Field Instructor's Role

Your field instructor is responsible for filling out the form and for returning it to your school within the calender guidelines. Field instructors vary in the manner in which they approach the task of evaluation. Some instructors will fill out the form during a conference with you, and review each item, eliciting your input as well as providing their own. Some will have an evaluation conference, and then fill out the form independently. Others will fill out the form themselves, and then schedule an evaluation conference during which they will review the form's contents with the student.

Evaluation conferences are in themselves learning experiences. Your field instructor will share with you his or her appraisal of your work, and together you will discuss the distance you have traveled since the inception of your practicum. If there are items on the evaluation form that have not received the necessary attention, your field instructor may suggest that these be addressed in the future.

Your Role

Self-evaluation and self-monitoring are an integral part of social work practice. These occur routinely on a daily or weekly basis. Did I adequately demonstrate caring and empathy? Was I sensitive to my client's cultural beliefs? Did I locate the best possible resource? How does my dislike of this client manifest itself? What should I do about it? Is this plan truly best, or is it my favorite because I am most familiar with it? How can I manage my workload so that I never keep clients waiting?

These and many other questions are a kind of self-evaluation. There is another kind of self-evaluation that examines work over a longer range. How have I improved my listening skills? What have I done to increase my self-confidence on field visits? Can I demonstrate increased awareness of cultural life-cycle events? What special projects have I completed? This kind of evaluation presumes a starting point — the beginning of field, a new quarter or semester, a new year — and explores and evaluates change and growth.

In general, the first kind of self-evaluation and self-monitoring is a part of weekly supervision. The latter kind occurs less frequently, and assumes a longer range perspective. It is this second kind of evaluation that occurs during formal field work evaluations.

You should prepare yourself for formal evaluation by setting aside some time for self-reflection. You may need to do this outside of your field agency, for the requirements of your caseload and the pace of agency practice may not be optimal for the kind of reflection needed. Think about the school's criteria for assessment. Do you feel that you have met the expectations? Do you feel you are where you should be in terms of the school? What are your strongest points? What are the areas you might need to continue to develop?

Think about your field placement. Are the opportunities for learning being provided so that you can meet the school's criteria? Is the placement receptive to you as a student? Are exploration and creativity in approaches valued?

If you "discover" things in this process that had not occurred to you, write them down. You may want to share some of your insights with your field instructor at the time of your evaluation!

Your evaluation conference should be approached in a confident, professional manner. You should feel free to share your thinking and to expand upon, object to, or suggest different views on material that your field instructor discusses with you, so that together you may arrive at a good understanding of your progress as well as your future educational goals.

C. **The Learning Contract: Your Personal Criteria**

In Chapter 9, we presented the learning contract as a basic educational tool. Your learning contract presented your overall learning goals, and some of the objectives you wished to achieve. Unlike the school's evaluation form, your learning contract is unique to you, and is tailored to meet your personal educational needs. It takes into account your starting point — which may be different from that of your classmates, your learning style, your personal professional goals, and your special interests. Although you shared your learning contract with your liaison and with the Field Work Office, it remains a personal document.

Your field instructor assisted you to formulate your contract, provided input, and agreed with the goals and objectives you set. Thus, the contract also becomes a part of the evaluation process for field. Were you able to achieve your objectives? Which approaches worked for you, and which didn't? Did you set objectives which could not be achieved in the space and time allotted to them? How might you rephrase or restate your objectives?

Evaluation times include reviews of your learning contract and a discussion of your progress toward your personal learning goals. It is also often a time to revise your contract. Revising your contract will be discussed below, in Chapter 13.

D. Step One: Self-Evaluation

As noted above, you will need to prepare for your evaluation by spending some time in self-reflection and self-assessment. You may find it helpful to have a copy of the school's evaluation criteria and a copy of your learning contract with you. The former will provide you with some general objective guidelines to use in thinking about your learning. The latter will give you a blueprint of the personal goals you have set for yourself.

As you reflect, be kind to yourself. Remember, you cannot become a seasoned professional overnight! It takes years of training, and years of experience, to achieve a high level of competence. The task of your educational experience is to break down the concept of global professional competence into smaller, manageable pieces. As you progress, you will build upon these pieces, developing a structure that is both that of a professional and that of the special unique person that you are.

The school's criteria are the building blocks that are necessary at this stage of your educational experience. Those in your learning contract are the ones that you, with the help of your field instructor, believe are important to you. Review each one, remembering that each person reacts differently to different learning tasks. Are they meaningful to you? Have you progressed toward their achievement? Have you enjoyed and blossomed with some, and stumbled over others?

You may want to share some of your thoughts with your field instructor.

E. Step Two: Evaluation in Supervision

It's impossible to avoid a few butterflies in your stomach as you approach your evaluation conference. It's stressful to be evaluated, and some students may feel uncomfortable with the "judgement" feeling that comes with evaluation. Remember that your field instructor is familiar with this process, and identifies easily with your feelings. He or she was a student once too; and all social workers, as we have noted, are evaluated on a regular basis. Your field instructor will work hard to put you at ease, and to help you relax!

Your field instructor will probably take the lead in setting up a structure for your meeting. She or he may prefer to begin with general discussion, and proceed to more specific items. Some field instructors begin by asking the student to read the school's evaluation form, and then use that as a springboard for discussion.

Your evaluation will probably include areas which are not listed on the school evaluation form, but which are relevant to your placement, as well as the objectives and goals included in your learning contract. You and your field instructor may choose to revise your learning contract as a part of your evaluation conference, or to set aside time at a later date for this important task. You may find yourself discussing some of the problems and issues in your field placement agency, or some of the dynamics of your supervisory relationship. You should feel comfortable sharing your impressions with your field instructor.

Evaluation conferences generally last about an hour — the same amount of time as supervision. Good preparation (on both your parts) can help make this important part of your education a wonderful opportunity for growth.

F. Step Three: Reviewing Your Field Instructor's Written Evaluation

Whether your field instructor fills out the school's evaluation form with you, before your meeting, or after its completion, you will be given the form to read prior to its being sent to your school. Should you object to any item in the evaluation, you will have the opportunity to discuss your objection with your field instructor. If he or she agrees with your appraisal of your work, the form can be amended.

If it is not possible to reach an agreement, and you feel that an item has been evaluated unfairly, there is a space on the form where you may list any comments or objections. You may also attach a letter or comment sheet. Your own signature is a necessary part of the form's completion; this will ensure that you are aware of your field instructor's evaluation of your work.

When you have reviewed the form and are satisfied that it represents a fair evaluation of your learning, your instructor will send the form to your school.

G. Field Office Review

Your evaluation will become a part of your record in the field office. Field Office faculty and staff review each form, and assess the student's progress as reflected on it. The grade recommendations are reviewed, and students are cleared to move on to the next quarter or semester in field.

Where there are problems, or if you have attached an addendum to the form, the material is presented to the Director of Field or to a Field Advisory Board for review. Serious difficulties in field, though rare, may occur. In such instances, students are involved through conferences and discussions in planning for their future educational goals. If it is necessary for a student to repeat a field work placement, other parts of his or her curriculum, significantly practice classes, are also strongly impacted.

Field work evaluations often include a review of the learning contract. You may find that you review your learning contract more frequently than you use the school's evaluation forms. Reviews engender reflection and re-evaluation, and often revision of contracts. New objectives may be added, approaches changed, and specific skills integrated. Learning contract reviews are complex processes. Chapter 13 provides some suggestions for addressing this important learning assessment.

CHAPTER THIRTEEN

REVIEWING AND REVISING YOUR LEARNING CONTRACT

Your learning contract, as noted earlier, is your personal statement of your learning goals and objectives, and the methods, approaches, and tasks that you plan to utilize to achieve your objectives. A learning contract, however, is not cast in stone. Rather, it is a living, breathing, dynamic document that reflects your personal achievements, your aspirations, and your progress over the course of your internship. As you move through your field work placement, your learning contract moves with you. It demonstrates the completion of some objectives, the restatement of others, and the development of further, more advanced ones.

Don't keep your learning contract in a folder in the bottom of a drawer! Keep it close at hand, for it will serve as your personal guide as you move through your educational experiences in field work.

You should review your learning contract during your supervision conferences as often as necessary. The time for reviews is determined by the time frame you have stated in your objectives. If you have written:

> *"Familiarization with agency hierarchy and structure as demonstrated by ability to diagram structure in one month"*

you will need to go back to your learning contract in one month to see if you have achieved your objective. If you have written:

> *"Ability to initiate, structure, and hold two initial interviews as documented in client charts in three months"*

you will need to go back to the contract in three months to review this objective.

If you are in an academic-year-long placement, you may find that you need to review and revise your learning contract after one month, halfway through the semester (as part of your midsemester evaluation), and at the end of the semester (as part of your final evaluation). You may want to begin your second semester with another review to add new objectives and plans for the upcoming work. Schedule your reviews and revisions with your field instructor, who should always participate actively in your planning.

Your field liaison may ask to review your learning contract, as noted, during visits. He or she will also examine the contract to determine whether you have reviewed and revised it in a timely manner, and possibly offer suggestions for new objectives, new approaches, or an alternative way of measuring success. Some schools will request that a copy of your revised contract be sent to the field office on a regularly scheduled basis, as an additional measure of the work that you are doing in field.

A. <u>The Contract as an Ongoing Learning and Assessment Tool</u>

Review the sample contract that has been included in Chapter 7. You will note that, in addition to spaces for writing objectives and approaches, tasks, or methods, there is a final column entitled Evaluation. When you review your contract, you will place any notes, comments, or assessments relating to the objective under review into this column. This will serve as an on-going record.

Generally, it is best to group your objectives by time frame for ease of review. You may find that you have one or two one-month objectives. These might be familiarizing yourself with your agency, or learning about your agency's population. You may have one or two three-month objectives, such as one described above which addresses beginning interviews, or a skill objective such as using empathy or focusing skills. You may on occasion have objectives with a semester-long time frame. It is best to have shorter time frames: breaking your learning tasks down into smaller segments will make it easier to accurately assess achievement, and will keep you focused and motivated.

When the allotted time frame has passed, carefully re-read your objective and the approaches and methods you have specified for achieving it. Have you utilized the methods you have written? Which have been most successful in helping you toward your objective? Which have not been useful? Have you achieved the objective as you stated it, or have you achieved something similar, but not quite the statement you wrote?

When you wrote your learning contract, you went from general (your overall goals for your education) to more specific (your objectives) to most specific (your approaches, tasks, and methods). When it is time to review, you might want to reverse the process, looking first at the specifics, and then moving to the more general statements.

Thus, the approach
   "contact clients by telephone, and set up a time and place for interview"
is assessed before the objective of
   "ability to plan, structure, and hold an interview with a client"
which is assessed before the general goal of
   "assisting clients toward meaningful change in their life situations."

As you review your contract, you will find a real affirmation of growth and progress toward professional competence when you can say "Yes! I can do that now!" This will serve to reinforce the validity of the efforts you are making. It is very satisfying to be able to write "objective achieved" in the evaluation column, and to be able to cross off, or highlight, or otherwise note that this objective is attained and no longer needs your attention!

There will be times, however, when your review does not go so smoothly: you may find that you were unable to put your chosen approaches into practice, or that they didn't work as you thought they would. You may find that your objective, as you stated it, was not appropriate to your setting and to the experiences you are having there, or that you did not allot enough time to achieve it. Hopefully, these problems will not occur with great frequency as your field instructor will have provided some guidance from his or her broader knowledge of the opportunities you will have and the structure of the agency. However, sometimes, with the best of intentions, you may be unable to achieve your objective.

If this happens, don't be discouraged. It is not an infrequent problem, and not a very overwhelming one! You will need to assess the reason you were unable to achieve the plans you had set for yourself, and either restructure and redesign it or discard it as unattainable. Section C offers some suggestions and guidelines for addressing this type of problem.

B. <u>When a Learning Objective Is Achieved</u>

As you proceed through your field work placement, you will find that you are achieving many of the objectives you have set for yourself. The formal learning contract reviews will serve as confirmations of your progress.

As suggested above, you may want to begin with a quick read of your objective and then a careful study of the approaches, methods, and tasks you used. Evaluate each one. Which ones worked best? Which ones were easiest? Which ones did you enjoy the most? This reflection will assist you to understand the specific learning techniques that work best for you.

You may find that you learn well by reading, and that the books that you read about your population, or about public agencies, or about alcoholism really helped you in achieving your objective. Or, you may find that you learned a great deal by observation, and that shadowing your field instructor or another agency social worker helped you to understand your role and to prepare yourself for field visits, or for play therapy sessions, or for running meetings and focusing on change efforts. You may find that you seem to learn most successfully by doing, even if there was a measure of trial and error which might have been minimized by careful observation or reading.

You may also learn that you prefer to plunge right into the thick of things — planning and running meetings, doing outreach, visiting clients in the field, running groups. Or, you may find that you are more cautious about things — you want to observe, think, and reflect before beginning something new. That first interview may have occurred too soon, not soon enough, or just at the right time.

You may find that you work and learn best alone — reading and observing and reflecting and preparing yourself. Alternatively, you may find that other interns, or other social workers, help you. You may like the feeling of "everyone being in the same boat," and enjoy discussing your experiences, worries, and successes with others. On the other hand, you may be uncomfortable with the pressure that sometimes builds up when several people are trying to learn together.

Another place to explore is the way in which your field instructor interfaces with your learning. Do you like close supervision, and a great deal of support? Do you prefer to have your field instructor very involved with your projects and learning? Or do you find that stifling and need room to grow independently?

This reflective review of your approaches will be invaluable to you in helping you to plan your future learning goals, objectives, and approaches. You will find that if you select methods that work best for you, you will have a much higher degree of success, and enjoy yourself as well in the process!

An objective that has been achieved was generally written in a manner that enabled its achievement. The time frame was estimated properly, and the method used to measure success worked well. The approaches and tasks selected were appropriate to the objective.

When an objective is achieved, notation is made in the evaluation column which includes your reactions, and what worked best in helping you to succeed. Then you will need to indicate its completion in some clear manner. You may want to draw a line through it, highlight it, or, if you have placed each objective on a separate page, place it in the back or in another section of your learning contract.

Do not discard achieved objectives pages: they will serve as an important record of your overall progress in field work. You may want to review these achieved objectives as you prepare for your final evaluation, or as you write your reports upon termination of your field work placement.

C. When a Learning Objective Is Not Achieved

Objectives which are not achieved within the allotted time frame offer special opportunities for learning. You can learn from examining problems on two levels: in terms of yourself and your own learning, and in terms of gaining additional insight into some of your clients' experiences.

You will learn a great deal about yourself. You may find, for example, that you did not break your task into small enough pieces, creating an objective too broad and global for accomplishment. You may find that you did not allot enough time. You may discover that you <u>have</u> achieved the objective, but that the measure of success you selected was not appropriate. These problems all reflect difficulties in the manner in which you framed your objective statement. On the other hand, you may find that the approaches and methods that you selected did not work well for you in achieving your objective.

Most objectives can also be revised and rewritten to enable their successful completion. The first step is to determine the problem which has kept the objective from being achieved. When that is established, you may revise, rewrite, reframe, or restate your objective and keep it on the learning contract. Some objectives cannot be achieved successfully, often due to causes beyond the control of a student. If this is the case, discard the objective and substitute another! There may be several different kinds of problems with objectives.

Problems with Framing Objectives

Some of the most common causes of failure to meet an objective are due to the way in which the statement itself is framed. There are three principal areas of difficulty: problems with the objective statement, problems with the time frame, and problems with the criteria used to determine success or failure.

A few actual examples may help in understanding the kinds of difficulties which may occur.

Objective Statements

Problems related to the <u>objective statement</u> might include:
"Establish an ongoing trusting relationship with clients as demonstrated by documentation on three clients' charts in three months."
The time frame and the achievement measure are quite appropriate. However, this student was placed in a hospital clinic where clients were seen one time only before being referred to outside agencies. Her objectives needed to be focused on short-term crisis intervention skills, and on learning community networks!

Another example:
"Facility in establishing relationships with alcoholic clients as demonstrated by three to four return visits in three months."

Again, a good objective. Working with alcoholics was a special interest of this student, and she had requested a field placement in an agency serving alcoholics. However, she had been placed in an agency serving dually diagnosed clients, most with a severe mental illness. There were few alcoholics, as these were served primarily in another agency. Her objective could not be easily attained in her current setting.

Another student wrote an objective:

"Proficiency in running a task group as demonstrated by leadership and documentation of three consecutive sessions in three months."

His agency had a number of task groups going, and he was eager to get involved and assume a leadership role. However, all of the task groups had leaders at the time, and were in the middle of special projects. He could look forward to assisting the current leaders, but new task groups with new leaders were not going to be formed for several months. He wouldn't have an opportunity to lead such a group until the second semester of his placement. Other objectives that might have been more appropriate: learning the structure of the organization, learning the task group process, assisting in documentation, or chairing a subcommittee of a task group.

Time Frames

Objectives are sometimes not achieved due to problems with time frames. An example of these kinds of objective problems:

"Diagnostic ability as demonstrated by accurately diagnosing five clients using DSM IV in one month."

An excellent objective — but in one month? Unless this student was completely knowledgeable about the DSM IV, one month was much too brief a time to acquire that kind of expertise!

Another example, written on a student's initial learning contract:

"Ability to complete a psychosocial assessment of a client as demonstrated by the written assessment in one month."

Again, an excellent objective. However, as this was written during the first weeks of placement, before any clients were even assigned, the time frame was unrealistic. It is best not to formulate such an objective until clients are assigned, and initial assessments are in progress!

And a third example:

"Familiarity with community resources as evidenced by records of ten visits to outside social agencies in one month."

A wonderfully worthwhile and ambitious project! But this student was in her placement eight hours a week — approximately thirty-two hours over the period of a month. To achieve her goal within her month time frame, she would have to visit two or three agencies every day that she was in field. Even if she could do this — if the agencies were nearby and if she could successfully schedule all the appointments, she would not have any time for clients, meetings, supervision, or any other learning!

Measurement Criteria

A third kind of problem with objectives involves the criteria used for measurement of success or failure. The criteria must be measurable, and must relate directly to the objective. Sometimes finding appropriate criteria is very difficult, and it is easy to choose criteria that may be relevant, but not measurable, or vice versa — measurable but not relevant.

An example of a measurable but not relevant objective:

"Ability to use empathy appropriately during interviews as demonstrated by ability to sustain client contacts over four interviews."

The criterion this student selected is clearly measurable — you can examine records or appointment sheets to determine if a client has been seen four times. However, there may be a multitude of reasons for clients to continue to receive services which are not related to empathy at all, such as need for concrete service, legal requirements in the care of mandated clients or clients on probation, inability to terminate services, such as clients in institutions or nursing homes, or dependency. Clients may also choose to continue services for reasons other than the worker's ability to be empathic. The criterion chosen by this student is more appropriate to the measurement of client retention than of the successful use of empathy.

The opposite, criteria that are relevant but not measurable, can also occur. Another student, also concerned with learning to use empathy, develops a learning objective of:

"Ability to use empathy appropriately as evidenced by successful interviews with three clients in one month."

This kind of statement is especially confusing, because it appears measurable: after all, it specifies the number of clients and numbers are quite measurable. And empathy used will usually lead to successful interviews. The difficulty, however, lies in use of the word "success." What does the student mean by "success?" How would the field instructor interpret it? The liaison? Is the student's assurance of "success" enough of a measure?

It might be helpful to think about how something like "empathy" can be measured. We would need to know about the student's empathic responses in some objective manner.

A statement like this one might give us the information that we need:

"Ability to use empathy appropriately as demonstrated in five instances recorded in process recordings of three client interviews in one month."

This kind of criterion is relevant — it examines actual statements made by students during interviews, which have been presented in written form. It is also measurable — it asks for five examples of use of empathy in each of three separate interviews. Such a statement tests actual performance in a concrete and specific manner.

Problems with Approaches, Interventions, Methods, or Tasks

Even if you are very careful in framing your objective statement and use appropriate timing and relevant and measurable criteria, you may encounter problems in meeting objectives which are due to the methodology you have selected. Careful review of your approaches can assist you in determining if these caused you not to achieve your objective.

If your objective is the one stated above:

"Ability to use empathy appropriately as demonstrated in five instances on process recordings of interviews with three clients in one month."

your approaches *must* include:

- having interviews
- making process recordings
- assessing process recordings
- reviewing empathy responses with your field instructor

as a minimum. If you do not have three interviews, for example, you cannot meet your objective. Similarly, if you do not do any process recording, you cannot meet your objective. Assessment and review will validate your objective and ensure you have reflected and learned from your experiences.

If your objective is:

"Ability to work with a focus group in a leadership capacity to arrive at a plan as demonstrated by written plan approved by group members in three months"

you will need as part of your methodology such approaches as:

- assembling a goal-oriented focus group
- assuming leadership of the group
- assisting the group to explore a problem
- assisting the group to explore options
- assisting the group to formulate a plan
- preparing the formulated plan in written form and submit to group
- obtaining group approval of plan

If you skip the group process, and just write the plan yourself, you will not be meeting your objective. If you meet with the group and work with them, but do not write a plan and submit it to them, you will not be meeting your objective.

Another example, from child welfare:

"Ability to plan and effect the return of one foster child to a mother as demonstrated by the child's return to live in the maternal home in six months (more time is allowed as this is a complex process)."

Your approaches might include:

- Read laws and government policies regarding children removed from their homes
- Read agency standards and procedures for planning a child's return to his or her family
- Discuss criteria with field instructor to ensure understanding and to make a preliminary plan
- Meet with child's mother weekly until the child is ready to be returned
- Formulate a contract and plan with her for organizing her home, finding employment
- Discuss plan with child, and with foster family
- Document plan and progress in client's chart
- Assess progress with the mother by reviewing her contract

and so on. Each of these steps is necessary to the successful achievement of the objective.

Just as every objective is formulated somewhat differently, using your own words and your own priorities, so some of the approaches that can be used to meet the objective will also be tailored to your specific needs. If you already know all of the relevant policies about returning children to their parents, as in the example cited above, you may not need that approach. Some of the others on the list, however, are always necessary.

Always make sure that your approaches are relevant to your objective. Some approaches which sound worthwhile but which do not relate to the objective above:

- Explore agency criteria for foster parenthood
- Diagram agency structure and hierarchy
- Plan and execute an in-service on contracting with parents and children

If your objective has not been achieved, review all of the approaches and methods you have used to meet it, and ensure that they relate closely to the objective!

Problems with Unattainable Objectives

There may also be instances where you have selected an objective that is not attainable either because of agency structure and policy, your skill or knowledge level, the time available, or other reasons.

Before determining that an objective is not attainable, it is wise to explore all of the possible reasons for difficulty described above. If none of them applies, you may have an unattainable objective.

Sometimes the objective is not attainable due to problems in your field placement agency. A objective that may be unattainable for this reason is:

"Familiarity with agency policy as evidenced by completion of reading of policy manual and mission statement in one month."

Simple? Yes, and no, for you have little control over this objective's achievement. Many are the students who, following suggestions of their practice instructor, adviser, liaison, or field work seminar instructor, innocently wrote an early objective like this one only to find that no one knows where the mission statement is, or even if there is one. Alternatively, they may find that the policy manual is in a locked office and the only person who has the key is on leave of absence for six months in another state. You may be unable to reach this objective, through no fault of your own!

Another example:

"Ability to work with ongoing clients as demonstrated by carrying five clients seen weekly on caseload for three months."

Possible? Certainly. However, the student who wrote this objective found that his agency was in a very slow period, and new clients were relatively few. Because clients generally kept their same worker throughout their period of service, which was twelve sessions, there were no clients that the student could work with on a transfer basis. It took this student a month to get one client, and three months to get two. He was unable to achieve his objective as he had stated it.

Another example:

"Experience in leading a focus group which explores restructuring outreach services as demonstrated by documentation of group process weekly for six weeks."

This is a wonderful objective. However, the agency in which the student was placed had already explored restructuring and agreed upon a plan. They were addressing implementation, not exploration!

Difficulties in Skill or Knowledge Attainment

Sometimes, of course, objectives are not met because a student may not have achieved the skill of knowledge level requisite. In this instance, student and field instructor together should examine the objective. Can the time frame be expanded? Are the criteria too rigid for the student's educational level? Can the objective be broken down into smaller pieces so that interim stages can allow for success? Careful rephrasing often enables successful completion!

D. <u>Adding New Objectives</u>

As you review your learning contract, cross off some objectives as completed, and perhaps discard others that cannot be completed, the number of objectives left current will of course decrease. This is the time to add objectives.

As you progress through the course of your field placement, you will notice that the objectives that you select are more difficult, more complex, and require skills and techniques you have learned successfully from older completed objectives. Objectives are like building blocks: you begin with a basic, but strong, foundation. You build upward upon it, taking care to keep the building blocks aligned and balanced.

You should keep your learning contract to around five objectives. Too many water down your focus, distract you and render problems more likely. Too few give you fewer options for those times when you cannot move ahead with one of the chosen objectives. Add new objectives to retain the optimal number for your learning.

You may want to refer to Chapter 9, Developing a Learning Contract, to refresh your skills in writing new objectives, tasks, and approaches.

* Remember that there are many parallels between your experiences with your learning contract, and your clients' experiences with their contracts with your agency and with you. The same kinds of success increase motivation, and the same problems can generate disappointment and discouragement. Keep in touch with your feelings during the process of reviewing and revising your learning contract. You will learn much that will be helpful to you in your work.

UNIT SUMMARY

This Unit has provided suggestions and guidelines for special events and circumstances that occur on a routine basis throughout the course of your placement in order to assist you to maximize all of the learning opportunities your placement offers.

Chapter 9 presented one of the most important tasks of your field work experience: your learning contract. The sample form included may appear different than that used by your program, but will include many of the same concepts and expectations. Preparing a learning contract requires a great deal of thought and reflection.

Earlier, we discussed the various components of your field work education, and stressed the fact that all of the pieces fit together like a puzzle to form a whole which is your professional competence. Chapter 10 offered suggestions for integrating your learning by bringing classroom learning into your practicum, and bringing your experiences in practicum to class to share with your classmates and instructor.

Your liaison represents your school's Field Office in your agency. Chapter 12 addressed your relationship with your liaison, and prepared you for agency visitation. This is a special time to review and assess your learning, present your clients and your work, and work with your field instructor to ensure that the school has an accurate picture of your practicum experience. This chapter also suggested keeping in touch with your liaison over the course of the year so that the school is well aware of the details of your placement experience.

Grading and evaluation comprise a complex and sometimes difficult process in field. You can decrease your stress and anxiety by careful preparation for your evaluation conferences and for reading your written evaluation. Chapter 12 assisted you to review some of the methods that will be used to assess your progress.

The final chapter in this Unit addressed the review and revision of your learning contract, providing examples of objectives and illustrating some possible reasons for any problems you may encounter in meeting them. Suggestions for rewording, reframing, or disposing of unattainable objectives were also included. When objectives are achieved, new ones, more advanced perhaps and more complex, can take their places. Your learning contract remains as your careful documentation of your achievement in field work of the personal goals you have set for yourself for your learning.

This Unit has addressed some of the experiences and procedures you will encounter as you move through your field placement. Unit Four will bring us to the final weeks and days of practicum, and to the primary tasks of this stage of your learning: termination. Terminating with clients, often a complex, difficult, and emotion-laden process, will be discussed in Chapter 14. You will also, however, be terminating with your field instructor, and moving through the final assessment and evaluation of your field work experience as a whole. These final processes, which are important in affirming your progress and learning, will be discussed in Chapter 15, while Chapter 16 offers some suggestions for reflecting upon and relating to your field work experience after it has been formally completed.

UNIT FOUR

WHEN FIELD PLACEMENT ENDS

Carol Bisman introduces the subject of termination with a consideration of loss.

> Loss is part of life. One cannot live without experiencing loss — loss of capacities in aging or through an accident or illness, loss of friends and relatives through death or geographic separation, loss of pets by death or disappearance, loss of familiar patterns and habits through deliberate change . . . or through growth into another life stage of developmental phase. Loss is a part of living, growing, and changing.[1]

There is a sense in which the end of field work placement is built into the beginning. You, your field instructor, your colleagues at the agency, and your clients all know that you will be with them for a period of time only, and that this is not a permanent position.

You are aware of endings as you write your learning contract, with its time frames that cannot be extended beyond a certain date. You are aware each time you must tell a client, a group, or a community gathering that you are an intern, placed at your agency for a specific amount of time. You are aware each time you feel the pressure to accomplish your goals for yourself and for your clients.

There is a deeper level of awareness, and often a complex of emotions, that begins as you enter the last few weeks of your placement: a bitter sweetness that is always a part of ending. You are sad to be leaving your colleagues, your clients, the agency itself within which you learned and grew over the course of months. Yet, there is also a sense of accomplishment: you have completed the tasks you have set for yourself (for the most part); you have demonstrated readiness to move ahead with your education, or to graduate. You are ready to move on to the next stage of professional development.

Your field work experience stands apart as a special time in your life. It may have been a wonderful time; chances are, however, that there were a few rocky moments, a few difficult challenges, and a few problems encountered en route. These blend into the whole, and will become part of the memory of internship days for years to come.

Clients may have known you were leaving in an abstract sense, but now you must begin to address formally terminating your relationship, and planning for what will happen when you are no longer their social worker. There is a mutual loss involved, for most students become attached to one or several clients and regret leaving them. You must prepare not only your client for the separation to come, but yourself as well. Terminating with clients will be discussed in Chapter 14.

A part of the formal ending of your field work experience involves a final assessment and evaluation, a time for reflecting and for pulling together all of the threads you have woven into your new professional self, ensuring that what emerges has a clear pattern, and a clear form. Unlike earlier reviews and evaluations, the final evaluation asks <u>you</u> to evaluate as well: to evaluate your field instructor, to evaluate your agency as a field placement for your school, and to evaluate the work of your liaison. Suggestions for preparing for this final evaluation process are presented in Chapter 15.

The last day comes, perhaps with a farewell lunch, or agency gathering, or a final visit with your field instructor. You formally leave the agency and sever all ties. What becomes of your relationship with this world, which had been so central to your learning for so long? You may want to keep in touch with your field instructor, your colleagues. You may even want to keep in touch with your clients. Your relationship to the agency after termination is discussed in Chapter 16, and suggestions are offered which include relevant portions of the Code of Ethics.

This Unit has been organized to reflect the probable sequence of events in your termination process. Generally, students terminate with clients first, then field instructors and colleagues, as part of separating from the agency as a whole. While the final day of field marks the end of the student's actual commitment to the practicum, the process of reflection, the integration of learning, and the mental and emotional separation process generally extends well beyond that last day.

CHAPTER FOURTEEN

TERMINATING WITH CLIENTS

One of the most difficult tasks of ending your field placement is separating from clients. There is a special tie that holds students and clients together. Both have worked to learn, to grow, to adapt, to change, to face new challenges. Both have developed new skills, perhaps in understanding others, perhaps in trusting. Though one person was officially "in charge," the learning process helps to equalize the relationship in the minds and hearts of both student and client. In learning the professional use of self, you may have shared too much, bent rules at times, encouraged dependency, made mistakes (even terrible ones), gone far above and beyond expectations of service. These things, a natural part of learning, also create a special closeness.

"Since social work addresses people in their social context, loss is also one of the recurring themes in the social work relationship," Bisman states.[2] Whether the loss is due to a move, a divorce, a child leaving home, an illness or death, a change in patterns of behaving, or any of a thousand other possibilities, the feelings and effects surrounding loss are never far from the content of our work.

There are several portions of the NASW Code of Ethics which deal with termination with clients:

Section 2F9: The social worker should terminate service to clients, and professional relationships with them, when such service and such relationships are no longer required or no longer serve the clients' needs or interests.

Section 2F10: The social worker should withdraw services precipitously only under unusual circumstances, giving careful consideration to all factors in the situation and taking care to minimize possible adverse effects.

Section 2F11: The social worker who anticipates the termination of interruption of service to clients should notify clients promptly and seek the transfer, referral or continuation of service in relation to the clients' needs and preferences (NASW Code of Ethics).

You and your field instructor will probably initiate plans for terminating with your clients several weeks prior to your termination date. You will discuss each client in depth, and arrive at the best possible plan: the one that causes least disruption to the client's well-being. As you prepare yourself in supervisory meetings, you will begin to realize that separation and termination from clients, like other parts of the social work relationship, are a process with carefully defined components which provide the structure that will support you and your clients through the last interview.

You may have already experienced terminating with clients during the course of your placement. There are several reasons that the client-worker relationship may end: departure of the worker is only one of the possibilities.

There are five different kinds of terminations:

1. Premature, unilateral terminations by clients.
2. Planned termination determined by temporal constraints associated with an agency's function.
3. Planned termination associated with time-limited modalities.
4. Planned terminations involving open-ended modalities.
5. Termination precipitated by the departure of a practitioner.[3]

You may already have experienced several of these. You may have seen a client once, only to find that the client misses the next appointment and never returns. You may have worked on a project with a group of community members, and worked with the group to assess the project and to dissolve. You may be placed in a family agency with an 8-interview limit, and have planned terminations with families. You also may have had a mandated client for six months and arrived with your client at a point of planned termination as your work was completed and probation ended.

All of these experiences in terminating with clients will assist you in preparing for termination at the conclusion of your field placement. However, what makes these final terminations different is that:

•   They are all happening at once.
•   You are terminating with your field instructor and your colleagues at the same time.
•   You are also terminating with your agency itself.

It is important to remember that your first concern must be the well-being of each client.

The NASW Code of Ethics addresses termination of services to clients in Section 1.16. This section provides ethical guidance as you read this chapter and plan termination.

1.16 Termination of Services

(a) Social workers should terminate services to clients and professional relationships with them when such services and relationships are no longer required or no longer serve the clients' needs or interests.

(b) Social workers should take reasonable steps to avoid abandoning clients who are still in need of services. Social workers should withdraw services precipitously only under unusual circumstances, giving careful consideration to all factors in the situation and taking care to minimize possible adverse effects. Social workers should assist in making appropriate arrangements for continuation of services when necessary.

(c) Social workers in fee-for-service settings may terminate services to clients who are not paying an overdue balance if the financial contractual agreements have been made clear to the client, if the client does not pose an imminent danger to self or others, and if the clinical and other consequences of the current non-payment have been addressed and discussed with the client.

(d) Social workers should not terminate services to pursue a social, financial, or sexual relationship with a client.

(e) Social workers who anticipate the termination or interruption of services to clients should notify clients promptly and seek the transfer, referral, of continuation of services in relation to the clients' needs and preferences.

(f) Social workers who are leaving an employment setting should inform clients of appropriate options for the continuation of services and of the benefits and risks of the options.[4]

It is also essential that you be culturally sensitive and aware in planning termination with and for clients. Different cultures view endings differently, and termination can be perceived as a personal abandonment or rejection on the part of the worker. There may be difficulty in sharing or acknowledging reactions to termination. Clients may feel a sense of shame or embarrassment in having to reveal private information to another person. Clients unfamiliar with the workings of social agencies may misinterpret your termination and believe that all services from the agency are being terminated as well. Language barriers may also impede the termination process. (Individual clients may also have these reactions: they are not necessarily always culturally based. It is important to separate the two so that you can assist your client appropriately.)

Lum suggests viewing termination through two frameworks, particularly adapted to working with minority ethnic populations, but applicable to all clients as well. He calls the first phase "termination as recital," and kind of "review and playback" during which clients can recite the story of their experience and of the events that have occurred during the helping process. The second phase is "termination as completion," an assessment of the changes that have occurred, and the manner in which they occurred. Lum also stresses the importance of re-connecting clients with their ethnic-community networks, particularly kinship networks, neighborhood networks, and religious organizations. He states that these can serve to lessen the sense of abandonment and rejection that ethnic clients experience.[5]

A. Reactions to Termination

Clients are often vulnerable and have experienced many losses, and you must assist them to recognize and address their reactions to termination. Because introducing the subject of ending is difficult for you, you may find yourself postponing it from week to week, even though you know that this is an issue which will not resolve itself without your care and attention. While there may be some variation to the timing of introducing the subject of termination, variations should be grounded securely in client well-being rather than your (often natural) desire to avoid this difficult and painful subject. Postponing the discussion of termination will impede the client's ability to work through the experience, because there will be insufficient time to address feelings fully.

Client Reactions

"Most clients . . . .experience positive emotions in termination. Benefits of the gains achieved far outweigh (author's emphasis) the impact of the loss of the helping relationship."[6]
Clients feel a sense of achievement, an awareness of their strengths and eagerness to be "on their own." There is a confidence that comes from the successful completion of an

often difficult change process. Clients look forward to the additional free time in their lives, and may also value the income now freed for other uses.[7]

However, some clients experience negative reactions, and express them by excessive dependency, clinging to the worker and declaring an inability to function without continued help. Clients may bring in new problems, begging for assistance in addressing them. Others, fearful that the changes and progress made are not sufficient, will experience old symptoms and problems once again, requesting additional time to address them. Still others may be angry, frustrated, sad, or may withdraw from your carefully built helping relationship. If you are working with groups, extra time needs to be allotted to process termination, for members may have differing reactions that need to be discussed and resolved. If you are working with a community problem, and were spearheading a new project or development plan, you may find a loss in interest level and motivation. You may have been the central point around which community members gathered. When you introduce termination, they may feel helpless to continue to put plans into effect without your expertise and enthusiasm.

Whether your field placement was with individual, families, groups, organizations, or communities, your field placement was with people. Each person involved will need to work through the separation process and their individual reactions to your leaving.

It is difficult for students to remain objective in the face of such reactions. After all, we all have chosen to be social workers because we like to help others. Here are clients who "need" us. How can we leave them?

Student Reactions

Your reactions may parallel and mirror those of your clients. It is very important for you to be aware of the potential effects of clients' reactions so that you may prepare to assist the client as needed, and/or to let go comfortably.

As a profession, we all have a bit of the "savior complex." We may sometimes feel that our clients need us in order to be able to grow and function. We often instinctively welcome and foster their dependency. We look for client weaknesses, instead of recognizing client strengths even though we are very well aware that this is not helpful to our mutual task.

Self-awareness is essential! If we know we have this tendency, we can work to minimize its effect on our clients. During the process of termination, when many feelings are stirred up and emotions are close to the surface for both you and your client, it is even more essential to be aware of your own reactions.

If your client is pleased with termination, and has a positive reaction, you may feel unappreciated and unrecognized. "After all my hard work," you might think, "she just says goodby with a big smile and doesn't even care!" Or, "She doesn't even see how much she needs me. She thinks she can do it all herself, but I know she can't." You may even find yourself waiting for something to happen, to "prove" that the client really needs your services!

If your client has a negative reaction, you may also experience strong feelings. Students, and indeed all practitioners, sometimes feel guilty when they initiate termination, believing that they are "abandoning" a client who is in need of them. You may also experience a kind of co-dependency with your client — you have helped your client to grow and change, after all, and you too have grown and changed in the process. You need your client to need you, to feel dependent upon you, in order to validate all of the professional skills you have gained.

You need to work through your reactions to terminating with clients in supervision, and to monitor yourself so that you remain aware of your own emotional reactions to your client's reactions to termination. Good preparation will lessen any detrimental effects on your client.

When you and your client have worked through some of the stronger emotional reactions to termination, you can more the process forward to the next stage — evaluation of the service experience.

B. Preparation, Review, and Evaluation

In Unit Three, we discussed some of the important functions and tasks of evaluation, noting that there is a self-evaluation process, and then a process that occurs with your field instructor. Evaluation assists you to consolidate gains, assess progress, and determine directions for the future. Evaluation answers that all-important question: "Did the intervention achieve its purpose?"

Reviewing the work that you have done together and undertaking a process of evaluation performs similar functions in your work with groups, clients, and communities. Mutual discussion enables each member of the relationship to explore and assess both any growth, change, or progress, and the process of being helped itself. Some settings will also ask clients to evaluate your role using a form prepared by the agency.

An excellent tool to use during the evaluation process is your client's contract with you. The goals and tasks included provide a good focus for a discussion of outcomes. You may also use any baseline measures, referral reports, consultant evaluations, or initial assessments. Evaluation should focus on client goals, strengths, and positive achievements, while not ignoring possible disappointments and negative outcomes.

It is important that both you and your client prepare for evaluation. You might want to introduce the subject in a prior interview, and suggest that your client think about the work and the relationship, what has been achieved, and what work will continue in the future. You can introduce the idea of evaluation simply when you have worked through some of the emotional reactions by saying "Next week we'll be focusing on how this experience was for you. You may want to think about the way you were feeling when we began our work together, and some of the things that have happened since then. I'll be doing that too, and together we can see what has been accomplished and plan for what comes next."

You do not want to create additional anxiety and stress for your client, so it is important to present the evaluation not as a test of some kind but rather as a pulling together of your mutual thinking about what has been achieved.

Your role is to review your client's chart, to think about your work together and your relationship process, and to jot down notes if needed to help you remember the points you want to stress during your meeting.

C. Terminating Agency Services

The process of termination and evaluation is especially meaningful for clients who will be terminating their formal services from your field placement agency at the time that your internship ends, either because they have achieved the growth and change they wanted, or because it has been determined that no progress is possible. In addition to separating from you, these clients are also separating from the agency which has stood behind your joint efforts, and provided the resources necessary for your work. This can be a very positive process — and an integral part of the whole experience of receiving service. Even clients who are terminating because no progress is possible can benefit greatly from a careful and well-planned termination.

It is important that you build in supports and reinforcement plans to assist clients to function independently, to maintain the gains they have achieved, and to provide a source of assistance should it be needed in the future. Natural networks (family, friends) should be supplemented by community networks. Assisting your client toward utilizing community networks to meet needs is an important part of termination. These might include social groups, support groups, school or work, a person to contact in an emergency, and a plan for getting help if needed. Supports will assist your client to maintain gains made, resist outside pressures, and feel confident in functioning independently.

If your client is terminating because of an inability to use the agency's services or to work toward change, you can still assist him or her by providing alternative resources, or a way of returning to the agency for help should this be needed.

Often you may choose to terminate gradually, spacing the time between visits more distantly. This provides clients with an opportunity to "test" their independent functioning and recognize their ability to continue without services. After you have terminated completely, you may also want to arrange for follow-up calls to monitor your client after termination. These can be provided by your field instructor or by an agency representative.

D. Transferring Clients to Another Worker

There are many settings where clients receive services over an extended period of time, such as foster care, senior citizens services, services to the chronically mentally ill, case management services, probation and parole, and services to people in institutions such as prisons and mental hospitals.

It is important to be aware that there may be a whole different set of feelings engendered in both you and your client when termination with you means transfer to another worker.

Client Reactions

Your client may show some resistance to transferring to another worker. After all, you have, hopefully, built a good relationship over a period of time. Your client has grown to trust you, and has shared many confidences with you. He/she/they may feel that transfer means starting all over again.

Some clients, when confronted with the need to transfer to another worker, withdraw, or express a desire to terminate services all together. Clients who routinely are confronted with new workers may either passively accept what is occurring, or express anger and resentment at "the system" which creates this need.

Many field placements take new students annually. Long-term clients of such agencies may have become habituated to the seemingly endless turnover of students on schedule every December or May. Because the agency maintains a caseload for students, clients are often left without an assigned worker, or with only an emergency coverage worker for several months each year. It is natural that such clients feel resentment and frustration as the process repeats itself year after year.

Such frustration and resentment are not aimed personally at you, although it might seem that way. Beneath the surface, where you are the convenient recipient of their frustrations, such clients may feel deeply about what they perceive to be the reasons changes in workers keep occurring, and about what this says to them about themselves as human beings with special needs in our society.

Assisting clients to accept a new worker takes time: you cannot accomplish this vital task in one session, for clients need to take the experience into themselves and reflect on it. Some suggestions for helping clients to make the transition:

1. If possible (it rarely is) assist your field instructor in assigning new workers to your caseload, selecting the one you feel will work best with each client. You may be able to make some suggestions in certain circumstances.
2. If you know the worker, share something special about the person that the client can relate to. Tailor your choices to client needs and interests.
3. Express your positive feelings toward the worker.
4. Introduce the worker to the client, if your agency policy permits this. This should be a brief face-to-face encounter.
5. As you complete termination, make an appointment for the client with the new worker. Remain with them briefly, then leave them to begin alone.

   In both (4) and (5), brevity is essential. The client should not relate to both simultaneously, or carry over your relationship pattern to the new worker. The client should not have to "choose" which worker to address, face, or reply to.

6. Once disengaged, stay that way! Don't give in to the temptation to go back for "a last goodbye," or to make a lengthy phone call "just to check on how it's going."

Remember, your goal is to help your client to make a smooth transition. Jumping in and out of the client's life increases stress and anxiety, misrepresents your future role in his or her life, and delays the client's acceptance of the change in workers, which is inevitable!

Student Reactions

You will find that you have some different reactions to transferring clients than those you had in terminating clients from agency service. In addition to the feelings we discussed in section A.2., you may experience a high degree of ambivalence, feelings of insecurity, and nervousness.

You are glad that your clients will continue to receive the services he, she, or they need. You may even like the worker assigned to them, and believe that he or she will be able to continue the work that you were doing. However, it may be difficult to accept that someone else can truly help "your" clients. You may have developed a belief, over time, that only you understand them and can help them. Another worker is de facto a challenge to that assumption. You may find yourself secretly wanting the clients not to like the new worker, and to demonstrate their faithfulness to you as their only choice of helper. These are not uncommon feelings — but care must be exercised to keep focused on the goal of client well-being. Setting up clients to dislike their new worker or wishing them not to like him or her sabotages all of the hard work that you have done, and can be very destructive!

Another common reaction to transferring clients is a feeling of insecurity. After all, you are a student. You know you have made some mistakes in the course of your work. You also know that you don't have the ease and experience that a more seasoned agency employee might have. "What," you wonder, "will my client say about me? Will he or she tell the new worker about my mistakes? Will my client like the new worker better because she or he knows what to do to help?" These, too, are normal reactions, and experienced workers transferring clients are themselves not immune to them!

If you have trust and confidence in the relationship you have built with your client, and in your own developing skills and abilities, and trust the advice and mentoring you received from your field instructor, you will be able to work through these feelings and transfer your clients with confidence that you have helped them, and that continued help is available to them as needed. A positive attitude and a good transfer summary will go a long way in supporting your client's continued effort to change and grow.

E. Transferring Clients to Another Agency

During the course of your field work, or at the point of termination, you may need to transfer a client to another agency or resource. If the client's needs exceed your agency's allotted time frame, if you and the client believe he or she would benefit from a change in modality (such as from individual to group), or if you have determined that another resource could more appropriately address your client's problems, you might need to transfer your client to another agency.

Selecting a resource is a joint project: you do some preliminary work, then discuss possible options and choices with your client in order to support self-determination and informed decision-making. Once you have made the referral, you will need to prepare a transfer summary to accompany your client. The transfer summary should include all of the information the receiving agency will need to provide optimal service — but no more. There may be parts of your experience with your client that must remain confidential.

You may wish to make your client's first appointment for him or her, preferably in his or her presence so that input can be provided regarding times and dates. Or you may feel that it would be beneficial to your client to make his or her own arrangements, and simply provide a telephone number. In either case, you will need to follow up with your client to ensure that he or she has followed through on the referral and is actually engaged with another agency or service.

F. Making Termination a Positive Experience — for Both of You

You have guided your clients toward growth and change, supported their efforts, cheered their successes, and acknowledged their failures. It is up to you to take the initiative in making termination a meaningful opportunity for growth. In helping your client address the complex issues and emotions that separation and loss trigger in people, you will be gaining another important professional skill, for ending requires the same high level of skill and knowledge that is required of beginning.

1. Allow yourself enough time to begin to plan and reflect on termination before actually initiating the process with clients.
2. Process your feelings about termination with your field instructor, integrating any suggestions and advice into the reflection process.
3. Come to terms with your feelings, increase your self-awareness.
4. Review each case with your field instructor and develop a tentative termination plan.
5. Initiate discussions of termination with clients well before your last days and weeks in your field work placement.
6. Work with your client in addressing your client's reactions, taking care to be aware of what is happening in your own mind.
7. Initiate and participate in an evaluation of the client's experience which includes a positive affirmation of strengths, growth, and change, an exploration of what worked well and what didn't, what was learned, and how the gains made can be consolidated.
8. Allow space for your client to provide some feedback about the role that you have played in your client's work.
9. Engage the client in planning for the future: transfer to another worker, referral to another resource, complete termination, building in community supports and emergency planning.
10. If possible, ensure that your client is engaged with the follow-up plan.
11. Accept that your work is complete and that you have assisted your client to continue to progress. Say a positive goodbye!

---

[1] Bisman, C. (1994) *Social Work Practice: Cases and Principles.* Pacific Grove, CA: Brooks/Cole.

[2] Ibid., p. 107.

[3] Hepworth, D., & Larsen, J.A. (1997). *Direct Social Work Practice*, 4th Ed. Pacific Grove, CA: Brooks/Cole.

[4] National Association of Social Workers (1996) *Code of Ethics.* Washington, D.C.: Author.

[5] Lum, D. (1996) *Social Work Practice with People of Color.* Pacific Grove, CA: Brooks/Cole, Chapter 8, Termination.

[6] Hepworth, D., & Larsen, J.A., *Direct Social Work Practice, 4th Edition.* Pacific Grove, CA: Brooks/Cole, p 605.

[7] Ibid.

CHAPTER FIFTEEN

FINAL ASSESSMENTS AND EVALUATIONS

As your final day of field work approaches, you will have completed your work with clients, and your final documentation in records and charts. During the last days, your focus will turn toward yourself, your field instruction experience, and your field work agency.

Some of the work of the final evaluation and assessment process will be familiar to you. You have already gone through the process of reviewing your learning contract, working through the school's evaluation forms, and meeting with your field instructor to discuss your learning. Some of the tasks of the final days, however, will be new: instead of being assessed, you will become the one assessing. You will assess your field instructor, your liaison, and your field work placement.

These are essential tasks, for the insights that you provide the Field Work office at your school will help to guide future decisions regarding use of your placement and field instruction team. Students who follow you into the school's program may have access to your evaluations, and will be guided in their choices and experiences by your accounts. Just as you may have read previous students' reports about agencies prior to beginning your field work placement, so the students who follow you will be reading yours. Fair and accurate assessment helps your agency, your school, and your fellow students in their decision-making.

In this chapter, we will review briefly the process of field evaluations and learning contract reviews. We will suggest some possible structure for your final meeting with your field instructor, this person who has been so important in the work that you have done during your internship. Then we will explore your part in evaluating your experience, and address some of the problems and pitfalls you might encounter as you wield your own pen over the evaluation form.

A. <u>Your Final Field Work Evaluation</u>

The format and time span for your final field work evaluation may be similar to others you have had during your placement experience; however, your school or your field instructor may wish to vary these somewhat. One possible variation is to include all of your field work experience in the final evaluation rather than a quarter or a semester: the entire academic year can be reviewed if desired. Another might be to use all of the previous evaluations as a springboard, and include these as steps to the final evaluation.

Whatever format and time span are used for the final evaluation in field, the process will be the same as that outlined in Chapter 12, Field Work Evaluations. You will begin by reflecting on your experience, your learning, and your new skills. You will affirm the distance you have traveled, and begin to think ahead to the challenges that lie before you. You will meet with your field instructor, who will also have spent time reflecting and preparing for your evaluation, and discuss your progress. As in your previous evaluation, your field instructor may fill out the school's form with you, complete it after the conference, or bring it completed to the conference.

In all cases, you will have the opportunity once again to read and review your field instructor's appraisal of your work. You will sign the form, attesting that you are familiar with its contents. Should you have an objection to anything your field instructor has written, or wish to elaborate and/or clarify any statement, you may comment in the space provided, or attach an addendum.

Following the completion of your evaluation process, the evaluation form will be returned to the school for review.

B. Your Final Learning Contract Review

With your field instructor, and generally as a part of your final evaluation process, you will also review your learning contract. As you revised it over the course of your placement, you added objectives and time frames that reached toward the end of your field work placement. If you have kept all of the pages of your learning contract as suggested in Chapter 9, you will have quite a detailed and comprehensive record of your progress toward your personal professional goals.

As during earlier reviews, you will need to re-read your learning contract, and reflect upon the work you have accomplished. You will meet with your field instructor to discuss your objectives in detail. Your final learning contract review, like previous ones, will note progress, changes, and achievement of objectives in the evaluation column. However, no new objectives will be formulated and added to the contract. Your contract, complete, stands as your personal achievement.

Though the final review of the learning contract is primarily a look backward in time, you may wish to use the review to look ahead as well. Education, especially professional education, is a lifelong commitment. Whether you will be moving on to another placement or to employment, you will always be seeking to refine your professional competence. You can begin this forward-looking process by making some notes "for the future" at the end of your learning contract, and ensuring that you keep it to review when you begin the next phase of your education or career.

C. Your Final Supervisory Meeting

There may have been times when you waited for supervision breathlessly, needing help with especially difficult situations. There may have been others where you entered your meeting prepared and confident. At still other times, you may have experienced annoyance, anger, and irritation. You may have wished for the year to end. Most students experience both high points and definite lows during the field instruction process.

Your feelings about field supervision are intimately related to your feelings about your field instructor as a person. Your field instructor has been a role model for you, not only teaching but living and acting the role of a seasoned professional social worker. You learned skills and techniques, but also norms of comportment and ethical principles and behavior. If you have related well to your field instructor, you have modeled some of your behavior as a social worker upon his or her pattern. If the problems outweighed the positives, you may have been less willing to use him or her as a model to learn your new role.

Good, bad, or indifferent, your relationship with your field instructor changes radically at the point of termination of field. While you may choose to maintain contact within professional parameters, the teacher-learner relationship is completed. The necessity of relating is no longer applicable, but becomes a matter of mutual choice. Distance, interests, personality characteristics, and time commitments will affect the relationship you may have with your field instructor after completion of your internship. Chapter 16.C addresses the conditions for possible continuation of a relationship with your field instructor from practical and ethical standpoints.

Some people do not like to say the last goodbye, and find excuses and reasons to have "just one more short meeting." Others tend to avoid final anythings, and would prefer to skip the final supervisory meeting all together. Chances are good that most of us fall somewhere along this continuum.

Just as terminating with clients is experienced as a kind of loss, so, too, terminating with your field instructor will be experienced as a loss. Losses reverberate through us, calling up echoes of other separations long past. It is important to recognize these feelings, and to acknowledge their impact.

Your field instructor may take the initiative in planning your final session. He or she might plan a lunch meeting, or a special quiet time. Some field instructors prefer to continue the learning experience through the last session and will ask for an agenda as usual. Planning with your field instructor to mark this special moment in some way will help you both to feel at ease.

Your final meeting will probably be planned for your final day in field, and students often leave the agency directly from this last supervisory conference, having removed any personal possessions ahead of time. Others include goodbyes to colleagues and staff on this final day after saying goodbye to their field instructor. Most field instructors will leave your final moments at the agency to your own planning and discretion.

A part of the task of ending will involve you in a special evaluation process: you will be asked by your school to evaluate your liaison, your field instructor, and your agency. These are important tasks: while you yourself can use evaluations for personal learning and growth, you will also be providing your school with invaluable information to use in planning, and future students with information which can assist them in making some important decisions about field placement.

D. Evaluating Your Liaison

The Office of Field will provide a form with which you may evaluate the work of your field liaison. Generally, this is a graded checklist with space for you to write personal comments as you wish. Criteria that may be included:

- frequency of visits to field placement
- frequency of other contacts
- helpfulness
- knowledge about field placement agency
- knowledge of school expectations regarding field
- relationship with field instructor
- relationship with you
- accessibility
- advocacy, where needed and appropriate

It is important to take the time to evaluate your liaison carefully, fairly, and thoughtfully. Your report may be used in determining position, promotions, and/or suitability for liaison work. If your liaison has been especially helpful to you, or if you have had difficulties in working with him or her, you should include specific information in your evaluation. You may want to review Chapter 11 prior to filling out your liaison evaluation form.

After your final field work grade is assigned, your liaison will be given a copy of the form you filled out detailing your evaluation of his or her performance. This timing is to ensure that there is no possibility of your report affecting his or her assessment of your work, and is utilized with field placement evaluations as well.

Your field instructor will also be evaluating your liaison. Sample forms are included here to assist you in preparing for this responsibility. (All forms courtesy The Catholic University of America, National Catholic School of Social Service, Washington, D.C.)

SAMPLE FIELD INSTRUCTOR'S EVALUATION OF FIELD LIAISON EFFECTIVENESS

Name of Your Liaison: _____

A. The role of the liaison is clear: Yes ___   No ___

B. I had contact with my liaison this past semester: Yes ___   No ___

      _____ by phone   _____ by site visit   _____ by off-site visit

C. If you needed assistance, did you invite/contact the liaison?   Yes ___   No ___
   If not, please explain why you did not initiate contact:

D. Field liaisons are assigned the following functions: please indicate an evaluation of how your liaison carried out these functions.
Scale for evaluations of liaison functions:
1: Most Satisfactory   2: Satisfactory   3: Unsatisfactory 4: Not Applicable

General Functions:
_____ a. To evaluate range and quality of learning experiences and learning environment.
_____ b. To provide information, support and consultation to field instructor.
_____ c. To help field instructors develop their teaching skills.
_____ d. To assist in problem solving in all aspects of field placement.

Specific Functions:
_____ a. To establish a communication link between school and agency.
_____ b. To make site visits.
_____ c. To meet agency director or agency field placement coordinator.
_____ d. To meet with field instructor(s) and student(s), together or separately, or both.
_____ e. To discuss student performance.
_____ f. To participate in trouble shooting.
_____ g. To share liaison report forms and evaluation of agency with agency and/or field instructor.

SAMPLE STUDENT EVALUATION OF LIAISON EFFECTIVENESS

Name of Your Liaison: _____

A. Have you had personal contact with your liaison this semester?   Yes __ No ___

    1. If yes, check the following as appropriate:
    _____ Liaison seen in group meeting only
    _____ Liaison seen at field placement
    _____ Liaison seen in personal interview on campus

    2. If no, check the following as appropriate:
    _____ Student did not attend group meeting
    _____ Student did not request contact with liaison
    _____ Liaison not sufficiently available for appointments

B. Liaisons are assigned the following major functions, therefore, please indicate your evaluation of how your liaison carried out these functions:
Scale for evaluations of liaison functions:
1: Most Satisfactory   2: Satisfactory   3: Unsatisfactory   4: Not Applicable

    _____ a. To monitor and review students' field learning experience.
    _____ b. To assist in integrating theory and practice.
    _____ c. To evaluate student's performance (assessing strengths, weaknesses) in the field.

C. Did you have contact with your liaison this semester regarding problems or concerns related to your field experience?   Yes ___   No ___

Did your liaison make a site visit to your agency this semester?   Yes ___   No ___

D. Field liaisons are assigned the following functions related to the student in the field. Within the context of your knowledge and experience this semester, please indicate an evaluation of how your liaison carried out these functions.

    _____ a. To evaluate the range and quality of learning experiences and learning environment.
    _____ b. To establish communication link between school and agency.
    _____ c. To meet with field instructor(s) and student(s), together or separately or both.
    _____ d. To discuss student performance.
    _____ e. To assist in problem solving in all aspects of the field placement, when necessary.
    _____ f. To act as an enabler/facilitator in resolution of concerns related to field work.

Comments:

E. Evaluating Your Field Instructor

You will also be asked to evaluate your field instructor and the supervisory experience. The form for evaluating your field instructor may be combined with the assessment you will also be providing regarding your experience with your field placement as a whole. Again, take special care to be fair, accurate, and thoughtful. Your evaluation will be used by the Field Office to determine whether he or she should be asked to serve as a field instructor during the following internship period.

In evaluating your field instructor, try to be objective, and consider teaching skills, and learning imparted, rather than basing your assessment solely on personality characteristics. Some field instructors are formal and distant, but are excellent role models and teachers. Others are very friendly, but disorganized and unprepared for supervision. Still others are super organized and demanding of efforts that leave you exhausted, but teach you much. Some share their work and their professional lives with their students, while others prefer to maintain a separation between students and colleagues. Think about what you have learned from your field instructor as well as his or her teaching style. Ability to impart knowledge and skills is the primary criterion for successful field instruction.

Because your relationship with your field instructor was much more intense than that with your liaison, the form with which you will be working may be much longer, more detailed, and more complex. You will be exploring various components of field instruction, including:

- ability to teach, explain, describe
- motivation for field instruction
- interest in student learning
- availability and accessibility
- appropriateness of assignments and requirements
- ability to be a resource for you
- knowledge of agency, population, community
- knowledge of resources and networks
- relationship to you
- degree of ease with supervisory responsibilities

and many other criteria that are relevant to your experiences. The form will also allow for personalized input if desired.

Field instructor evaluation forms vary greatly among schools and programs. The form included here, which combines field instructor and field placement agency evaluations, can serve as a sample of the kinds of questions and format you may be asked to work with.

As you think about evaluating your field instructor, other issues may intrude upon your fairness, honesty, and accuracy. Will you need a recommendation from this field instructor when you apply for a job? Would you like to return to this agency as an employee when you complete your education? Was your field instructor very nice, but ineffectual, and are you concerned about hurting his or her feelings? Are you afraid that you will suffer in some manner if you write any negative comments? All of these and other concerns will affect your written evaluation. In trying to minimize their effects, and preserve objectivity and fairness, think about your professional role and responsibilities, and try to respond to the evaluation request with that foremost in your mind.

SAMPLE STUDENT EVALUATION OF PRACTICUM EXPERIENCE

Specify Your Field Placement: _____

Name of Field Instructor: _____

Name of Liaison: _____

Choose the response which best describes your reaction to this course of instruction.

A. Understanding of objectives of field education.

_____ Objectives never made clear   _____ Only indirect reference to objectives

_____ Objectives made somewhat clear   _____ Objectives reasonably clear

_____ Very clearly outlined from beginning

B. Clarity of the definition of your responsibilities for the field experience.

_____ Often in doubt about expectations   _____ Occasionally in doubt

_____ Usually had a general idea   _____ Usually knew expectations exactly

_____ Always knew exactly what was expected

C. Extent to which field learning tasks were organized.

_____ No apparent organization   _____ Less organization than desired

_____ Fairly well organized   _____ Well organized

_____ Extremely well organized and integrated

D. Rating of field instructor's knowledge of social work practice skills.

_____ Poor _____ Fair _____ Adequate _____ Good _____ Excellent

E. Ability of field instructor to provide a generic understanding of social work.

_____ Poor _____ Fair _____ Adequate _____ Good _____ Excellent

F. Extent to which field instructor stimulated curiosity about theory.

_____ Not at all _____ A little _____ Moderately

_____ Very good _____ To a most unusual degree

G. Extent to which field instructor related field learning experience to other concerns in your curriculum (helped with integration).
_____ Not at all   _____ A little   _____ Moderately
        _____ Very good   _____ To a most unusual degree

H. Extent to which field instructor presented or allowed more than one view in controversial matters.
_____ Sharply limited views   _____ Rarely presented differing views
_____ About average   _____ Paid considerable attention to differing views
                _____ Eager that all views be heard

I. Receptiveness of field instructor to expression of student views.
_____ Did not allow expression   _____ Seldom allowed student expression
_____ Average   _____ Above average   _____ Very receptive

J. Frequency of individual conferences to discuss.
_____ No individual conferences   _____ Rarely (less than 3 per semester)
_____ On an "as needed basis"   _____ Regularly scheduled, less than 1 per week
        _____ Regularly scheduled, at least 1 per week

K. Value of individual conference sessions.
_____ Practically of no value   _____ Occasionally valuable
_____ Generally valuable   _____ Almost always valuable
            _____ Outstanding in value

L. Frequency of group conferences to discuss student experiences.
_____ No group conferences   _____ Rarely (less than 3 per semester)
_____ On an "as needed basis"   _____ Regularly scheduled, less than 1 per week
        _____ Regularly schedule, at least 1 per week

M. Value of group conference sessions.
_____ Practically of no value   _____ Of little value
_____ Of moderate value   _____ Very valuable   _____ Outstanding in value

N. Value of your contacts with staff members other than field instructor.
        _____ Practically of no value   _____ Of little value
_____ Of moderate value   _____ Very valuable _____ Outstanding in value

O. Satisfaction with the procedures for evaluating your performance.
_____ Not at all satisfied   _____ Moderately satisfied
_____ Average satisfaction   _____ More satisfied than in other courses
                    _____ Completely satisfied

P. Your rating of field instructor in general (all around teaching ability).
_____ Poor _____ Fair _____ Adequate _____ Good _____ Excellent

Q. Your rating of agency for student learning.
_____ Poor _____ Fair _____ Adequate _____ Good _____ Excellent

R. Check each of the following activities you experienced in this placement:
_____ Individual Treatment   _____ Group Treatment
_____ Family Treatment   _____ Administration
_____ Community Organizing   _____ Interagency Relations
_____ Policy/Program Development   _____ Research
          _____ Other (specify) _____

S. What was your average caseload this year?
Number of Cases: _____   Interviews per week: _____
Long Term: _____   Other contacts with or for clients per week: _____
Short Term: _____

F. Evaluating Your Field Placement

Your school may ask that you evaluate your field work agency together with your field instructor, or separately. Separating field instructor and agency evaluation encourages you to consider these separately: it is, after all, possible to have a good experience with a field instructor, but a negative one with field placement, and vice versa. Where both evaluations are combined on one form, you will note that different questions and criteria apply to field instructors and agencies.

Perhaps the most important evaluation you will be asked to make as you complete your internship is the one which addresses the field work placement agency itself. Although your school may need to work around the difficulties in locating field work placements engendered by budget cuts, staffing cutbacks, and managed care (see Chapter 17), you may be assured that close attention will be given to your evaluation of your field work placement agency. Negative student experiences, especially repeated negative student experiences, often result in the termination of an agency as a school field work placement.

Reflect carefully upon your field work experience. How were you received by your agency? Were they receptive to students, interested in your learning and progress? Were adequate arrangements made for space for you? Did the agency's population provide for adequate learning experiences? Was the caseload assigned appropriate? Were agency policies supportive to your learning, or restrictive? Did you find any policies objectionable or discriminatory to clients, workers, or staff? Were you concerned about agency ethics? Did you note any unethical conduct? How accessible and safe was your agency for students?

Would you recommend this agency to a fellow student? Why? If you were searching for a field work placement, would you choose this agency yourself? Would you be willing to talk with prospective interns about your agency?

These are some of the kinds of questions you will be asked during the process of evaluating your field work agency. As with your field instructor evaluation, you will find that other considerations come to mind. Will you want to apply to this agency for a position upon the completion of your studies? Are you staying on as a part-time employee, or more difficult yet, are you a regular employee of this agency with field work arrangements added on? Are you concerned about the accuracy of your impressions, and unwilling to put them in writing? Are you uncomfortable about exposing agency ethics and politics? Worried about the public nature of this field placement evaluation, and about who will read it and what will be said about its contents? Did you like your field instructor but find agency policies cumbersome and difficult to work with? Or, conversely, like your agency's mission and programs, but dislike your field instructor?

Are you concerned that you will be asked to support and defend what you wrote? That people at your agency will be angry with you or dislike you? That students who follow you will walk into difficult situations because you withheld information out of fear of repercussions? That you will overemphasize either the positive or the negative based on your personal values and feelings rather than on objective criteria?

All of these considerations, as well as many others, will impact upon your written field work evaluation, just as others impacted upon your field instructor evaluation. Be sure to allow yourself enough time to sort through all of your feelings and impressions, and think about your priorities. As with your field instructor evaluation, you need to focus on your professional ethical obligations. Where are your responsibilities in this matter? With whose well-being should you be most concerned?

Evaluations are a part of professional functioning. These are your introductions to this important dimension of social work. If you find that you are unsure of how to proceed with any concern or circumstance, remember that there are members of your field education team who may be of assistance. Your adviser, for example, may have the objectivity of distance. Your practice instructor may have experiences drawn from other students or direct involvement. The Director of Field is also available for consultation and always interested in your input in these important matters. Share your concerns with any of these professionals, or another faculty member, and they will be happy to assist you.

CHAPTER SIXTEEN

NOW THAT YOUR PLACEMENT IS COMPLETED

Because the experience was so intense, you will always have clear memories and strong feelings about your field work placement. Years, even decades, later you will still recall with great vividness and intensity your high points, your problems, and your favorite clients. The lessons you have learned in field (both planned and unplanned) will be a part of your professional self throughout the course of your career.

Because of the strong impact of your field experience, it is important to process it and reflect upon it when it is first completed, while the memories are freshest. Processing will help you to understand and integrate the whole experience, and will also give you many opportunities to think about yourself: how you learn, what you like in supervision, and what you could never accept in regular employment.

If you are going on to another placement, you need to think about the kinds of new experiences, populations, and problems that would be most beneficial to your professional growth. You will also want to know what you do not want in your next placement. If you are going on to employment, you may want to think about agency policies and procedures and your needs in terms of congruence between your values and those of your agency. You may want to consider caseload size, and supervision issues. Sorting out your thoughts and feelings about your field placement will help you to know your professional self.

Processing can also assist you in your formal evaluation of your liaison, field instructor, and field placement agency. Generally, however, you will only have time to begin to think about your experience before the due date of your assessments and evaluations. The more you have had time to consider your placement in depth, the more accurate you will be on the formal evaluations.

A. Processing Your Experience

Field placement may seem a global kind of experience, and the thoughts and feelings attached to specific events and people may at first be difficult to separate and sort out. It is easier to process your experience and learn from it if you break it down into separate discrete parts. Though there will always be some overlap, structuring your process might be helpful.

The list included here is meant so serve as a guideline only. You will want to personalize your list to your own experiences and interests. It will be helpful to include:

1. Your agency's location: Was your agency accessible to public transportation? Did it have adequate parking? Was it comfortable and safe to get to? How important were these to you?

2. Your agency's physical setting: Was your agency warm and welcoming, or cold and impersonal? Was there adequate space for you? For regular employees? Did the space foster good communication and interaction?

3. Your agency's receptivity and atmosphere: Did your agency welcome students, and integrate them warmly into agency processes? Did people seem to like each other?

Were other workers friendly — to you and to each other? What was the relationship between professional staff and employees? Did you feel comfortable in this atmosphere? If not, what bothered you? What kind of atmosphere would you prefer in another placement, or in regular employment?

4. Your agency's ethics and politics: (this is of *major* importance!!) How did your agency's stated mission and values fit in with your personal values? Were there any areas of difference? How did you respond to these? Did you observe any unethical behavior? Were you comfortable in responding? If not, why not? Were the reasons valid and would they apply in other circumstances? Were there many conflicts, unfair treatment of some people, power politics, or other problems? How did they affect the atmosphere and the work of the agency? How did they affect you?

5. Your agency's population: Were you comfortable working with your agency's clients? If you were not, were you able to work through some of the problems you felt? Do you enjoy working with this population (children, mentally ill, Hispanics, new immigrants, the elderly, terminally ill, alcoholics, etc.) If not, why not? What kind of population would you enjoy working with?

6. Your caseload and clients: Was your caseload appropriate to your student needs? Did it offer a wide variety of learning experiences? Was there ample time to do the work you wanted with each client? Were enough clients assigned? What are some of the most important things you learned from your clients? Who did you like best and least and, most important, why?

7. Your other activities and responsibilities: Were you able to attend staff meetings? Inservices? Ethics committee meetings, or advisory board meetings? Were you asked to give a case presentation, or other presentation? Did you enjoy doing that, or was it difficult for you? Would you enjoy doing presentations in the future? Were you able to keep up with documentation? Did you feel the requirements were too great? Too skimpy to give a real picture of your clients and your work? Were you comfortable with the responsibilities and opportunities offered?

8. Your field instructor: (also of *major* importance!) What did you especially like? What didn't you like? What would be very undesirable characteristics in a future field instructor or supervisor? How would you describe your field instructor's personality? Teaching style? Mentoring? Ability to be a professional role model? Interaction with you? Availability and accessibility? Affinity for students, and understanding of student issues and problems? Sensitivity? Directiveness? Expectations of you?

9. Your colleagues and fellow students: How important were these to your learning, and to your overall experience in the field? Do you prefer close collegial relationships, or are you more of a loner? Do you learn well with a group? If you had other students in your field placement, was this a positive aspect of your experience? Would you seek another placement with other students, or would you prefer to be the only student? Did you observe any unethical or improper behavior? If so, how did you handle it? Were you comfortable with your responses to the problem?

10. Your liaison: How important was the role of your liaison to your overall experience? Was he or she available and accessible to you? Were confidences maintained, so that you were able to develop trust and share any concerns about your placement?

11. The field work office: Were you placed appropriately, efficiently, and with consideration of your special interests and abilities? Was the Field Office responsive to your concerns and problems? How accessible was the Director of Field? Did the Field Office provide all the necessary forms and reports in a timely manner? Were field work books, manuals, or other written material assigned and available to you? Were you satisfied with the methods your school used for evaluating your work and assigning a grade?

12. Your own personal reactions to the experience: **(most vital of all!)** Did you enjoy the work that you were doing? How do your personal values, interests, and beliefs fit in with what you now know of the profession as a whole?

And lastly, that all important question:

Did you make the right choice of career, and are you doing what you want to do?

Some of these questions can probably be answered quickly and easily. Others may require serious thought and consideration. Don't try to process your field work experience in a day or a week — it will take time to sort out your thoughts and feelings, for the experience was of long duration, complex, and intense. You may choose to share some of your thoughts and ideas with fellow students, and to compare experiences. This, too, will add to your learning and growth.

B. Relationship with Colleagues

Over the course of your placement, you may have developed close friendships with colleagues and fellow students. What happens when your field placement ends?

Professional Colleagues

Your continued relationship with professional colleagues will depend on your mutual choice. If you have developed a close personal friendship, you can continue to see each other outside of work. You can also meet them for lunch. You should not "drop in" unannounced, in the same way that you "dropped in" to a colleague's office when you were taking a break or had a question during your field placement, as this can disrupt the office routine and your colleague's schedule.

If your relationships with colleagues have not extended beyond professional parameters, they will probably terminate with your placement. You can keep in touch on occasion, send a holiday card, or stop by during a visit to your field instructor or agency director.

If you plan to ask a colleague to serve as a reference for you, you should ask him or her in a timely manner, provide the necessary forms and stamped envelopes, and let the colleague know how to reach you. You may ask a colleague for a general reference to keep, or for a specific reference for a job, placement, or school. In contacting a colleague you have not seen or talked with for an extended time to ask for a reference, help jog his or her memory by sharing recollections of mutual experiences, and ask if he or she would be willing to serve as a reference. It is always best not to assume that a colleague will do this!

Fellow Students

If there were other students in your field placement, your relationship with them may have become very close and intense. You will have shared many experiences, feelings, and concerns. As with colleagues, your contacts beyond your field work agency's parameters will vary according to the kind of relationship you have established.

If you were placed with students from other schools, you may continue the friendship, or terminate it. If you were placed with students in your own program, you will probably continue the relationship unless there were special problems. You will be encountering them in classes, and around the campus. You'll see them in the cafeteria and library. There will always be a "special" bond between you which is different from your relationship to other students in your program. The degree to which you will continue to seek each other out will depend upon the kind of relationship you developed in field.

C. Relationship with Field Instructor

There are many possible variations in the relationship you will have with your field instructor once placement is terminated. During the course of your field placement, the boundaries of your relationship were clearly determined by the NASW Code of Ethics, which proscribes dual relationships between field instructors and students. Because of the power imbalances between students and field instructors, the danger for harm and exploitation is always present.

However, the guidelines are less clear for relationships after field work is completed, and you will need to determine your ongoing relationship with your field instructor, if any. This can easily become a part of your final supervisory conference: you will set the conditions for any continued relationship best while you are still at your agency.

If you have had a difficult relationship with your field instructor, you will of course prefer to terminate it completely when your assigned work and school requirements are completed. If you have maintained a comfortable professional relationship, you may wish to remain in contact. Your field instructor may be willing to continue to mentor or provide some guidance to you, but care should be exercised not to continue the student-field instructor relationship in a manner that would impact negatively upon your future supervisor-supervisee relationships. In the same way that it is in the best interest of clients to make the inevitable change to a new worker, it is in your best interest to be able to approach your next supervisor-supervisee relationship with a willingness to engage fully.

This does not mean you can't stay in touch with your field instructor, if this is your mutual choice! Many students find that occasional phone calls and visits are a comfortable way of maintaining this relationship, at least for a period of time. Your field instructor will be genuinely interested in your future plans, and in the progress of your education, and you may be eager to share your experiences.

More frequently than colleagues, students turn to field instructors to serve as references. Again, it is best not to assume that your field instructor will write a reference for you. However, it is unlikely that your field instructor will forget the details of your field work experience, or be unwilling to write you a letter of recommendation. You may want to include a discussion of this in your final supervisory conference as well.

Because personal friendships and intimate relationships were proscribed during the period of your internship, you will want to consider engaging in such a relationship with your field instructor carefully. While the "official" power imbalance no longer exists, there is still the potential for harm to you. You are used to accepting your field instructor's guidance and advice, and he or she is used to having it accepted. Although your field instructor can no longer affect the course of your education or professional career, there may be an underlying residue of concern about this on your part. Proceed with caution, if you must!

D. Relationship with Clients

A one-word answer will suffice here: DON'T! Why not? you may ask. If you want to stay in touch and "just see how the client is doing," or "be there for my client, who needs me," or "really like my client as a person," what harm can there be in continuing the relationship when the formal client-worker relationship ends with the termination of field placement?

There are two primary reasons for wanting to continue a relationship with a client after terminating a formal contact. The first is the desire, sometimes experienced as a feeling of obligation, to continue to help your client. Students have often regarded termination upon completion of field work as a form of abandonment. They have read the Code of Ethics statements regarding abandonment, and believe that it is vital to clients' interests to continue to work with them outside of agency parameters. That "savior complex" can be felt very strongly, and you might sincerely believe that your presence is absolutely necessary to your client's well-being, which is your professional obligation.

The second reason students desire to continue relationships with clients outside of the agency is a sincere attraction and affection for a client. You may have, in the course of your work, found many areas of similarity and common interest with your client. You may enjoy your client's company, and feel that you could develop a close and meaningful friendship. You may feel a strong attraction, emotional and/or sexual, and recognize that your client shares your feelings.

While both of these reasons are appealing and may seem valid and justifiable, there are strong reasons to reconsider initiating a relationship with your client after formal termination. Dual relationships with clients and with their relationship networks, as well as sexual relationships with them, are clearly proscribed in the Code of Ethics during the course of service. There is a great potential for harm and exploitation in such relationships. This potential still exists when the formal helping process is ended.

While friendships with former clients are not specifically proscribed, sexual relationships are clearly so:

> Social workers should not engage in sexual activities or sexual contact with former clients because of the potential for harm to the client. If social workers engage in conduct contrary to this prohibition or claim that an exception is warranted because of extraordinary circumstances, it is the social workers — not their clients — who assume the full burden of demonstrating that the former client has not been exploited, coerced, or manipulated, intentionally, or unintentionally (NASW Code of Ethics, Section 1.09.c).

It is not clear how long a period of time is involved in this proscription. There may no longer be civil liability after a period of time. For example, in California and Minnesota, civil liability ends two years after the termination of professional services. Beyond civil liability, however, is the legal and ethical concern regarding potential exploitation. This cannot be limited in time, but must depend upon individual relationships.

There are many reasons for extending this policy to friendships, helper-helpee, and casual relationships with clients as well. Some of these include:

Impeding Continued Work

If you have transferred a client to another worker, contact with you on any grounds may impede or postpone the development of a meaningful helping relationship with the new social worker, and thus the client's continued growth and goal accomplishment.

Fostering Dependency

Clients who plead with you to maintain contact with them, and to continue to "help" them may feel extremely dependent upon you personally. Such feelings of dependency undermine the client's strengths and coping abilities. It is preferable to address this request and expressed dependency in terms of a termination reaction, and work through it with your client.

Blurring Professional Boundaries

A professional relationship is very different from a friendship. Goals, relationship patterns, and material shared differ markedly. Your client is accustomed to relating to you as a professional. Changing the relationship changes the balance between you and may harm or diminish previous gains and achievements.

Lingering Power Imbalances

Although you and your client may believe that you can form a balanced friendship relationship, this is very rarely so. You know much more about your client than your client knows about you. Your client has accepted your help and perhaps your advice on serious, fundamental life issues. You have assumed the role of expert. With a change in relationship, these power imbalances are likely to continue, often in insidious or inadvertent ways.

Undermining Your Agency

Your client, though assigned to you, is a client of your agency, whose mission it is to provide the services your client has needed. Its programs and policies are designed to assist your client toward growth and change. Providing help outside of your agency's parameters undermines its function. In addition, your agency has provided the all-important grounds and terms of your work with your client. It has determined who does what, when, and how. Relating outside of your agency leaves both you and your client without these necessary protections.

Unpredictability of Future Needs and Wants

As noted above, your agency has provided the boundaries and conditions for your relationship with your client. When you continue the relationship outside of agency's auspices, you create unlimited possibilities for difficulty. Suppose your client wants the relationship to develop into something other than you had envisioned. Suppose you wish to terminate the relationship after a period of time. Suppose your client becomes excessively demanding of time and attention. Brings other, perhaps unwanted, relationships into your relationship. You will limit your own freedom, and that of your client, to live as you each choose by attempting to sustain a relationship outside of your agency.

Misinterpreting Grounds for Continuation

You may wish to continue with your client because you believe it is essential to your client's well-being, and you wish to be of continued help. You may believe that your client "needs" you. Your client, on the other hand, may view your continued interest as an invitation to a casual friendship, or even a sexual relationship. Conversely, you may view continuing on a casual friendly basis as friendship, while your client may view it as an opportunity to continue to depend upon your professional services. It is easy to see the potential for serious problems here — without the structure of the agency's program to set the terms of relationship, anything can be presumed!

Violating Agency Policy

Although you are no longer affiliated with your agency, you need to continue to honor its policies and accepted practices. Most agencies have clear policies regarding extending relationships with clients outside of agency auspices. Your loyalty, fidelity, and obligation to your agency ask that you continue to observe these proscriptions.

Exposing Yourself to Potential Lawsuit

Although the precedents for lawsuits in such circumstances are not clear, we are living in an increasingly litigious society. Social work malpractice suits have increased greatly in recent years, and continue to increase. Continuing a relationship with a client beyond termination may be considered to be outside of the boundaries of formal professional practice, and not commonly accepted by social work professionals. Any actions which are apart from the accepted norm for professional behavior leaves the worker open to possible legal actions.

The temptation to continue with your client is often <u>very</u> strong, and difficult to resist. If you feel this pulling at you as you terminate with your agency, it is important that you discuss the problem with a professional with whom you have developed a trusting relationship, such as your field instructor, your liaison, your adviser, your practice instructor, or other faculty member.

Endings are inherent in beginnings — true. But that doesn't necessarily make reactions simple or predictable. Careful thought, planning, and consultation will assist you in making the termination experience another good opportunity for learning and growth.

Unit Summary

The end of field placement is a special time. Elation at successfully completing a major portion of professional education, excitement in thinking of the extra free time, and affirmation in the completion of serious responsibilities mix with sadness in ending relationships with clients, a feeling of loss of a meaningful experience, and uncertainty about ongoing relationships with field instructor, colleagues, and fellow students. Anxiety about future course and field work mixes with the positive acceptance greater professional competence. As with all endings, emotions can seesaw up and down.

In all endings there are the seeds of a new beginning. In order to process the experience of termination, so that the new beginning may build upon it, it is important to consider the various tasks of termination, process the field work experience, and think through future relationships with agency, field instructor, colleagues, and clients.

In this Unit, suggestions for terminating productively and affirmatively have been offered. Chapter 14 addressed termination with clients, and presented some of the reactions clients and students experience during this time. Termination in itself can be a growth opportunity both for you and for your clients, and possible approaches were discussed to enable you and your clients to address termination issues openly and successfully.

Although terminating with clients is often the most important part of completing field work for many students, the termination process involves several distinct processes and responsibilities. You will have your final evaluation, your final learning contract review, and, at the last, your final meeting with your field instructor. As you terminate your placement, you will also be asked to evaluate the agency, your field instructor, and your liaison for your school. This is an important step, for the information you provide will guide the field office in decisions for the future. It is important to approach these tasks openly, honestly, and with care and reflection. These final procedures were presented in Chapter 15.

What happens after you have walked out of your field work agency that last time? How can you ensure that you have integrated your learning, and focus on future goals as a continuum of your past experiences? Chapter 16 discussed processing your experience, as well as offering suggestions for continuing relationships with colleagues, field instructor, and fellow students. These will be based very much on the kind and degree of relationship you have evolved over the course of your placement. A final section presented the possibilities for serious problems that can occur if you wish to continue your relationship with clients after termination, and strongly urged careful consideration. Relationships with clients outside of the formal professional boundaries can be harmful and exploitative for them, and potentially very risky for you.

The final Unit will present some of the common problems that students encounter during the course of their field placements, and offers suggestions for addressing them. Rarely are problems so serious and pervasive as to be unresolvable, although this does occur upon occasion. Most students do encounter some minor problems or difficulties during the course of placement, and this section can serve both as a preparation and as a reference for some of the situations you might encounter.

UNIT FIVE

IF PROBLEMS OCCUR . . .

Even in the best of all possible worlds, problems do sometimes occur. Most are relatively minor, and can be addressed and resolved with a minimum of difficulty. Occasionally, students encounter a major problem that is an obstacle to learning, creates undue stress, and appears intractable. Problems often have the unique quality of spreading and expanding at a geometric rate if they are not addressed promptly. If you find that you develop a problem in your field placement, it is best to address it quickly. This is often much better for you personally as well — holding an unresolved problem over a long period of time can be debilitating and can adversely affect your professional growth.

Some problems are obvious and their cause is clear. Others may appear broad and general, and you may have difficulty in pinning down the source of your concern and discomfort. An example might be your awareness that agency staff and employees appear unhappy with their work, are resentful of the director and of each other, and complain constantly about the agency. Nothing seems to get done efficiently, and there are cliques and sub-groups among employees which severely limit interaction and cooperation. Clients are impacted because service delivery is compromised. A problem like this may also have a strong effect upon your learning. However, there is rarely one single, clear, obvious cause. The situation has probably built up over time, and there are now several conditions that contribute strongly to the overall disaffection and alienation.

It is important, in such cases, to spend some time thinking about your problem, so that you can attempt relate to at least some of it to a specific issue, person, policy, or condition. You may find that this diffuse problem seems to have multiple causes, or that it is extremely complex with layers of issues which are interrelated but also separate. The original cause or determining factor may be buried so deeply in the agency's past or even present experience that you may be unable to determine it.

If your problem presents such difficulties when you attempt to analyze it, you may need to break it down in some way so that you arrive at a portion or aspect of the problem which you feel <u>may</u> be the central one but, if not, is an important part of the problem. It is helpful to define your problem in such a way that it will be possible for you to address it. The more specific and concrete your description, the more amendable to thought and possible resolution.

When you have determined your problem as best you can, your next step is to choose a course of action. This is often a very delicate and complex process: what you do will depend not only on the nature of the problem, but also on the personalities involved, the possible effects of various courses of action, and your own needs. There are generally several options available to you, and you must select among them carefully.

Because you are working with other people, within a formal organization with a structured hierarchy and policies, and often under conditions which are stressful, the possibilities for difficulties are almost unlimited. The wonder is not that problems occur — but that there are not many more of them!

We will be exploring some of the kinds of problems students often encounter in the course of field placement in this final Unit. Chapter 17 will introduce some of the realities of field placements at the dawn of the new century. It is important to be aware that budget cuts, managed care, and the burgeoning of for-profit agencies and programs have a very strong impact upon field placements. These, in turn, have impacted upon field work programs in many ways, creating "real" circumstances and choices which may be quite different from the "ideal" field placement you may have wanted, or that your Field Office describes.

Chapter 18 will discuss your field placement setting from the perspective of your agency's attitude and approaches to student interns. Agencies vary widely in the kinds and degrees of accommodation they make for students, and the way in which they see students' roles in overall agency functioning.

Chapter 19 addresses concerns about caseload, such as too many or too few clients, inappropriate assignments, abuse of time schedules, and concerns about clients. Problems with insufficient or inadequate supervision, issues with field instructor competence and ethics, and personality clashes with field instructors are addressed in Chapter 20. Chapter 21 includes issues with colleagues and fellow students, and Chapter 22 addresses agency ethics and politics, which often tend to have a major impact upon field work students.

Despite the seriousness of some of these problems, it is possible to bring most of them to a reasonable resolution without a major disruption in your learning process. Suggestions for addressing and resolving problems are included in Chapter 23. Chapter 24 addresses personal safety and the role of school, agency, field instructor, and yourself in maintaining safe conditions while at work.

While most of the problems you will encounter are resolvable, it is important to recognize that not all can be successfully addressed within the context of your field placement. If the problem is not with your willingness and ability to assume your role in the learning process, and is not amenable to any of the suggested solutions, it may be necessary to terminate your placement and initiate one with another agency. This will involve the same process originally undertaken when you were placed, but close monitoring by the Field Office will expedite the necessary change and ensure that your learning proceeds as needed.

CHAPTER SEVENTEEN

"REAL" AND "IDEAL" PLACEMENTS

In the ideal world, schools are able to visit and explore a variety of potential placements for students. They can use an established set of criteria in the selection, and ensure that field instructors and agency directors are carefully oriented to the school's program. They can require advanced degrees, years of supervision, and years of experience as qualifications for field instructor appointments. They can expect that students will have their own office, or at the very least their own desk, and telephone access. They can ensure that students have just the right kind of caseload — not too many cases, not too few, varied to ensure optimum learning. They can "match" students and field instructors through an interview process to ensure that a good working relationship can be established. In the ideal world, agencies are always dedicated, apportionment of services is always fair and according to the requirements of the program, budgets are ample to fully meet the needs of the client population, confidentiality is always respected, and colleagues work together to ensure the best services to clients.

In the real world, outside forces and events shape agency programs, and an ever fewer number can accommodate students, forcing schools to scramble and sometimes to compete for field placements. In the real world, student's "desks" may be lunchroom tables, file cabinets, or a corner of a field instructor's desk. Students may wait months for cases, or immediately be given the caseload of a seasoned full-timer. Field instructors may be unavailable, or overworked and distant. They may dislike the agency or their jobs, and communicate their attitude through the student-field instructor relationship. They may leave or be fired in the middle of the student's internship. Colleagues may attempt to establish alliances with students to undermine the field instructor's authority. Agencies may assign cases by assigning seasoned professionals to clients according to ability to pay, rather than according to client needs, leaving students with caseloads of complex and often intractable problems where poverty is often a strong component. Agency politics intrude upon student assignments and client problems are discussed in hallways where other clients are able to hear.

Welcome to the real world!

While most students find their field placement to be an excellent experience, most also are confronted with problems and issues during the course of internship which require that they adapt, confront, and resolve. Ethical issues, field instructors, and problems with agency policies are some of the most frequently encountered problems. Students, whose learning is freshest, and who are new to agencies, often become aware of long-standing problems or issues that agency staff have long ago learned to accept, circumvent, or ignore.

Should you "go with the flow," or "stand up for principles and rights?" Risk your grade and status, or keep quiet and wait to leave? Your answer may depend on the particular circumstances you are encountering, your personal values, and your willingness to compromise or adapt.

We begin by exploring some of the forces outside the agency which strongly affect all field placements today. Outside pressures will affect a great deal of the agency's day-to-day functioning.

A. <u>The Effects of Budget Cuts</u>

Many agencies grew and expanded their programs and services during the Kennedy and Johnson administrations, a period when many people believed that society's problems could be resolved if sufficient funds were allocated. As a society, we would eradicate poverty, improve education, make our streets safe, and find jobs for everyone. Everyone would own their own home, have two weeks of vacation, steak twice a week, and a large-screen TV. Teens would not get pregnant and gangs would be seen only in old movies. Life would be so good there would no longer be people needing to abuse substances, steal from others, or live on the street. Prejudice and discrimination would vanish as everyone learned to love and respect everyone else, and economic and social distances would disappear. We would become a "Great Society."

Congress allocated a seemingly unending stream of funds for programs which were going to achieve all of these goals — immediately!

A marvelous time to be a social worker! Jobs abounded, programs flourished, and new opportunities arose daily. Clients could continue to receive services indefinitely, if they were "needed," and the decision to continue or terminate was made between client and worker only.

So then what?

Society, through representatives in the Congress, wanted to see results. And, though some important gains were indeed achieved, they did not meet expectations. The major societal problems seemed intractable. As eligibility criteria for programs broadened in the belief that this would finally resolve problems, the numbers of people requiring services grew far beyond those originally projected, until the funds required to maintain them became greater than society was willing to provide.

The era of great social programs came to an end. Some programs were eliminated, and agencies closed their doors. Others lost massive amounts of funding, and were forced to cut back on services and on the numbers of people served. Caseloads increased as many more people remained eligible for needed services than could be accommodated. Numbers of professional staff were cut back, and the use of paraprofessionals or untrained workers to provide services increased. Paraprofessionals and untrained workers, however, needed supervision, and overworked professionals found an ever-expanding number of duties in their job descriptions.

In addition, program criteria began to require "proof" of services rendered and goals achieved in order to receive continued funding. This required detailed documentation of services as well as planned, goal-oriented, time-limited services. The way in which services were rendered changed radically as caseloads and assignments increased. Documentation requirements continued or increased, however, so that workers found the proportion between the hours of documentation and the hours of direct service overly weighted in favor of documentation. This often led to frustration and disillusionment.

Overburdened workers, documentation requirements, budgetary cuts — all of these contributed to a general decrease in the numbers of agencies able to accommodate students. Students carry a small caseload. They require hours of supervisory time. They require space. These have become luxuries many agencies can no longer afford, shrinking the pool of potential placements markedly.

B. The Effects of Managed Care

"Managed care" is the term used to describe health and mental health services which are paid for by a third party. The service provider (the social workers) and the service consumer (the client) constitute the first two parties. Third party payers such as the government pay for services through major programs such as Medicare and Medicaid; private insurers such as Blue Cross and Blue Shield, HMOs, and PPOs are also considered third party payers. Because third party payers provide the funding for services, they also have the power to determine the direction of service, the time frame, and the modality used.

Third party payers, whether governmental or private, have a goal of cost containment. They themselves are accountable to Congress, a Board of Directors, or other governing and overseeing body. Parameters for services are often determined outside of the programs themselves; the programs administer and oversee their implementation. There is often a limit to the total amount of funding available for distribution, and third party payers are responsible for the overall utilization and allocation of the funds.

In order to meet their own goal of cost containment, third party payers limit the amounts and kinds of services provided. "Open-ended" therapy, a frequent practice in years past, was one of the first affected by managed care, which carefully limited interventions to the minimum possible. Individual treatment is more costly than group treatment. Thus, workers are encouraged to develop group programs which could provide services to a number of people at the same time. Case management enables workers to carry much larger caseloads. Thus, clients with complex chronic problems previously served through individual, intensive, long-term casework services are served through case management with crisis interventions as needed.

The kinds and duration of services are determined by diagnostic categories, and are set by the third party. Thus, it has become necessary to "label" clients according to DSM-IV criteria, raising serious ethical issues. Labels follow clients, often throughout their lives. A more serious label, or a certain kind of label, may warrant the approval of more services. If you believe your client needs the additional time and services, should you determine a more serious "label" to enable them to qualify? What of confidentiality, when your records and the "label" you have assigned are perused by third party employees, often non-professionals, via computers? If this information is available to third parties, informed consent requires that you share information and documentation with clients. Is such a degree of sharing always in the best interests of the client?

In the "real world" of managed care, hospital patients are discharged before they are ready, people with chronic mental illnesses are given time-limited interventions, complex assessments are completed during single interviews, and case management services are limited in number of permissible contacts. Workers must learn skills that can assist them in negotiating the managed care environment in order to obtain the services needed by their clients. Advocacy becomes an essential part of social work, and a thorough knowledge of community networks and resources becomes vital.

Loewenberg and Dolgoff suggest that there are three sections of the Code of Ethics that address some of the ethical issues encountered in managed care, and provide some direction:

Section IA.2: The social worker should not participate in, condone, or be associated with dishonesty, fraud, deceit, or misrepresentation.

Section ID.1 & 3: The social worker should be alert to and resist the influences and pressures that interfere with the exercise of professional discretion and impartial judgement required for the performance of professional functions.

Section IIF.9: The social worker should terminate service to clients, and professional relationships with them, when such service and relationships are no longer required or no longer serve the clients' needs or interests.

These provisions of the Code often present difficulties for the social worker attempting to comply in a managed care setting.[1]

C. The For-Profits
Groups of mental health professionals often band together to provide services to clients. Under names such as "Counseling Center," "Recovery and Rehabilitation Services," "Psychological Services," "Turning Point," "Progress Unlimited," or "Potential to Achieve," such private groups of practitioners often include psychiatrists, social workers, psychologists, and counselors.

For-profits provide income and revenue for the owners, who may be the professional staff or an outside organization. Their sources of funding include managed care organizations and fee-for-service. Clients of the for-profits are often not the traditional social work population of the poor, the oppressed, minorities, and the chronically mentally ill, many of whom require services that enable basic survival. Rather, for-profits generally serve the middle classes, whose problems involve self-esteem, marital discord, acting-out adolescents, and job-related issues — the segment of the population who is generally well insured and/or able to pay privately for services. Some for-profits also accept a percentage of clients on a sliding scale of fees. However, in order to remain viable, they must focus efforts on clients able to pay for services.

Because they do not serve traditional social work clients, and because the for-profit orientation seemed at variance with basic social work values, for-profit agencies were rarely selected as field work placements. As traditional agency placements have undergone continued attrition, however, schools have been forced to explore for-profits as field placements as well. The possibility of using for-profits as internship placements has stirred heated debate in the profession as a whole, and the impact is felt well beyond the faculties and administrations of the social work schools themselves. Some schools have decided to use the for-profits, while others continue to hold to the more traditional sources of placements.

Concerns about using for-profits as field work placements have focused on three areas:

Will students learn the requisite skills for working with social work's traditional populations?

If for-profits serve primarily the American mainstream, how will students placed where clients tend to be fairly homogeneous learn the skills needed to provide services to the poor, the oppressed, chronically mentally ill, immigrants, undocumented aliens, the elderly, people in prisons, people for whom English is not the native language, and others? Where will they learn the important techniques needed for multicultural counseling? How will they experience a broad range of degree and type of social problem? How can they develop empathy and understanding for people whose basic survival needs direct their behavior and responses to all situations?

A vital part of social work education involves advocacy, networking, and utilizing community resources. For-profit clients generally do not need these kinds of services, and students will not have the opportunity to develop skills in these areas.

Will students learn and integrate the core values of the social work profession into their professional development?

The NASW Code of Ethics states that the mission of social work is embodied in six core values. Restated here, these are:

- service
- social justice
- dignity and worth of persons
- importance of human relationships
- integrity
- competence

(NASW Code of Ethics, Preamble)

Service as a value demands service to all who are in need, not only those who can pay for social work services. For-profits focus on a small portion of the population in terms of providing services. Ability to pay determines who is accepted for services, not need. The core value of dignity and worth of persons asks social workers to respect and consider all persons, not only those who can afford service, and learning to respect people in circumstances which are often degrading, debilitating, and destructive to them is an important part of social work education.

Social justice demands that all people have access to needed goods and services in society, regardless of their personal characteristics, origin and history, place in society, or financial resources. In this sense, for-profits could be considered as not socially just. Will students learn to advocate for equal services and programs without exposure to all segments of society?

Field instructors and colleagues serve as role models to students. Will social workers in for-profit settings model the kinds of behaviors students need to learn?

If students observe workers turning away or terminating clients who are unable to pay for services, giving preferential treatment to those who pay privately and fully for each therapeutic session, or assigning cases based on financial considerations, what will they learn from this kind of role modeling? For-profit agencies that have students often assign to them the clients who pay the lowest fees, and reserve the best and most experienced workers for full-fee paying clients. The clients who can afford to pay the least often have the most severe, complex, and critical problems, leaving students to struggle while experienced workers address less critical problems.

Social workers in for-profit agencies have, in a sense, determined that their own needs (for a good income) and their personal interests (serving middle-class clients) are worth at least equal, if not greater, consideration than the traditional social work commitments. Will students thus learn that their own needs should be placed ahead of those of their clients?

Reisch sums these problems up well:

Their professional code of ethics obliges social workers to make clients' interests paramount. Evidence exists, however, that for-profit organizations are more likely to market their services to those clients most likely to benefit the organization rather that those clients most likely to benefit from its services.[2]

Placement in a for-profit demands that both the school and the student reflect carefully upon these issues in order ensure that the core values of the profession, and the necessary skills, are accessible to the student for integrating into professional competencies.

D. **Personalities and Places**

Budgetary cuts, managed care, the use of for-profits as field work placements — all of these impact on the people and places used for field work placements.

In addition, there are the "traditional" problems related to differing personalities, interests and priorities, and in location and facilities. Some agencies are located in poor or high-crime areas, which may be less safe and thus create stress for the student. Some may be virtually inaccessible to public transportation, while others involve feeding parking meters every two hours. Some may be far from the students' home or place of employment, if the student is also working part-time. While schools try hard to consider the special needs of each student, the increasing scarcity of field work placements often limits choices significantly, and students find they must incorporate compensating for distance or inaccessibility in addition to meeting the demands of field work.

Schools are also limited in their ability to control the selection and suitability of field instructors, and in matching interests and personalities between field instructors and students. Agencies may be friendly and pleasant places to work, or produce anxiety and stress due to work loads, politics and bickering, differing priorities and interests among workers, and many other causes. Even with the best of intentions, schools cannot accurately assess the suitability of every aspect of every field work agency, and students may find that personalities and circumstances may be difficult at times.

E. Organizational Change

It is also important to recognize that agencies and programs have a very strong stake in self-preservation, which is usually manifested as a strong inclination toward the maintenance of the status quo and a resistance to any change. Stability ensures continuation of services to clients, the identifiable existence of the agency as an organization, and, perhaps most important though least discussed, the assurance of job security for employees.

We can gain some insights into the way organizations function using the ecological perspective — the same perspective we use in conjunction with the life model to think about goodness of fit between individuals and environments.

When an organization develops, it establishes a niche for itself in the community network of other agencies, in its neighborhood, and among the resources available to sustain it. Agency policies, programs, employees, and resources are all in harmony. The agency, like any organism, reaches homeostasis.

A change in organizational structure, a diminution of funding, a new director, a move to a new location, a shift in program focus or in service delivery systems are all perceived as a potential threat to the organization as a whole, and thus to its staff. It disrupts the homeostasis and produces turbulence. The organization will mobilize its forces to resist the changes, to maintain the status quo, and thus to preserve itself. When changes are imposed from without, and do not involve the agreement, or even the awareness, of employees, anger and resentment added to uncertainty about the future may be felt throughout the organization.

Most agencies and programs are able to motivate themselves toward the change eventually. In common with all living organisms, organizations have the ability to adapt to changes in their environment and reach a new state of homeostasis. If the surrounding environment is extremely hostile (such as if program funds are completely cut), or if the organization is not flexible enough to adapt, the disruptions can prove fatal.

Today's climate is tough on agencies and programs. Change, from within and from without, occurs frequently, at times disrupting services, lives, and communities. Field placement agencies are not immune to these changes.

As a student, you may find that your agency is in the midst of restructuring, adding a new service or closing an old program, moving, or even of closing down. While this is extremely rare, there have been instances in which a field placement agency or a program in which a student is placed closes down completely, thus forcing a change in placements. More commonly, your agency may be in the midst of restructuring its hierarchy, modifying programs or service delivery, cutting back on services and/or employees. Your field instructor and colleagues may be immersed in this process.

It is possible that their immersion can affect your placement, which ideally requires continuity and order, and the ability of others to focus on your learning experiences. It is best to regard it as a challenge and as a wonderful opportunity to learn another aspect of professional functioning and responsibility.

The concerns presented here are some of the major issues that affect the development of problems for students in field work placements. In the succeeding chapters, we shall focus on several kinds of problems and circumstances that may create difficulties. Remember to view the problems you encounter within the broader contexts suggested here.

---

[1] Loewenberg, F.M., & Dolgoff, R. (1996) *Ethical Decisions for Social Work Practice*. Itasca, IL: F.E. Peacock, p. 186.

[2] Gamrbill, E., Prguer, R., Eds. (1992) *Controversial Issues in Social Work*. Boston: Allyn & Bacon, p. 33.

CHAPTER EIGHTEEN

RECEPTIVITY OF SETTING

We begin our exploration of the kinds of problems you might encounter in field with a closer look at your field placement agency setting, and its receptivity to you as a student intern. Agencies that accept student field work placements in general are committed to their roles. They accept their responsibilities in terms of preparing future professionals, and welcome the opportunity to share facilities and resources with students. Many agencies have accepted students for years, and have a tradition of this kind of professional service. Others are eager to expand their professional commitments. Still others enjoy the status of having students. Some value the fresh, cutting edge knowledge and theory students will bring, and view students as an excellent training resource for staff. Government-supported agencies and programs may have student training as a part of their required activities, and special programs place students in these settings. Thus, most agencies and programs are genuinely interested in their interns, and are committed to making the learning process meaningful.

Notwithstanding all of the above, problems can occur. Some, such as lack of space, may be a condition which cannot be remedied. Others, such as the use of students for the agency's own ends and purposes, create ethical issues for students and field instructors alike.

A. <u>Your Personal Space</u>

In the "ideal world," you will have your own office, or one to share with fellow students. You will have a telephone, and comfortable furniture. Such a placement is described in a liaison's summary to the field office:

"The student's office is private and convenient to the waiting room. There is soft lighting, and the comfortable furniture creates a warm and inviting atmosphere. He has personalized it with posters and a wonderful brass table, set next to the client's chair. There is a bookshelf containing literature relevant to the placement, populations, and problems served by the agency in the office as well."

Most students will read this description and realize that there is no connection (though this placement does in fact exist) between it and their own situation. In general, students share offices with other students, with colleagues, or with their field instructor. Arrangements are adequate, if not luxurious like the one described above.

Other descriptions, from the "real" world, include:

"The field instructor's office includes a brown two-drawer file cabinet on one side of the room. This has been fitted with a small lamp, and a folding chair. The student shares her field instructor's office, and must leave the room when the field instructor makes confidential calls or interviews clients. The student may sit at the field instructor's desk when she is interviewing."

"The student's office is in the agency's lunchroom. She uses the lunchroom table as her desk. She must clear off her work, and vacate the table, between 11:30 and 1:30 daily, while staff use the room for lunch breaks. There is no telephone available and the student must ask the permission of a colleague in the next-door office to use the telephone. The student must arrange with the field instructor to use her office for interviews, and these must be scheduled far in advance."

"The student has her own desk, chair and telephone, and the agency has even made a lovely nameplate for her. Her space is in the administrative area. The office is a large, open space divided into cubicles by moveable walls. The student's desk is not in a cubicle, though she does have two walls. There is little privacy for interviews and the student says she and her clients must whisper to ensure confidentiality."

"The school is delighted to have a student, and his reception has been warm and welcoming. Space is at a premium, however. The field instructor shares an office with the assistant principal. The student's office is in a large utility closet, which has been cleared for his use. He has a desk and chair, and a chair for clients. He is unable to close the door, as there is no air circulation, but has placed the desk in a way that maximizes client confidentiality."

"The student's office is large and comfortable, and there is even an Oriental carpet on the floor. One wall is lined with windows that look out over the hospital campus. There is a desk, chairs, and a couch in the office, and a two-line telephone. However, the field instructor's office is located in another building, a five minutes' outdoor walk from her office. Patients are in the field instructor's building, and are seen in the day room or in a small cubicle adjacent to the nurse's station. All writing and documentation must be done there as well, as hospital policy precludes taking any charts out of the hospital building."

"The agency has a long and distinguished history, and has been in this location for 85 years. They are proud of the many years that they have served as a field placement to area schools. The student has been assigned a small area in the large storage room at the back of the agency. While the rest of the area contains what appears to be old desks and other office equipment, and is unlighted, the niche carved out for the student has been fitted with a grey wooden desk and matching chair. A comfortable chair for clients is placed next to the table. Although there is no readily available telephone, the student has ready access to clients at this senior center."

People vary in their ability to adapt to less-than-ideal circumstances, and students in these placements did have to adapt themselves to their agencies' space limitations. If you find that the arrangements that have been made for you are totally unworkable, you may want to discuss these with your field instructor or with your liaison. In most cases, they will do whatever is possible to make your working environment functional for you.

B. The Place of Students in the Overall Agency Plan

As noted earlier, agencies make a choice to seek and accept students. The agency's Director is generally primarily responsible for field placement arrangements, and must in all cases approve them. Most agencies will welcome you; some will even have a tea or a small party to recognize your presence as a part of them.

Preparations for students must include accommodations other than physical space. Clients must be assigned. Supervisory time, often extra supervisory time, must be made available. Professional and non-professional staff must be informed and involved. They must be willing to answer questions, share information and resources, and, at times allow students to shadow their activities in order to learn. Staff must be willing to engage fully with students, while knowing that these placements are limited in time. Each agency is its own unique world: it welcomes students at its own pace, under its own terms.

There are times and situations where a student may not feel especially welcomed at their field placement agency. Heavy caseloads, budget cuts, and insufficient staff cause worker overload, leaving little time and emotional energy to invest in a student. Very rarely, the decision to accept students will have been made by an agency Director without the knowledge and/or support of the agency's professional staff. Decisions made in this manner by an unpopular Director can adversely affect a field placement.

If your agency is a new field work placement, colleagues and staff may be uncertain of where you fit in to the overall agency structure. Are you a guest? Are you an employee? How much should be shared with you about agency problems and concerns? Where are your confidentiality limits? Will the things that you hear be reported to your school's Field Office? Be discussed in your classes? If this is your first field work placement, you might have some confusion about your role and the agency's expectations which can complicate these issues even more!

Even experienced field placement agencies will vary greatly in the way that students are expected to fit into the overall agency structure. Some expect that you will honor and abide by all of the policies that apply to regular employees. This may appear very positive at first, but can create some problems. If everyone is expected to attend all staff meetings, and they are held on a day that is not a regular field placement day for you, are you obligated to attend? If all employees are required to have late office hours one night a week, must you have them as well? What about school vacation days that are not agency holidays? Your school may have a policy about that, but your agency might disagree. What do you do?

Other agencies may regard you as separate from the regular staff. You may be excluded from certain kinds of meetings. Because you are not there every day, and your time with the agency is limited, lunch groups, coffee breaks, and special agency events may not welcome you. When guests visit the agency, you may not be introduced. Desiring acceptance in your new professional role, you may find these painful circumstances. Generally, your best resource is your field instructor, who should set parameters and serve as an example to others in your agency in establishing a clear role for you.

C. Demands for Extra Time and Services

Students may also encounter a demand for extra time and services from the field instructor, or the expectation of extra time and services from the agency's director and/or staff.

The days and times that you are expected to be in field work are determined by the school, and, as noted in Chapter 1, Section D, are established by the Council on Social Work Education. A part of your school's agreement with your placement agency stipulates the school's expectations in this regard. The curriculum is planned so that classes are scheduled on non-field days, and allowances are made for you to have adequate time for the library, for studying, and for personal commitments. Individual adjustments in the school's plans for field work scheduling may be made based on student need or agency requirements, but these are planned from the outset, and all parties are well aware of the arrangements. Outside of scheduled class and field hours, you should be free to plan and live your life as you choose.

However, some agencies expect that you will remain at your placement beyond the required numbers of hours, or return to placement at times not officially scheduled. These expectations may result from agency need, their perception of your best interests in terms of learning, or the services you are expected to provide to clients. At times, your agency may require your presence. Uncertain about the regulations, eager to please, afraid of causing a problem which will impact on the rest of field placement, many students silently comply. Some of the more common kinds of time problems students have encountered include:

"I work my two days every week, on Mondays and Thursdays. But staff meetings are on Wednesdays, and they say I have to be there, or I won't know what is really going on. My field instructor says I need this learning experience."

"They always expect me to work late. I'm supposed to leave at five but I can never seem to get out of there until six-thirty. There are so many meetings all day I can't get my work done, so I have to stay late to do it. Everybody there stays late. It's expected of me."

"I was assigned clients who work all day and I can only see them at night. Not all the clients at the agency work like that. But my caseload demands that I work at night if I want to have any client contacts or really get involved."

"I have such a huge caseload (see Chapter 19B) that I can't get my work done in the time I'm supposed to. I don't want to complain and I don't want them to think I'm too slow, so I just come in on Saturday and catch up with my recording and documentation. My field instructor doesn't even know I do that!"

"We're open on evenings and weekends too and we all have to take turns doing intakes. The turns are assigned in rotation, and when your turn comes up, you have to be there no matter what. They don't let you trade with anyone because they say it messes up the schedule. Sometimes my turn is at night, and last week it was on Sunday."

And a personal favorite:

"My field instructor says I have to come in to this meeting every month. I told her I have a class scheduled right at that time but she says it doesn't matter, and I have to come anyway. She says that my learning in field is much more important than classroom learning anyway. But I'm going to miss one class a month, and it's a once a week class. That's 1/4 of my learning. How am I going to do my assignments? What should I tell my instructor?"

Agencies who have these expectations often take the position that if students really wanted to learn, they would take every opportunity offered gratefully, no matter what the inconvenience or personal cost. Students may feel guilty, and be ashamed to protest.

In addition to demanding extra time, agencies may demand extra services as well, with the same stated motivation of providing wonderful opportunities for students to learn. Students may be given the "assignment" of taking notes and preparing them for distribution for every staff meeting, or be asked to answer telephone calls "to learn about the kinds of questions people ask when they call here." They may be asked to take the agency's clients to all medical appointments (often in their own cars, on their own insurances!), in order to have this "extra" opportunity to talk with them.

Extra services may provide opportunities for extra learning, in some circumstances. In others, however, students' learning time is devoted to meeting agency needs, not their own.

D. Demands for Inappropriate Services

Very rarely, students are asked to perform services that are not appropriate to their learning and that seem to serve the needs of the agency exclusively. While "helping the agency out" in times of need is certainly understandable and acceptable, agencies who regard students as secretaries, maids, or fill-in professionals are abusing their placement status. A special story from a liaison's agency visit provides a dramatic picture:

"The student seemed a bit uncomfortable, but I couldn't tell why. I asked about her cases, and she said she didn't have any yet, but had been allowed to watch therapy sessions through a one-way mirror. I asked her how she was spending her days. She replied that she was working in the agency's little convenience shop, counting candy bars, toothpaste, and other stock. When I expressed amazement, the field instructor maintained that learning about the kinds of items clients bought in the shop was a part of learning about the client population. When I requested that the student be relieved of this assignment and given a caseload appropriate to her learning needs, the field instructor said she would do this as soon as they hired a girl to run the gift shop!"

While this story is extreme, it is absolutely true! The student's placement was terminated, and she was placed with another agency. However, this student <u>had not complained to anyone</u> about her assignment, which did not become known until the liaison visit midway through the semester. Uncertainty, fear of repercussions from the field instructor, and a desire to comply with the agency's wishes kept her silent.

Another student's experience, as told in a worried phone call to her liaison during the <u>second week</u> of her first field work placement in a mental hospital setting:

"My field instructor is going on vacation for a month, starting on Monday. He says I am going to be responsible for his whole caseload while he's gone. He has thirty cases, and I think a lot of them are violent. I'm scared to be alone with them. Besides, I don't know anything yet. I won't know what to do. He says I can ask his friend whose office is down the hall if I run into problems. But I don't even know if I'll know it's a problem!"

And two more:

"They told me that every day I have to pick up all the toys in the playroom after the last client has left and clean up the room. I found out that the secretary used to do that but she complained and said that it was not part of her job, so they assigned it to me. I don't know what I'm supposed to learn from <u>that</u>! I'm paying hard-earned money for my field work experience. I want to see clients, not pick up toys!"

"I asked the student to tell me about her caseload. She seemed a bit uncertain. The field instructor told her to tell me about Mrs. S., whom she had driven to the doctor this morning, and who had told her about her problems with her daughter. I listened to the story and then asked the student when she would be seeing Mrs. S. again, and what her plans were for helping her. The student told me she had written a note about the problems in Mrs. S.'s chart, but that she wouldn't be seeing her again. She always saw clients only once, because she only drove them to the doctor's office. Sometimes she got to see them more than once if they needed to go to the doctor more often. The field instructor said that the agency scheduled all its clients' medical visits on field work days so that the student would be able to take them and talk to them on the way. I asked about the vehicle and the insurance and found out the student was using her own car and her own insurance. She was the agency's official driver!"

While these kinds of situations are uncommon, you must be careful to assume some of the responsibility for making sure that the work assigned to you will meet your learning needs and is appropriate to a student professional. If you encounter problems such as these, you should contact your liaison, the Field Office, your adviser, or your practice instructor <u>as early as possible</u> so that adjustments can be made and your learning is not compromised. While some of the problems related to caseload, field instructor, or colleagues can loom larger in a student's perception, the agency's receptivity to student placements is always an important consideration in assessing and working with field placement problems.

CHAPTER NINETEEN

CASELOAD AND CLIENT CONCERNS

Many of the problems students encounter in field work placements involve caseloads and clients. Too small, too large, not challenging, too difficult, caseloads and assigned projects are often not exactly what students expect or desire of internships. Clients, too, often cause difficulties that students worry over frequently. Most client problems can and should be addressed in supervision, but some may make you hesitant, uncertain of how to proceed.

A. Client Problems

The problems that you encounter with clients should be addressed with your field instructor during the course of supervisory sessions. Some of them will be related to your level of knowledge and experience, while others clearly require prompt attention and action.

Problems such as the client's refusal to establish a relationship, discomfort with interviewing, or the development of appropriate interventions are not "problems" per se: rather, they are an expected part of your learning tasks and may be addressed through school and field work knowledge and experience.

Other kinds of situations that might need to be discussed with your field instructor include:

- your client wants to establish a social, rather than a professional, relationship
- your know your client, or your client's family, or people in your client's social network outside of your agency relationship
- your client obtains your home number, or address. He or she may or may not use it to contact you.
- your client is aggressive, threatening, or destructive
- you are afraid of your client, or of someone in your client's relationship network

Some very challenging problems might occur when clients attempt to form an alliance with you which undermines agency policy, mission, and practice. A client may tell you (in confidence, of course) that he or she is sneaking out after curfew in a residential setting, or is keeping more than the agreed-upon amount of outside earning for personal use, or is abusing drugs when policy requires complete abstention. Clients may say that they are telling you this because they "trust you," or because it was "just this once," or because they need your help.

Some examples:

"I just have to tell you but don't tell anybody. I got a part-time job today. I'm going to be working with a building contractor. He said he'd pay me in cash each day that I work. He calls in the morning and I just go where he sends me. Maybe I can really get out from under and get my family back together. The contractor said that if I do good work, he can hire me full time after a while. Then maybe I can get off assistance, too."

"I had a really hard time Friday night. My husband called and started to hit on me wanting me to come back to him. Every time I talk to him I flip out. I just can't handle having anything to do with him. So I had a few drinks. It was just this one time. I haven't touched a drop since. You won't tell anybody, will you? I know I'm supposed to stay dry but it was just this one time. He was really bothering me and it just made me so nervous."

"I had to leave them to go to work. I know I'm not supposed to leave them. The lady from Protective Services said I can't leave them by themselves. It was just for two hours, after they came home from school. They were all right. Nothing happened. I promise I'll never do it again, even if it means I can't keep my job. It's so hard because I need to work to support them and then I can't leave them to do it. I'll never do it again. You just can't report me! They'll take them away if you do! They said I could only have one last chance. I'll never do it again. I swear!"

"Johnny came over the other night. He said he just had to see the kids. They were really glad to see him too. Jeannie just laughed and laughed and hugged him and you know how quiet she's been since he left. Lorrie got to sit on his lap and 'have a story,' just like she used to. Maybe I don't need the court order any more. I don't think he'd do anything to them, and I could always be there too. I know the girls miss him, and he does truly love them. What do you think?"

In each of these stories, the client is trying to create an alliance with the worker, by asking the worker to collude in withholding information from the agency or the courts. In each, the client's story sounds reasonable, and the worker can easily empathize with the client's problem. In the second and third story, the client promises never to do the action again — never to take a drink, never to leave the children. When something that violates rules or policy happens "only once," we tend to have a different feeling about it than we would were the behavior chronic. Also, if we believe that the end, such as that of financial independence, is a worthwhile one, we may feel that almost any means are acceptable if they will lead to it.

The client has told us these things because he or she "trusts us." We are proud and pleased to be trusted, and to have established such a good client/worker relationship. And we do, after all, have an obligation to the client that is primary. We want to maintain confidentiality, too.

Yet, there are many pitfalls to honoring the client's requests. A major problem is that colluding with clients in this manner violates the NASW Code of Ethics, which states:

<u>Section 4.04</u>: Social workers should not participate in, condone, or be associated with dishonesty, fraud, or deception (NASW Code of Ethics).

In addition, the client has agreed to the conditions of service, with any accompanying restrictions or limitations, preferring these conditions to any other options available. (Even "non-voluntary" clients have options — jail or agency program, hospitalization or abstention, etc.) In violating the agreement, however minimally or excusably, the client has not met the terms which permitted the choice he or she has made.

As professionals, we also serve as models for our clients — of honesty, integrity, hard work, caring, empathy and understanding, and many other things. What message are we sending when we agree to participate in dishonesty? What kind of behavior are we modeling?

What of our responsibilities to our agency, our colleagues, and our field instructor? If we do not share this information with our field instructor, he or she can still be held legally responsible for our behavior and actions, under the terms of *respondeat superior*. Agencies lose funding when the policies and conditions stipulated in programs are violated, and thus we could be placing many people's well-being at risk. Colleagues who refuse to collaborate with clients in this way may be harmed by our actions as well, for their clients may hear about our actions and expect the same from them, harboring anger and resentment if they are treated differently.

These are issues that require serious thought and reflection. You also need to remember, as we noted earlier, however, that if you seek advice on this issue, (which is generally the best option) you will lose control of it. Whomever you choose to tell — field instructor, colleague, adviser, practice instructor — is placed in the same kind of ethical dilemma as you. He or she may chose to advise and keep silent, or may feel a personal obligation to report. The decision is no longer solely your own.

B. Insufficient Cases or Work Assigned

Some students find that their caseload, projects, or work assignments are not sufficient to provide a good learning experience. An initial delay in the assignment of work is not uncommon, but when the situation continues for an extended period of time, it becomes a problem requiring attention.

It's easy to become stressed over caseload assignments. You may be ready to begin your first day, and find any delay wasteful and annoying. Conversely, you may be nervous about interviewing your first client, or holding your first meeting and find yourself searching for reasons to rationalize postponing it even further. In your classes, you listen to stories from students who have begun to see clients, who have large caseloads, or who have been assigned a major project.

Initial Assignments

Schools and field placements vary in their timing in the assignment of cases and projects to field work students. Some schools require that students be assigned "their own" cases in a month, or in six weeks. Others have no specific requirements beyond "in a timely manner," and leave the timing of assignments to the field instructor. You may find that you arrive at your placement, and are given a list of cases which will be your own. Your agency may have a required orientation program, or period of familiarization with the agency prior to the assignment of cases and problems. Your field instructor may believe that a waiting period is important, to provide time for you to become comfortable in the agency, and to have begun your classroom practice learning.

On occasion, there may be a more difficult problem: your agency may be in a period where there are few clients, when projects have been completed and new ones not begun, or where the work available is not appropriate to your needs and ability. These problems, which are inherent in the agency structure, should be discussed with your field liaison and the Field Work office, so that arrangements can be made, in another placement if necessary, which will enable you to begin your learning experience.

You should be fully engaged in your work within several weeks of beginning your field work placement. Your school has some checkpoints built in to check on your progress in terms of field work assignments: your practice instructor will ask students about caseloads and assignments, you will have written assignments which require that you have specific experiences involving clients and projects, your liaison will be in contact with you and will be visiting, and there are midterm caseload report forms that many schools require through the field office. In the unlikely event that all of these systems fail, you should take the responsibility of bringing your problem to the attention of the Field Work office.

Ongoing Caseload Insufficiency

Each of us is unique in terms of the workload we can and desire to carry and the way in which we relate to too much or too little work. However, problems can occur if caseloads and work assignments are so small that they do not engage your time and attention during the hours of field. It is frustrating to be sitting around your agency the required number of hours, reading a book or gazing out of the window. The problem is compounded as you hear almost daily recitals of the exciting work other students are doing at their field placement agencies.

You have been assigned one family. True, you are working with several family members, with the children's school, and with the mother's parole officer. Your field instructor may feel that this is a sufficient assignment for you for the entire period of your placement, but you may disagree. There seem to be long stretches of hours and days when there is nothing to do. You want another family, but the field instructor is adamant: students always carry only one client family.

You are placed in a crisis intervention agency, and your assignment is to field phone calls and respond to the initial problem, then to refer the client to an ongoing worker. This was challenging at first, and you did feel that you learned about the agency's population and the kinds problems clients experienced. However, no cases are assigned to you, and you have no ongoing responsibilities. Is this all I'm going to do? you wonder.

You are placed in a judiciary setting, and are assigned one parolee. Your task is to assist him to return to the community by finding housing, employment, and developing a supportive social network. You work hard with him for a period of time, and help him to develop a community support network, but then all of your goals are met. You continue to see him, just to "check up" on things, but your interventions are over. Yet, no new cases are assigned and your field instructor continues to encourage you to see your client every few weeks.

You have been promised three to five children to work with, doing play therapy. One child has been assigned. Your field instructor keeps telling you that children will be assigned "soon," but "soon" never seems to come. You see your one child each week for a hour. You write in his record for, at most, another hour. You have read everything you could find on play therapy to be ready. You go to every meeting. Still, the empty hours stretch out. Will "soon" ever come? How long should you wait?

You have joined an ongoing organizational restructuring group. Each member has specific responsibilities, and your field instructor is the group's leader. The group comes together at 4 p.m. each day to discuss progress and plan for the next day's work. You attend each meeting, sit next to your field instructor, and participate by offering comments and supporting plans. Everyone involved with the project is pleasant and easy to work with, and they appear genuinely happy that you are a part of the group. However, you have not been assigned any responsibilities of your own. You have nothing to report at the meetings, and the hours until 4 p.m. are often empty. Sometimes you ask another group member if you can watch or help with his or her work. Your field instructor is satisfied with your participation and work, and encourages you to assist other group members with their work.

It is important that you address insufficient caseload promptly so that this problem can be remedied before many hours of field placement and opportunities for learning have elapsed. Shyness, uncertainty, and fear of creating a difficult situation should not prevent you from sharing your concerns with a member of your field education team. If you are hesitant about the potential effects of sharing your concerns with your field instructor, the problem can often be resolved without a direct confrontation, or without your field instructor's awareness of your concern. A liaison visit, carefully phrased questions, and a tactful review of the school's goals for your learning can resolve the problem in most cases.

C. <u>Over-Assignment of Caseload or Projects</u>

From famine to feast! Problems can also occur if your field instructor and/or agency's expectations of the work you can perform are unreasonable for the number of hours and learning you have available. Overload creates stress and burnout, and may also impinge upon your personal time as you try to meet expectations in terms of visits, progress, and documentation for each case. Students whose caseloads are too large may also be unable to spend the time in processing and reflection that are an important part of integrating knowledge and experiences.

If you have been assigned a caseload, or been given responsibility for a project, whose demands exceed your field work hours, you may have even more hesitation in expressing your concerns than if you have been given insufficient work. In addition to fear of repercussions, discomfort with confrontation, or shyness about complaining, addressing caseload overload carries some special difficulties for students.

After all, you think, I'm new to this, and I don't know what's expected. What if this <u>is</u> an appropriate caseload? What if this project is what students are expected to do? What if I'm just having a hard time because I'm too slow in getting the work done, or if I have to ask questions about things that I am expected to know and that slows me down? What if I can't get it all done because I rewrite all my documentation to be sure it sounds just right? Should I just try to work faster? Should I stay later, or come in to catch up at another time?

If I complain, will they think I'm weak, inept, inefficient, or acting like a baby? Should I just keep quiet, do it all, and not rock the boat? Everything else seems to be OK — I'm getting along with my field instructor, the other workers like me, and I'm doing well in school. Is it worth it? And, if they take away some of my workload, someone else will have to carry it. Everyone may be overworked as it is. Will I be creating a lot of resentment? Will they think I'm not doing my share? That I'm not dedicated to my work? Or, worst of all, that I shouldn't be a social worker?

Different students in different placements carry very different caseloads, so it is usually hard to make any comparisons with classmates. If you are uncomfortable raising the issue with your field instructor (a not uncommon feeling), you can always discuss the problem with someone at school — you practice instructor, liaison, or adviser are good choices. They will have a good "feel" for what you are doing, what the school's expectations are, and whether your field work placement is expecting more than is appropriate from you. If your workload does appear unreasonable, they will try to determine the cause of the problem.

In some cases, over-zealous field instructors assign large numbers of cases believing that this will provide wonderful opportunities for students to work with a variety of clients and problems. They regard the size of the caseload as a positive, rather than a negative, experience. Alternatively, field instructors may assign cases based on the number of hours you spend relative to the number of hours regular employees spend, without regard to the extra time for each assignment required by your status as a student learner.

The size of your caseload may be determined by the agency's director as well. Some field work agencies may have an ulterior motive for taking students: they may have insufficient staff to meet their program needs, and use students to make up the deficit. Your work then becomes necessary for agency functioning, rather than an optional choice which is made to be of service to the profession.

D. Inappropriate Responsibilities Assigned

On occasion, you may find that work that is assigned to you appears inappropriate to your level of skill, your learning needs, or the time available. Such circumstances as the assignment of complex mental health problems requiring high levels of professional expertise, clients who must be visited in places and circumstances known to be extremely unsafe, clients whose potential for violence is severe, clients requiring daily support and intervention, or projects so complex that little progress can be achieved in the duration of the field work placement are examples of inappropriate assignments. Generally, it is the degree and severity of these situations which make them inappropriate for student assignment.

Clients with complex problems who can be helped with the skills that can be developed over the course of placement, a colleague to accompany students on visits to unsafe areas, visits to areas that are generally not considered extremely dangerous, violent clients who are seen in close proximity to staff able to intervene, and projects that may not reach completion, but can make clear, definable, measurable progress can all be appropriate assignments for students.

If you are uncomfortable with any case or project assigned to you, discuss the problem with your field instructor. He or she may be able to explain the rationale and justification for the assignment, alter or adapt it, or refer it to another worker. If the problem appears unresolvable, you should contact another member of your field education team.

Because of the amount of time, energy, and financial resources that you are investing in your professional education, it is important that the caseload assigned to you meet your learning needs in an appropriate manner. Ensuring that this will occur is the responsibility of your school and your field placement. However, ultimately, you will know best what will provide optimum opportunities for your growth. Each student is a unique individual with different interests, tolerances, and learning styles. You can best ensure that the clients, caseload, and assignments provided for you will meet your needs.

The next chapter will present some of the more common problems students encounter in working with field instructors. Because field instructors control caseloads, assignments, working conditions, and grades, problems with this relationship can become extremely frustrating and stressful. It is important to address them in a manner which will resolve the issue — at least to the point where you feel that you can continue to learn and grow professionally.

CHAPTER TWENTY

FIELD INSTRUCTOR PROBLEMS

The relationship between you and your field instructor is crucial to your learning and well-being within the agency. As in any relationship, the particular personalities, issues, and conditions of the relationship will affect its development. You will probably have had the opportunity to meet your field instructor during the early interview process, and you and he or she will have had a chance to make a beginning assessment of the potential for working well together.

As your relationship develops over time, and with the intensity inherent in the learning process, both you and your field instructor may find that there are areas which require some consideration and adjustment. It is important to keep good lines of communication open with your field instructor: this is your best way of ensuring that problems, if they occur, can be easily and quickly resolved.

Some possible problems:

- your field instructor is late, or unavailable, for supervisory time
- your supervisory time is interrupted frequently by telephone calls, emergencies, and other demands upon his or her time during supervision
- your field instructor is much more casual than is comfortable for you about supervision and about your relationship
- your field instructor is more formal and distant in your relationship than is comfortable for you
- your field instructor does not offer you the kind and degree of support you would like or feel that you need
- your field instructor introduces personal matters into your relationship by sharing personal information or eliciting such information from you
- your field instructor provides too much — or too little — control over your activities
- your field instructor is not available to you in emergencies outside of planned supervision
- your field instructor is consistently late or unresponsive in meeting the school's expectations in terms of evaluations and reports

Much rarer, and more difficult problems:

- your field instructor does not keep the content of supervisory conferences in confidence
- your field instructor engages in unethical, or illegal activities
- your field instructor expects you to engage in such activities as well
- your field instructor discounts or undermines your concerns about safety issues
- your field instructor expects you to perform tasks that are inappropriate to your educational level and learning objectives

- your field instructor expects you to carry responsibilities that properly belong to him or her
- your field instructor sexually harasses you, or uses sexual language or expression
- your field instructor appears to be biased against your cultural, ethnic, or socio-economic group, or against another personal characteristic

The possibilities are endless . . .

Most of the common problems noted in the first list above can be addressed directly with your field instructor during the course of supervision or in a special meeting if desired. You may, after some reflection, decide you can "live with" certain characteristics of your supervisory relationship, and that learning to work with others who may be very different from you is a valuable experience in preparation for professional functioning. Remember that you will always have a supervisor, and that, over the course of your professional career, you may need to work with many different kinds of people!

If you decide to share your concerns with your field instructor, always do so in a calm, clear, and professional manner, and support your position with examples. "You are always late for my supervision conference" may feel like a personal attack, while "I notice that we've been late starting our supervisory time. I know that you have many other demands on your time. How can we set this up so that you can do the work you need to do, and I receive the supervision that I need?" enlists cooperation and support. "What can I do to help you prepare this evaluation form?" will probably work better than "I'm going to get an F in field if you don't send this in right now" — though in extreme circumstances you may have to allude to this possible consequence.

If you encounter any of the more difficult problems suggested above, or any other serious situation, you may wish to consider your course of action very carefully. It is generally best to begin discussion of these issues directly with your field instructor. However, you may wish to ask your field liaison or your adviser for suggestions, or for support in talking with your field instructor. Knowing the school's position on your problem may give you the additional confidence that you need to address it.

Because of the range and variety of potential problems students encounter with field instructors, it is impossible to address each one here. A few of the more common problems have been selected to assist you in considering how to handle problems with your field instructor. Almost any problem can be addressed through the process presented in Chapter 23.

A. Insufficient Supervision

Supervision is an essential learning tool. A school acknowledges its central role by carefully selecting field instructors, providing them with orientation (written and/or in meetings) to the school's program and expectations, and offering continued support during the field placement process. The school's agreement with agencies generally stipulates that students receive an hour of individual supervision weekly, or, in some BSW programs or part-time programs, an hour of supervision for every sixteen hours of field work.

However, students sometimes encounter field instructors who, for various reasons, do not provide the supervision necessary. If you are not receiving the amount of supervision your program has stipulated, or that you need, you may first want to explore the circumstances and try to determine the reasons for the problem. Circumstances and reasons can suggest the best course of action. Some common circumstances:

- The field instructor does not schedule regular supervision time, but arranges for supervision "when I have time," often at the last minute.
- The field instructor cancels supervision regularly.
- The field instructor believes that group supervision is more effective and provides no time for individual supervision.
- Supervisory time is interrupted by frequent phone calls and/or staff so that there is little continuity to any discussion. This problem is compounded if the field instructor does not extend the time of supervision to make up for the interruptions.
- The field instructor is often unavailable at the last minute.

There may be reasons for any of these circumstances that, the field instructor may believe, justify them fully. He or she may believe that this is compensated for by the quality of supervision, or by the availability of colleagues and others to provide guidance.

Some of the reasons might include:

- The nature of client population creates frequent emergencies, which cause unpredictable schedules.
- The field instructor has multiple responsibilities that overlap and conflict with each other so that each one must be short-changed somewhat.
- Agency policy, and the field instructor's position, require that he or she be available by phone and in person as needed at all times.
- The field instructor has taken too many students and is unable to provide enough time to work with each individually.
- The field instructor's other agency responsibilities are too heavy to allow time for a student.
- The field instructor's schedule varies for a variety of reasons.

Problems with insufficient supervision are usually obvious early in the field placement, and need to be addressed quickly, before patterns develop which make change more difficult. You can encourage regular, uninterrupted supervisory time by:

- Suggesting that a regularly set time would help you to plan for supervision.
- Providing your field instructor with a written agenda a day or two prior to each session.
- Asking to reschedule at the time that your field instructor cancels a session.
- Suggesting that you have concerns that you would like to discuss privately, or that you are uncomfortable violating your client's confidentiality regularly in group supervision.
- Sharing that you have difficulty concentrating and maintaining focus when there are too many interruptions.

- Last choice, the most confrontational — remind your field instructor of her agreement with your school for supervisory time.

If none of these approaches seem to resolve the problem, contact your field liaison.

B. Inappropriate Degree of Supervision

Inadequacies or inappropriate supervision may be more difficult to perceive early in a practicum. You are uncertain what to expect, and the parameters of the student/field instructor relationship may not be clear at first. You may be unaware of any deficiencies in the direction and supervision provided to you. Additionally, your need for guidance will increase as you become more involved with clients and projects and acquire knowledge through your classes at school, so that inadequacies may not be apparent during the first weeks. You may wonder if minimal guidance, or micro-management, is actually beneficial to your learning.

It is important to distinguish actual difficulties from teaching style. Your field instructor may use several strategies in working with you. Some may work well, others may not. You will need to think through this distinction carefully before determining that the supervision you are receiving is inadequate, overly controlling, or incompetent.

Inadequate Supervision

Inadequate supervision leaves you with no guidance in circumstances that create danger and/or ethical problems, or leaves you unsure of how to proceed in dealing with a client's problem.

You see a client who threatens to "beat the hell" out of his fourteen-year-old son next time he is late for curfew. You believe that you need to intervene immediately to protect the son, because his father has a history of violence. Actually, his violent behavior is the reason that you are seeing him, but this is the first time that he has voiced a threat. Should you report him? Should you call CPS? Should you warn the son? Should you try to have him come in again and explore this further?

You ask your field instructor for guidance, only to be asked "Well, what do you want to do about it?" When you say you don't know, the field instructor suggests that you both think about it for a while, and discuss it again in a week.

Your client has told you he has violated the curfew of his residential program, but was not caught sneaking back into the building. He asks you not to tell, and says he won't do it again, but you decide that you must seek guidance from your field instructor, and inform him of the violation. "Well," the field instructor says, "we could tell the Head of the school. But maybe we should let it go this once. What do you think? It was just one time. On the other hand, a rule's a rule. Let's move on to the next problem."

One instance of this kind of problem may not be enough to assure you that there is a real concern about supervision. However, if you notice avoidance, unwillingness to give direction, or insufficient direction given on numerous occasions, you will need to address this difficult issue.

Overly Controlling Supervision

On the opposite end of the scale, you may find that your field instructor attempts to manage every minor detail of your caseload or project, leaving you with responsibility only for implementing his or her plan. There is no space for you to problem-solve, take the initiative, or take (reasonable) chances. Direction is provided in every minute detail.

You are preparing for your fourth visit with your client. You have been working on exploring her problems, and have decided to focus on increasing job skills with the goal of employment. As you are discussing the client with your field instructor prior to the interview, he says, "Now, you have to be very careful here. You have to keep the momentum going so that she will move ahead with learning her job skills. You should focus the interview on job skills right away. You want to know exactly what job skills she would like to acquire. The two of you can make a list of them, and then you and I can go over them and decide what to do next. Then you can make an appointment for her with the vocational program at the rehabilitation center. Here's their number, right here. You should call them while she is in your office. You call and speak to the intake worker, and make an appointment. Be sure you check with her to see if this is a good date and time for her. Get directions, so she will know where to go. Do you think you can manage all that?"

You are about to have your first interview with a newly assigned client, your third. You have read the client's chart, and learned that, like your first two clients, he is coming to the agency for substance abuse counseling. Your field instructor stops by your office to "check in" with you and to "make sure you are ready." "Now remember," she says, "go out to the waiting room to get him. Introduce yourself and just say something casual. I know — ask him if he located the agency easily. Then take him to your office. You'll want to close the door to be sure that he feels that he has privacy. Then ask him to tell you about himself. Remember, you can't believe anything he says — people like that never tell you the truth about anything. But you don't want to confront him so soon. Just nod your head and don't say much. He'll probably talk on and on and you won't have to do too much. You should take some notes, though, so you and I can go over them. We can look at his record and see if we can untangle the truth from the stories he tells. Don't worry. Just listen. We'll sort it out together later."

You need guidance, yes, and advice. But you also need room to breathe, room to grow, and room to explore and experiment. If you were the student in the second story, you might be asking yourself: "What if I did confront him? After all, I've read his chart. I'll know if he's lying. What would happen? And I don't like to take notes. I think it distracts clients and it distracts me too. I'd rather sit down right after the interview and jot things down. I <u>know</u> I should go to the waiting room to get him, but I'd rather ask him if the sun is out. I <u>know</u> I should close the door. Doesn't she think I can do anything myself?"

Field instructors may micro-manage because they feel you need the guidance, to provide support, or to maintain control over your learning and your caseload. Overly controlling field instructors actually impede progress. You may want to raise these concerns tactfully in supervision. You can also demonstrate to your field instructor that you are able to handle your work by developing and implementing plans spontaneously, or by moving further or faster than she had planned. As the field instructor gains confidence in your ability, she will (hopefully) be able to relinquish some of the control. If the problem persists, you may need to discuss it with your liaison.

C. Incompetent Supervision

Also usually not noted until a student is working with clients or immersed in a project, incompetent supervision poses a danger of harm to yourself or others and must be addressed immediately. Unlike inadequate supervision, where you may want to see if there are several instances, or a pattern, in what is occurring, incompetent supervision requires prompt remedies.

You are working in a family reunification program. You have been seeing a mother, and have made plans with her for the return of her children. She has met all of the goals you have set for preparation, and has been having weekly visitation with her children at the agency. Everything seems to be proceeding well according to plan, except that when you checked in on the last visit, you noticed that the two-year old daughter was crying, and was lying on her side on the floor with her knees to her chest. The five year old was standing in a corner, looking on with apprehension and fear clearly in her face. When you asked what was happening, the mother told you that they were playing a game, and the children agreed. You are worried about their interaction and potential danger to the children when they return to the mother. You seek out your field instructor, who tells you that, if the mother has met all of the requirements of the program, and is prepared to take her girls home, things will work out all right.

You are working with the homeless, and have been talking with a woman about her medical problems. She has agreed to go to a clinic if you arrange an appointment for her. You arrange the appointment, but do not see the woman on the street for several days. You are afraid she is ill. She has told you she sleeps in a tent and cardboard "city" on an empty lot, under a freeway overpass, in a desolate part of town. The only way to reach the area is by walking along a dirt road which goes along the freeway supports for a mile. Should you try to go there to see how she is, and to tell her about her medical appointment? Your field instructor appears quite vague at first, but then says that you certainly should try to find her. She is your client and you owe her loyalty and fidelity. Besides, she could be in need. You describe the tent city and its access, and express some concern for your safety. The field instructor says that personal physical risk is a part of social work and that, if you want to be a social worker, you should put your client's interests first, not your own.

You are working with several focus groups to develop a plan for addressing teen pregnancies in a Hispanic community. You have a group of pregnant teens, a group of parents, and a group from the local church, and a group of high school teachers who are not members of the Hispanic community. Each group has expressed its ideas to you about how to address this problem. You are unsure of what to do next, and consult with your field instructor. She tells you that you should get all of the groups together, have a town meeting, and come up with a clear plan to which all have agreed. You protest, saying that their views are too divergent, that one of the girls' parents are in the parent group, and that some of the teachers don't know about the girls' pregnancies. The field instructor insists that you proceed with your group meeting, despite your protestations of potential cultural insensitivity. During the meeting, the parents of the pregnant teen who are present are shamed and begin to shout at her that they are disowning her, the church leader gives a long speech about the lack of good values in girls who become pregnant, the parents are ashamed to discuss the problem in front of outsiders (the teachers) and do not participate, and the girls finally walk out en masse. When you share the details of the debacle with your field instructor, she takes a self-righteous position, saying that there's nothing you can do to help "those people" anyway.

If circumstances like these occur during your field placement, you should contact your field liaison immediately for assistance and intervention.

D. Inaccessibility of Field Instructor

Field instruction may be excellent during scheduled supervisory times. However, you may find that your field instructor is not accessible to you at other times when consultation may be needed. She or he may be out of the office on your field work days, or have regularly scheduled conferences most of the day. She or he may have clearly indicated to you that she or he expects that you will function independently outside of the scheduled supervisory hour. The field instructor's door may be closed as an indication that she or he is busy with other things, and should not be interrupted.

Where do you go if there is an emergency? Who should you turn to if you have a question? You may want to ask your field instructor these questions. A procedure may be set up which enables you to contact the field instructor if there is a need, or brief times of availability may be provided, such as the first 15 minutes of every field work day. Alternatively, your field instructor may designate another worker to assist you and provide the guidance or information that you need during the times that she or he is not available.

E. Personality Clashes

There is an indefinable something that happens between people in a relationship. Sometimes it is instantaneous, sometimes it does not occur until each have become more knowledgeable about the other. You click, or you don't. If you don't, you may just feel impersonal and uninvolved, or you may dislike the other person. Generally, because this is an interpersonal feeling, you will be aware of your own feelings and those of the other person as well. You will have noticed this special quality of relationship in social and business relationships before entering school, with classmates, and with instructors. You will notice it with your field instructor as well.

You may have gotten some "vibes" — those often accurate instant impressions — the first time you met your field instructor. If the vibes were good, you entered field placement with some degree of comfort in regard to your field instructor relationship. If they were bad, you were apprehensive and worried.

First impressions do matter. If yours were negative, try to explore the reasons for your reaction, and approach your field instructor with as positive an attitude as possible. If you find that your problems increase, develop over time instead of instantly, or occur after some specific event that seems irremediable, you will want to consider how to address these.

You and your field instructor might disagree over the management of your caseload, your responsibilities to the agency, the role of supervision, the confidentiality of what is discussed in supervisory meetings, your choice of colleagues to have lunch with, or the function of your liaison. The possibilities range from serious ethical issues grounded in value differences to personal tastes and preferences. Often, there is no one single way to do things, and both you and your field instructor may have valid reasons for the positions you espouse.

The Japanese play *Rashomon* is a wonderful example of the problem that may occur. In the play, a murder occurs, which is witnessed by three people. When they are interviewed separately, each gives the version of events that appeared "real" to them. Each version was "right," but none was complete. It depended upon the viewpoints and perspective of the observer.

Einstein's Theory of Relativity demonstrates this as well. Events, objects, colors — everything in our world, is affected by our viewpoint. There is light, and there is shade, at the same time. There is fast, and there is slow, also at the same time.

In the same way, your field instructor may view a certain exchange or idea, problem or recommendation one way, and you another. There is not necessarily a "right" and "wrong" in every case. There may be just a difference in perspective.

A problem with a field instructor has the ability to permeate every aspect of your field placement, even every aspect of your professional education. The difficulties are compounded because of the power imbalances between you. If you have different perspectives, but one of you has the power to fail the other, how do you resolve differences? If you believe that your field instructor dislikes you, or you dislike your field instructor, who will remain silent, and who will speak?

There are a number of ways you can deal with personality conflicts and other differences between you and your field instructor, some more constructive than others. Several are suggested below, in Section F, Ethical Problems, and in Section G, Optimizing Your Relationship.

F. Ethical Problems

There are times when you may observe your field instructor doing something that you might consider unethical conduct for a professional. You are in school, and the NASW Code of Ethics is fresh in your mind. Your field instructor, however, may have over time developed ways of working that are expedient if not professional, may have become casual about some professional issues, or may be concerned about job retention or promotion.

These problems are often difficult and painful, and can occur in any professional relationship. They are presented more fully in Chapter 21. However, there is a greater stress, and a greater risk, in acting upon possible ethical problems in relation to your field instructor. Your first resource in other cases — your field instructor — may not be a possibility. Should you report your field instructor's behavior? To whom? Are you being overly concerned over issues that may be minor, and are considered as an accepted practice?

Before doing anything, you may want to be sure that there is a problem. Think on what you have heard or observed. Could there be any reasonable, rational explanation? If you believe there is not, you have several options. You may raise the issue in supervision, say that you are sure you misunderstood, or that there must be a good reason for what you saw or heard, and ask your field instructor to explain his or her reasoning. If you feel unable to discuss the concern with your field instructor, the best option is to present it to your field liaison, or other field work education team member. This ensures confidentiality and objectivity, and does not affect your relationship with your field instructor immediately. Another option is to contact his or her supervisor and share your concerns. This may promptly involve your field instructor, however, and could create a confrontation especially if you have not first discussed your problem with the field instructor directly. You may also choose to share your concern with a colleague. This is probably the least desirable course of action: a colleague cannot address the issue, nor effect any changes. He or she can advise you, but the advice may be colored by his or her own values, or even more problematic, his or her relationship with your field instructor.

G. Optimizing Your Relationship

The field instructor-student relationship is the basic vehicle for learning in the field. Wherever possible, it is important to develop and maintain a strong, productive, and positive relationship. However, occasional problems sometimes occur during the course of field placement. Students may choose to address these in several ways. Only you can determine which way works best in your situation, with your field instructor and your specific problem.

Confronting

You may choose to <u>confront</u> your problem with your field instructor during supervision. If you choose this approach, try to plan ahead. Write down some specifics, and concrete examples that illustrate the difficulty and your understanding of it. Approach your field instructor and ask for an appointment to discuss a problem. Wait until the appointment, or until your field instructor indicates readiness to discuss things with you. Try to remain calm and pleasant, and simply state what you have observed and your reactions to it. Listen to your field instructor's response, and reflect on his or her perception of the problem. Discuss issues and attempt to reach a resolution.

Circumventing

You may choose to <u>circumvent</u> the problem as much as possible by minimizing your contacts and relationship with your field instructor. Students who choose this approach often find another mentor, usually a colleague, to whom they can turn for advice. This relegates the field-instructor-student relationship to a formal arrangement only, not the best solution. However, there may be circumstances where this approach may work best. Under certain circumstances, (such as severe time limitations in availability) your field instructor may him or herself support your arrangements.

Denying

You may choose to <u>deny</u> the problem. You accept your field instructor's ideas, behavior, and personality characteristics, and tell yourself that everything is really all right. This approach is difficult to maintain over long periods of time, or with certain kinds of problems.

Adapting

You may decide to <u>adapt</u> to your field instructor's personality, ways of doing things, or approaches to you. If the differences are not vast, and if their effect on your learning relatively minor, this approach often works best. There is a learning experience here as well: because supervision is a foundational part of the practice of social work, you will need to adapt to many different styles, personalities, and viewpoints during the course of your professional career. Learning how to adapt, as well as the areas in which you cannot adapt, can prove valuable to your future.

Avoiding

You can also <u>avoid</u> the problem by minimizing contact, curtailing discussions of certain issues or problems, and confining your relationship to strictly necessary items. Unlike the option of circumventing your field instructor, avoiding may leave you with little guidance and supervision, and affect your work with your clients.

Withdrawing

Very rarely, students <u>withdraw</u> from the relationship with their field instructor. They may proceed through supervisory meetings by rote, with little affect and less involvement. It is difficult to maintain this kind of approach without affecting your relationship with clients, as emotional and physical withdrawal from your placement will be reflected in the way you relate to them. Building your own world with your clients, apart and without guidance from your field instructor, can be harmful to clients and to yourself as well.

The extreme of withdrawal can occur if a student chooses not to attend supervision, or to stop attending field work altogether.

> ** You should never terminate your relationship with your field instructor or with your agency without informing the school and following the school's procedures. Failure to do this can result in failure, or in dismissal from school.*

It is unusual for students to have a field placement where their relationship with the field instructor is positive at all times. Problems, mostly minor, are likely to occur. When they do, don't panic. Careful reflection and planning will help you to resolve your problems and continue to have a productive and meaningful relationship.

Some of the problems you might encounter with your field instructor are more general than those presented in this chapter. The next, which addresses collegial issues, may provide some assistance to you in working through field instructor issues as well.

CHAPTER TWENTY-ONE

COLLEGIAL ISSUES

There are many similarities between your relationship with colleagues and with your field instructor. Although collegial relationships do not carry the same potential for stress and anxiety, and the power imbalance is less pronounced, you will still have opportunities to learn a great deal, share a great deal, and enjoy working with colleagues. Relationships with other social workers at your agency may be more casual than the relationship you have with your field instructor, and more one between equals. All relationships with colleagues, whether they are field instructors, regular agency employees, or fellow students, require careful consideration to ensure that professional obligations are honored and collegial rapport maximized. You may find some of the problems and suggestions offered here helpful in addressing concerns with a field instructor as well.

A. Provisions of the Code of Ethics

Section 2 of the NASW Code of Ethics defines the professional relationship with colleagues. Some of the provisions have been discussed in earlier chapters about field instruction and supervisory relationships. The focus here will be primarily on those provisions which relate to collegial relationships in general.

Some of the points which may provide some guidance in working with colleagues are: treating colleagues with respect (2.01a) avoiding unwarranted negative criticism, and cooperating with them in the interests of client well-being (2.01b & c). As in all professional relationships, it is expected that you will keep confidential information (2.02), cooperate with members of multi-disciplinary teams of which they are a part, and attempt to resolve any disagreements within the team (2.03). Workers are also asked to seek consultation when needed (2.05) and refer clients to other professionals when specialized knowledge would serve the clients' interests (2.06).

Social workers also must be careful not to take advantage of a dispute between a colleague and an employer, or two colleagues, for their own gain (2.04a & b). Sexual harassment is of course not permitted (2.08).

Impairment and incompetence (2.09 & 2.10) are also addressed, and the Code suggests that, if a worker has knowledge of these kinds of problems, that he or she attempt to discuss them with the colleague first, assisting the colleague as able to remedy the circumstance. If the situation persists, workers should "take action through appropriate channels," such as "employers, agencies, NASW, licensing and regulatory bodies, and other professional organizations."

Similar measures should be followed if a worker becomes aware of unethical conduct (2.11). However, the worker is also responsible to "take adequate measures to discourage, prevent, expose, and correct" the conduct (2.11a), and be knowledgeable about procedures for addressing ethical problems and complaints (2.11).

B. Relating Professionally

You will be working with colleagues in many capacities during the course of your field work placement. You may share cases, each focusing on different areas of functioning, members of a family, or of a group. You may serve with colleagues on interdisciplinary teams or join with them for case conferences, meeting to discuss the progress of a client or a project, develop a plan for change, or assess results of interventions.

There may also be times when colleagues take on a mentoring role, assisting you to become familiar with an agency process, accompanying you on your first home visit, or allowing you to observe their professional functioning.

Your professional relationship will be affected by agency practice, personalities and personal preferences, and, often, by a colleague's relationship with your field instructor. If there is a positive collegial relationship between them, there will probably be an immediate positive relationship between that colleague and you as well.

Your field instructor will assist you in defining and developing professional collegial relationships. He or she will take the initiative and be involved in the choice of colleague and the nature of the learning and guidance that is provided. If he or she does not take this initiative for any reason, or if there are problems between you and your field instructor, you may need to take the initiative yourself.

There are circumstances when you may want to seek out a mentoring relationship with a colleague yourself. If your field instructor is not offering you the supervision that you need, and you are unable to resolve the problem, you may turn to a colleague. Often this works well, but sometimes it can aggravate and accentuate the problems with your field instructor.

> ** If you find that you are considering seeking guidance and supervision from a colleague rather than your field instructor, think this through very carefully, and proceed with extreme caution!*

Turning to a colleague for professional advice with your caseload or your learning can create a distance between you and your field instructor. There are often several ways to approach any one problem in your caseload. If your field instructor suggests one, and your favorite colleague a different one, what would you do? Your field instructor may become aware that you are seeking (and receiving) supervision from someone else. Resentment, frustration, and a feeling of abandonment will create a further problem. If it is obvious to others at your agency that you are seeking guidance from a colleague rather than your field instructor, your field instructor may feel humiliated or embarrassed, again, further aggravating the problems in your relationship. If you find that you are seeking guidance elsewhere without your field instructor's awareness and consent, eventual discovery will increase the potential for a negative reaction from your field instructor.

It is important to remember that your field instructor will still be evaluating your learning and performance, and is still responsible for your caseload and assignments. It is best to be very cautious about circumventing him or her in this manner. If you feel you do need additional guidance and/or support from a colleague, discuss this with your field instructor and attempt to enlist his or her help and support.

C. Relating Personally

Colleagues are not only a professional resource. You are functioning with them closely during the hours that you are at your field placement. As in any other life situation where there are people interacting on a regular basis, personalities, character traits, interests and abilities, experiences, and many other things will lead to developing a close relationship with some, and a friendly but formal relationship with others.

You may find that you develop a close friendship with a colleague, and that this extends eventually outside of agency boundaries. You need to be careful to ensure that this relationship does not affect your professional comportment with clients and other colleagues while you are in field placement. It is important to treat colleagues professionally and *equally* when relating on professional matters. Forming an "alliance" with a colleague undermines your independence as a professional and can create difficulties for you with others.

It may be tempting to confide problems in a colleague, or to turn to a colleague for advice about an issue of concern in your relationship with your field instructor. Sometimes, this will be helpful and productive. However, there are many dangers inherent in these kinds of practices: you must be aware and careful regarding interpersonal relationships within your field placement agency. You need to avoid forming an alliance with a colleague which will harm your relationship with your field instructor by providing negative information, undermining your field instructor's advice or authority, or circumventing the avenues for communication which have been set up to best support your learning.

> *Always remember that you may not be aware of a colleague's own agenda in regard to intra-agency politics, and may unwittingly harm your field instructor, yourself, or others.*

D. Observing Unethical or Unprofessional Conduct

In most cases, the kinds of problems you will encounter with colleagues do not affect you personally — you just become aware of unethical, incompetent, inappropriate, or unprofessional conduct. The lack of direct involvement and/or impact may make it easier for you to ignore the problem or behavior — after all, you might wonder, is it really my job to address this, when there are other people who are aware of these issues as well? When I'm "just a student?" Am I really even sure that this is unethical or unprofessional?

If you observe unethical or unprofessional conduct, you need to consider your own responsibilities for action. The Code of Ethics specifies that you must intervene, at least to the degree of discussing the matter with the person involved, and possibly beyond that in reporting the matter to your field instructor, the agency's director, or outside regulatory bodies. As a student, this can often be a difficult and painful ethical dilemma.

You may observe behavior in colleagues ranging from improper accounting of time, to misuse of funds, to substance abuse, or to unprofessional relationships with a client. Again, it is important to stop and reflect upon the problem before deciding upon any course of action (or inaction). Who is affected? Are clients being harmed, or placed in danger?

Some common problems you may encounter include:

- observing confidentiality violations
- observing, or being told about, misuse of time, such as field visits which include stops at the grocery store, or that take "all day"
- observing, or being told about, outright deceptions, such as accounting for visits not held, or phone calls not made
- observing, or being told about, misuse of agency resources, or violation of agency policies
- being made aware of information about your field instructor which is not helpful or appropriate
- being co-opted into an alliance with a colleague against your field instructor
- being co-opted into agency politics
- observing, or being made aware of, a colleague's substance abuse or impairment
- being asked to participate in unethical or illegal behavior because "we all do that"
- a colleague or group of colleagues sexually harasses you, teases you, or uses offensive or derogatory language

These are difficult and painful problems — you want to maintain a good relationship with colleagues, but you do not want to participate in any questionable behavior. You may decide that there is a difference between your active participation, and just awareness of something improper. Or you may decide that you must always act in support of professional behavior.

The most extreme course of action, whistle-blowing, should not be undertaken without careful reflection and consultation.. Going public is a serious step and every recourse should be explored prior to embarking upon that course of action. Reamer and Siegel both suggest that, while action is often merited to address unprofessional, unethical, or illegal collegial behavior, "going public" should be undertaken only as a very last resort, if at all.[1]

Your field instructor (if he or she is not involved) is often an excellent resource for advice in these situations, though you must consider the effect of your revelations, especially when they impact directly upon him or her. You may also share your concerns with your liaison, or with your adviser, and, of course, with your practice class.

If you decide that action is warranted, you should if at all possible discuss the problem personally with the colleague. Make sure that you choose a time and place that will enable privacy and uninterrupted discussion. Avoid being confrontational, and recognize that perhaps you are misunderstanding or misinterpreting. Be open to listening to your colleague, and reflect upon his or her "take" on the issues you have raised.

If you are able to offer any help or suggestions, you should do so. You may want to encourage the colleague to develop a plan of action to remedy the situation. As with all goal-oriented planning, suggest and build in a time frame. If the time frame is not met, you may want to speak with the colleague again, or to raise the problem with your field instructor, the agency's director, or other appropriate resource.

If the colleague refuses to recognize that there is a problem, or becomes angry with you, do not persist. It is best in such cases to bring your concerns elsewhere.

If the problem is widespread within your agency, if it involves a group of people, if it impacts upon you directly in a difficult and unwarranted manner (such as sexual harassment, or the request to collude in unethical behavior), it important to seek help and advice promptly, for such actions and behavior cannot be permitted to continue.

> *The unethical, unprofessional, incompetent, inappropriate behavior of any social worker or group of social workers affects every social worker. It is a part of your professional responsibility to address this!*

There are some rare instances when such behavior is widespread within your agency. Agency ethics and politics will impact you, other employees, and every client of your agency. If you are placed in an agency where unethical behavior occurs, or where agency politics hamper services to clients, program delivery, and employees, it is important that you consider your role as a student in the agency. This will be discussed further in Chapter 22.

E. Relating to Other Students

In most instances, you will enjoy the contact with other students who are placed at your field work agency. However, there may be problems in these relationships as well. Students who share a field instructor may compete for time and attention, or favored student status, a kind of sibling rivalry with the field instructor in the parent role. Students may undermine each others' efforts, or compete for scarce clients and assignments, or for the best and most interesting learning experiences. They may form subgroups and alliances which are harmful to you, or to each other. There may be personality clashes among students as well. Differing learning styles, field instructor relationships, assignments, and other problems may create difficult situations, and create stress and anxiety.

You may also become aware of unethical or improper behavior, such as any of the possible circumstances listed in D above. Suggestions for resolving them are similar; however, with fellow students the school becomes an additional resource in a more immediate sense.

This chapter has focused primarily on individual relationships between you and professional colleagues and other students at your field work placement. The next chapter will explore the kinds of difficult and challenging problems which affect your entire agency, or a large group of people within it.

---

[1] Gamrbill, E., & Pruger, R., Eds. (1992) *Controversial Issues in Social Work*. Boston: Allyn & Bacon, p. 66-67.

CHAPTER TWENTY-TWO

AGENCY ETHICS AND POLITICS

Some of the most difficult problems students encounter during field work placement involve agency ethics and politics. When possibly unethical practices or policy violations occur, they often involve the active or tacit cooperation of many people. Professional staff are aware, and are either turning a blind eye or actively participating and colluding in these problems.

Students who are new to the field of social work feel justifiably overwhelmed when they encounter these broad ethical issues. Who am I, you might think, to question something that even the agency Director knows about? I must be wrong. Maybe I just don't understand what is happening. And, anyhow, even I'm pretty sure I'm not wrong, what do I do? If everyone is participating, who would I even talk to? Who would understand?

Agency politics presents a very rocky terrain for students to negotiate. You are new to the agency, and you are there only temporarily. You want to do your work, learn as much as you can, and move on. When the political climate impedes this, it is difficult not to get caught up in it, generally to your detriment. Agency politics can swirl around your field instructor, your office mate, the colleague with whom you become closest. It may affect your own caseload, your field instructor's time and ability to guide you, whom you are expected to have lunch with, and with whom you become friends. It can even affect the evaluation of your work.

Agency politics are often insidious and covert. In many agencies, there is little open discussion and no acknowledgment of problems. Yet politics can affect every client and every service provided by the agency.

A. Agency Ethics

Each of us individually, each organization or service, each institution, in fact, our very government, are governed by ethical principles and values. Our nation's values are embodied in the Constitution and other founding documents, and expressed in our laws and public policies. Our institutions' and organizations' values are embedded in mission statements and policies. Some of these are dependent upon and consonant with government policies and values, while some are developed to address the unique circumstances of the institution or organization. Our personal values are generally developed through learning, reflection, and experience. We absorb values from parents, teachers, peers, and society, and modify them to reflect our own unique life experiences.

Our personal values reflect what we consider to be the best within us: for example, I can say that I want to be honest, brave, considerate, gentle, sensitive, just, spiritual, prudent, fair — any or all of these and many others. The key to understanding how this all works, though, lies in those three little words want to be. These values reflect the person that I aspire to be, the person I hope to be, the person I want others to see me as being. However, I know that, in the practice of my everyday life, I am not always able to act in consonance with these values that I believe to be so important.

There is an ideal me, the person that lives according to all of my values and the principles that flow from them always. There is also a real me, the person who actually experiences each day and must often choose between values, do the expedient, protect the interests of my loved ones and myself, and who cannot always act in consonance with every ideal value and principle. The closer the congruence between the values of the ideal me and the practices and behavior of the real me, the more in harmony with myself I will feel, the fewer conflicts I will experience, and the happier I will be.

This kind of ideal-real divergence occurs in government as well. We can think about the ideal values embodied in the constitution, such as freedom, equality, justice, and fairness. Five minutes listening to CNN Headline News or glancing at any newspaper forcefully reminds us that although as a nation we try to live up to our ideal values, in practice the complexity and competing interests in society forces choices and priorities that often are far from these ideals, and which at times seem to reflect the interests and values of those in power rather that the ideals of our foundational principles.

Organizations and institutions also have these ideal-real conflicts and pressures. Social agencies have ideals which are clearly formulated in mission statements and policies. When these ideals are put into practice, however, they are often affected by the needs of clients, the social work staff, the interests of those in power, and funding sources. The need to survive as a viable agency can often cause divergence between mission and ideals and actual agency practice. Expediency, self-interest, and the effect of power groups affect agencies in the same way that they affect individuals and governments, so that compromises of various sorts are made which move the agency away from the ideals it espouses.

There are almost unlimited possibilities of less-than-ideal ethical practices in agencies. Some of the more commonly encountered problems are suggested here to serve as examples of the kinds of issues students might encounter at their placements.

Misuse of Public Resources

Almost all social agencies receive some funding through government sources. This funding is generally allocated as part of a specific program, and thus designates the population and conditions of the services clients receive. The terms and conditions are thus determined outside of the agency, and often by governing bodies or policymakers who do not have a complete and thorough understanding of the issues and problems involved in administering the funds allocated.

Agencies want to keep their funding. They want to continue to exist, provide services, employ staff. However, funding sources do not simply allocate. They also require accountability, review, and evaluation. Agencies who do not meet the requirements of funding sources will lose funding much more readily than funding sources will change their requirements. Periodic reviews become sources of stress and apprehension for all as agencies try to meet the requirements and successfully renew grants and allocations.

Sometimes, ethical problems arise in the process. Two examples will assist in illustrating the problems that might be encountered:

An agency located in a Hispanic area of a major urban center has a major grant through a program designed to meet the needs of the Hispanic community. The grant addresses the substance-abuse problem in the community by specifying the provision of services to Hispanic substance abusers. Funds provide bilingual counseling services, vocational training, education, and substance-abuse testing for Hispanics including special services for pregnant teen substance abusers. The program has been very successful and is a well-respected and utilized resource in the community. It has operated for 15 years.

However, in the past two years, the number of clients served has begun to fall. Hispanics are moving out of the area to a more affluent section of the city, and the proportion of Hispanics among the population in the area served by the agency has fallen. Thus, the number of clients needing the agency's service who meet the original program criteria have also fallen. A local hospital has opened a clinic for substance abusers which provides only testing and counseling and does not offer bilingual services. However, some of the agency's potential clients have turned to the clinic instead.

The agency wants to remain viable. The staff also believes that there is a segment of the population whose needs cannot be met through the hospital clinic: people who need additional services, people who do not speak English, or teens who need the special services the agency provides. They believe that it is vital to retain the funding for the program.

There are other residents in the community who could benefit from the agency's services. These are non-Hispanics: they are whites and African-Americans. They have similar problems and needs and could use the existing resources appropriately, except for the bilingual services. However, the funding is very specific: it is for Hispanics only.

Slowly and insidiously, these other clients are beginning to be served by the agency. Statistics are blurred or altered so that these clients do not appear as non-Hispanics. The numbers are going back up, and continued funding for the program is assured. The staff is pleased and plans to continue to serve non-Hispanics.

The student placed in this agency has ethical concerns on two levels:

1. She is aware of collusion to defraud, clearly against the NASW Code of Ethics. She also is aware that the intention of the funding source is being violated and ignored, and thus that the dictates of society (who ultimately provide the funds through taxes) is not being honored. She is also aware that needed services to a population who was not receiving them — the whites and African-Americans — is benefitting these clients. What is her obligation?
2. She knows that she will also be assigned non-Hispanic clients and ask to "bury that small detail" so that it will not be obvious to reviewers. Should she participate?

The second example is very extreme and dramatic. However, it also illustrates the kind of problem students might encounter.

A student is one of four students placed with an adoption agency which serves clients by assisting them in making arrangements to adopt children from a South American country. The agency provides the home studies, locates the children through a government agency in that country, and assists with the arrangements for visiting, paperwork in the country of origin, payment of fees to the government of the children's country, and transportation of adoptive parents and children back to the United States.

For many years, the agency had a monopoly on intercountry adoptions from this country. However, recently two other agencies have asked for similar arrangements and are beginning to refer large numbers of adoptive clients to the governmental agency responsible for arrangement in South America. The governmental agency has said that it wishes to work with only one agency for reasons of expediency and efficiency, and will select the agency with the largest number of potential adoptive parents.

All of a sudden, a numbers war has erupted among the three agencies. The Director of the student's field placement agency calls a meeting of all staff and students. After asking the staff for absolute confidentiality, he says that it is necessary to take extreme measures to protect the agency's clients and the services provided by the agency. He then distributes adoption application forms to each member of the staff and to each student. He requests that each staff member and student fill out a form as though they were applying to the agency to adopt a child. They are asked to make up a name but to use their own social security number. The Director says that he understands that their participation in this action cannot be required, but that it is necessary for the agency to increase their numbers immediately in order to successfully compete with the others.

The student is aghast. She is even more amazed when <u>all of the staff members and the other three students</u> dutifully begin to fill out the requested forms. She sits in silence staring at her blank form as the other forms are passed to the Director. She does not speak, and no one speaks to her as the meeting concludes and everyone returns to work.

Obviously <u>very</u> unethical behavior. But what to do? Upon reflection, she decided that her options were:

1. Do nothing
2. Confront the director
3. Confront the field instructor
4. Whistle-blow with regulatory bodies
5. Contact NASW
6. Discuss the problem with her school

What would <u>you</u> do? The student's response is at the end of this chapter.

Failure to Provide Appropriate Services

This is a problem which affects individual clients. However, it often also becomes a widespread agency practice. Client needs may be adjusted to fit agency services at times when they might best be served through other resources in order to "keep the numbers up." Alternatively, clients can be provided fewer services than needed in order to conserve resources.

A client come to a mental health clinic complaining of severe depression. She has a history of mental hospital admissions, and wants to try to remain in the community during this episode. She was last discharged two months prior to this interview. The client seems unaware that, because she was discharged so recently, she is eligible from extensive aftercare services from the hospital through a new program. The clinic has a waiting list for individual therapy of about two months. However, they also offer group services which clients can attend either while waiting for a social worker to be assigned or simultaneous with individual treatment. The intake worker refers the client to group services and places her on the individual treatment waiting list. She does not offer or discuss referral to the hospital's aftercare program, which might meet the client's need for immediate service and might have numerous resources and services designed for the client's specific needs.

Another client also comes to a mental health clinic seeking service and complaining of paranoid ideation and fears of persecution. While obtaining the client's history, the intake worker learns that she is also on heroin. The clinic's policy precludes service to dually-diagnosed clients, and there is an agency which does provide service to these clients locally. However, the intake worker assigns the client to an ongoing worker and does not refer the client to the agency which would best meet the client's needs, thus violating both agency policy and primacy of client interest obligations.

A social worker in a long-term care facility becomes aware that one of the residents is displaying symptoms of serious mental illness, which include self-mutilation, refusal of medication, episodes of tearfulness, and hallucinations. She reports these behaviors in multidisciplinary care meeting, but finds that other members of the team do not feel that this resident needs a referral for psychiatric evaluation, as they believe that her behavior can be well managed and contained within the facility. At the worker's insistence, a psychiatric consultation is arranged. The psychiatrist recommends ongoing treatment. As patients pay a global fee for all services, approval for this must come from the Administrator. The Administrator consults with the Director of Nursing, who maintains her original position: the resident's problem does not need to be addressed and can be contained easily within the facility by the facility's staff. Additionally, the social worker is specifically asked not to intervene in the functioning of the facility, contact the resident's family, or spend extra time herself with the resident. Budgetary constraints and the need to distribute resources equitably among all residents are given as the reason for the restrictions.

Another kind of problem occurs when an agency does not distribute its services equitably. Some services are provided to some clients, and not others. The reasons for these differences appear to be some client characteristic such as race, religion, ethnic group, sexual orientation, gender, marital status, disability, mental status, or other criteria. These differences are often so subtle as not to be noticeable at first. If a student asks about them, a "rational explanation" is often given.

A student placed in a public agency which includes a housing division is working with a single mother of three children who are living in foster care. The mother is working hard toward family reunification. She has found a job, established a good relationship with her children, and is taking a class at night school. She has the money in the bank for beds, furniture, and equipment for the children, and is ready to bring them "home." Her problem: she has no "home," and is currently living in a rented room with a girlfriend. The student approaches the director of the housing division to ask for priority assignment of an apartment for this mother, only to be turned away, because "as soon as these girls get their kids back, they lose their jobs and can't pay the rent. I need these apartments for older couples, who have social security and no place to live. She can go and find housing out in the community. I've tried giving them apartments and I see what happens. And then we have to move them out and clean up the apartment and start all over again. I want people in these apartments who can pay and are going to stay long-term. Too hard to have all that turnover." Discrimination? Yes. Valid? Is discrimination ever valid? Is the director of housing prejudging and making assumptions, or is she acting in the interests of agency efficiency? Is that a valid reason to discriminate?

Inequitable Assignment of Workers

This kind of situation often occurs with students who are placed in for-profit agencies, but can also occur in social agencies which use a sliding scale in fees. It is easy to see how a problem can occur:

- Clients pay a fee based on ability to pay, insurance reimbursement, or program membership. All of the clients in an agency can be groups according to the amount of fees paid per contact.
- Clients' problems vary greatly in severity, complexity, degree and kind of skills required to address them, and need.
- Workers range in experience from seasoned workers who have been with the agency for twenty years or more and are perhaps supervisors or unit directors through workers with less experience, recent graduates, and, at the bottom of the experience scale, students.

Three continuums can be created: a fee continuum, a client problem continuum, and a worker experience continuum. Who <u>should</u> get the seasoned, experienced workers? Who in fact <u>does</u> get them?

This often impacts upon students because, as the least experienced, they are assigned the clients who pay the lowest fees, or who do not pay any fees. Often, these clients also present the more complex and intractable problems, problems that require skills, knowledge, and experience that students may not have. Students can then feel inadequate, and get justifiably frustrated as they observe skilled workers with clients who seem to have less severe problems. "How can I help this client?" they wonder. "This client needs somebody that 'knows what they are doing' and who can really intervene successfully. This is not a client for me. It's not fair to the client!"

Students often express their feelings to the field instructor. Some field instructors will agree and attempt to change the student's assignment. Others will try to provide extra help and guidance. Still others take the position that these are excellent learning cases for this very reason: their complexity and intractability are wonderful opportunities for the student.

Some students are not comfortable complaining; they are afraid that such complaints can be used to suggest that the student him- or herself is incompetent, overly reticent, or unwilling to take risks or challenges. They suffer in silence and try to provide the best possible service to the clients.

In many cases, agencies will say that assignments are made as space opens up in caseloads, or randomly, or in rotation. They will deny that there is any deliberateness to the way clients and workers are assigned. In the face of such denial, students may choose to withdraw their efforts to change the system in order not to risk their own place in the agency, their relationship with their field instructor, or their grade.

Labeling and Billing Practices Issues

Because managed care requires diagnostic labels, and some labels carry the potential for additional fees and/or interviews, abuses in labeling of clients also occur. Some of these abuses have as a goal the provision of needed services to clients whose managed care organizations are not willing to pay for them without a more serious diagnosis; thus, workers' perception of clients' best interests often motivates labeling practices. While such actions are dishonest and fraudulent, and arguably serve to perpetuate managed care abuses, one can at least rationalize that they are, in the opinion of the worker, in the client's best interests. This doesn't avoid or excuse the unethical behavior but, according to the student's personal values, may mitigate it somewhat.

What of agencies where billing practices are outright fraudulent? Where clients carry labels totally unrelated to their conditions, and where they are not even aware of having been given such labels? What about agencies where services are billed which are not provided?

A student placed in a child welfare agency which is reimbursed by client home visits is assigned several cases. He visits the families at home weekly. Because of the degree and severity of problems, he also maintains supportive contacts by telephone daily, calling from home or school on the days that he is not at his field placement. The clients are doing well and the situation appears stable with this phone call regimen.

The monthly statistical forms which the agency uses to bill for services rendered, generally to government contract programs, include spaces for numbers of home visits per client, but no spaces for telephone calls, which are not reimbursable. In conference with his field instructor, the student is requested to consider all telephone calls as home visits ("after all, you spend a lot of time, and the clients are at home") in order to boost the reimbursements for this client. When he questions this, the field instructor says that it is agency policy to consider all "lengthy" phone calls as home visits. The additional billing, the field instructor says, enables the agency to assist clients with transportation, and to provide babysitting during parent job interviews — both needed and worthwhile services. Should the student comply with the field instructor's request? One of the options that would circumvent the problem is to stop the daily supportive phone calls. Is it justifiable to place the client's stability at risk?

And, too, what should the student do about the knowledge that this is a common agency practice?

Another student, placed in a private counseling service that specializes in family therapy becomes aware of an agency billing practice that is unethical. Most of the families seen by this service carry private insurance which will reimburse for individual, but not family, therapy. The agency routinely bills for each member of the family separately, thus engendering a much higher reimbursement composed of several individual reimbursements. The administration and social workers take the position that family therapy is the treatment of choice for the kinds of problems that the agency addresses. Their obligation to clients is to provide the best possible service. They can provide this "best service" to clients only if they bill for each family member separately.

Although the student was made aware of this practice, special care was taken not to involve the student in any way by assigning clients for whom this billing practice was used. The student was not asked to participate — she was just made aware. Her field instructor ensured that she was protected from "the real world of managed care" during her placement, but yet was informed of this "real world" that would be waiting for her when she completed her course of study.

Clearly unethical practice. But should the student place the agency's clients at risk? Should she whistle-blow when everyone was so nice and so protective of her? When the managed care companies were, as a group, abusive of their clients anyway? Wasn't it better for the needed services to be provided, and the managed care company could take care of itself?

Confidentiality Violations and Disrespectful Language

A frequently encountered problem students observe in field placements is the often wholesale violation of client privacy and confidentiality. While some sharing of information is necessary within an agency, such as that between supervisor and supervisee, worker and consultant, and worker and agency director if necessary, in some agencies it appears to be acceptable to discuss clients casually with colleagues, in the hallways and common areas, and even where other clients can hear what is said. The rationale is that all the staff are involved with all the clients and have both an interest in their well-being and a meaningful contribution to make. Schools, mental hospitals, residential treatment centers, extended care facilities, and prisons are especially prone to these kinds of confidentiality violations. Students who notice even the agency director, or their field instructor, involved in such confidentiality violations, and for whom the Code of Ethics is an integral part of learning, are justifiably shocked. Should they speak up?

Another client-related agency problem with ethical dimensions involves the way that workers refer to clients with each other. Workers in certain settings tend to depersonalize clients, use humor, or make derogatory references to clients. Social workers in acute hospitals, mental hospitals, hospices, courts, and other settings which are extremely high stress often seem to engage in this kind of speech to relieve tension and to separate what is happening to the client in some manner from themselves. They are not alone in using this technique to relieve the tensions under which they work daily. Physicians, nurses, physical therapists, probation officers and others who work in high-stress settings use some of the same kinds of mechanisms to relieve tension. It prevents burn-out and keeps people functioning, performing necessary services under often difficult circumstances. Does this excuse the behavior? What about the core professional value of dignity and respect? And, most troublesome of all, what about settings where these kinds of behaviors occur which are <u>not</u> high stress or particularly difficult?

Ethical issues of all kinds abound in agencies, and you will surely encounter a number of them over the course of your field placement. They are often uncomfortable and upsetting, and students wonder how they can address these complex problems and still learn the skills they need to work with clients and on projects. Yet, addressing serious ethical issues is also an important skill that will prove essential in your professional career.

B. Agency Politics

All places of employment have a degree of internal politics, and social agencies are no exception. Politics influence promotion, appointment, office space and location, job assignments, intra-office relationships, and salaries. They often determine who sits with whom at lunch, and who votes with whom at staff meetings. Some agencies appear to be stable, and the politics are kept under control. Others are veritable hotbeds of political actions and power plays, and these at times can have a strong impact upon students in field placements.

You will probably not become aware of the politics in your agency for a number of weeks or even months. In some agencies, you will never feel the effect of agency politics; in others, it will be noticeable every day.

When you begin at your agency, and possibly for the entire time of your placement, you may notice that you are affected most by the politics that affect your field instructor. People who like and support her or him, will like and support you. Unfortunately, the reverse can also be true. If your field instructor is very unpopular, not respected, or "out of the loop," you may find others treating you in the same manner, at least initially. It will take time for you to develop your own place and unique identity in the agency's structure. This may seem very unfair to you — and it is!

A student was placed in an agency with a field instructor whose colleagues believed him to be eccentric, and teased and avoided him. In reaction, he had become used to staying in his office all day, from the time that he arrived until the time that he left. He ate lunch in the office, took coffee breaks in the office, and had clients escorted to him rather than receiving them in the waiting room. A desk had been placed in his office for the student. He enjoyed students: they were his only source of socialization at work. His expectation was that the student would remain with him in the office for lunch and coffee breaks, and that she would not interact with other staff. He expected that she remain in the office during his client interviews, and that he remain during hers, thus hampering her spontaneity and both of their clients' confidentiality. He was warm and friendly toward her, and she was immediately aware of his vulnerability. Yet, she was uncomfortable with the lack of space and privacy, and wanted to have contact with other workers. She felt disloyal when she tried to make other contacts and to leave the office for lunch.

Another student was placed with a field instructor who was engaged in a strenuous competition with another worker for the directorship of a new agency program. The other worker was the intake worker at the agency, and was in charge of all case assignments. In vain, the field instructor asked for clients for the student. None were forthcoming. When the field instructor was finally forced to go to the agency's executive director to discuss the problem, the intake worker's fury was broadcasted to all listeners. She later assigned cases to the student — but each one was a deadbeat client who either never showed up, or came in once and disappeared.

Still another student was placed in an agency which served as a field placement to two schools. One school had six students in placement, while the other had only one, the student. The other six students were assigned two to each of three field instructors. The three field instructors arranged special learning programs, visits to other agencies, and social activities for their six students. They soon became a close group and enjoyed social occasions outside of the field placement agency as well. The student was kept completely separated from the group; she was not invited to participate in any of the programs, visits, or social activities. While she knew intellectually that this was not personal to her, it still made her days of field work a painful experience in isolation.

As she explored this problem with her field instructor, she discovered that her field instructor, too, was isolated from other staff. She was the only member of the agency staff who was from out-of-state, the only one who had not graduated from the public school of social work in the neighboring city. The school of social work they had all attended, not coincidentally, was the same school of social work that had placed the six students. Apparently, over the course of years, this field work agency had trained social workers from this particular school, hired them upon graduation, and helped them eventually to become field instructors for the next group of students.

The field instructor approached her colleagues and asked if "her" student could be included in the learning activities and in visits to other agencies and resources. She received a grudging agreement. The student began to attend; however, she was never included in any of the social activities, and there was minimal efforts at conversation. Eventually, she stopped attending and withdrew from the group.

It is easy for a student to get co-opted into agency politics on various levels. One area that is especially difficult involves colleagues and field instructors, and was discussed in Chapter 21. Students also get involved in issues between colleagues, and in problems that involve the agency's director as well. An unpopular, incompetent director can create an atmosphere where politics, control, and power plays are daily tossed from worker to worker.

If at all possible, it is best to remain detached from the internal politics of your field placement agency. Unless you believe the situation is unethical, harms clients, or is illegal, it is generally best to try to remain on good terms with everyone, and to exercise care in deciding with whom to share any confidence, impressions, or feelings. This may be difficult, and even impossible at times, but remaining detached will generally help you to sustain a successful placement.

* Student's action in the case of the adoption agency:

She decided that she would not report the agency, nor take action against any of the staff or the director. However, she decided that she could not continue to work in a field placement in which the director requested such unethical practices, nor with a field instructor and colleagues who participated fully in them.

She discussed the problem with her field liaison, asking for confidentiality. As the liaison was extremely uncomfortable with strict confidentiality, they agreed to a time frame — the end of the semester, just four weeks away, after which the liaison would be free to discuss the problem with the Field Work Office. She approached the field work office using an urgent reason and requested an immediate transfer of field placements. This was granted when it became obvious that this excellent student would drop out of the school's program completely if she were forced to remain at the adoption agency.

The other students continued in the placement. At the end of the semester, the liaison informed the field office of her discussions with the student and the promise of temporary confidentiality. The other students were contacted for corroboration of the problem. The placement was closed.

Do you agree? What would you have done?

CHAPTER TWENTY-THREE

ADDRESSING AND RESOLVING PROBLEMS

In the preceding chapters in this unit, we have discussed some of the common kinds of problems you might encounter during the course of your field placement. As noted earlier, it is the rare student that doesn't encounter some problem at some point along the way. Learning to address and resolve problems in the professional setting, in a competent, expedient, and effective manner is in itself an important skill for students to acquire, one that will be used throughout your career.

Most of the problems you encounter will be resolvable without drastic action or radical changes in your field placement arrangements. If you are one of the rare students that encounter a severe and seemingly intractable problem, more serious steps may need to be taken to resolve it and to ensure that your field work learning experience continues.

This chapter will suggest a general process for addressing problems. Your procedure may vary somewhat, depending upon the nature of the difficulty, the personalities of the people involved, the extent of the effect of the problem, and your own personal choices in problem-solving.

A. Reasoning and Reflection Must Come First

Before you decide on a course of action, it is important to stop and reflect on the problem. Ask yourself these questions:

- Is it really a problem? What is the source, the kind of problem, and what are its effects upon you and upon others?
- What does the Code of Ethics say about the problem? Does it have some specific advice, or do some areas of possible confusion or conflict remain?
- What are some possible resolutions you can think of? What is it that you would like to achieve in order to resolve your problem?
- Whose interests are primary here? A client's? Your own? A colleague's? The agency's as a whole?

* Doing nothing about the problem is also an option:
one that carries both positive and negative possibilities.

B. Gathering Information, Documenting the Problem

Concurrent with A, above, but extending beyond A in time, you will need to gather information and document the nature and extent of the problem. "Feeling" that there is something wrong may be intuitively accurate, but will not suffice if you must take action or discuss the problem with others.

You "feel" as though you are not getting enough supervision time. You don't seem to get the guidance you need and feel as though you are just floating along. In order to begin to address this, you will need to keep a record of your supervision times, interruptions, and canceled meetings. You do not necessarily need to use this documentation in a discussion, but it is important to have it to render your position more clear, and help you to see that your "feeling" was right.

You may notice that a colleague is always on the phone making personal calls, and that she is seeing few clients. You are aware that this is unethical and perhaps reflects the serious personal problems that you know are occurring in her life at that moment. You think you should talk with her: it is, first of all, your ethical responsibility as her clients may be harmed by her behavior, and she is misusing agency time and resources. Additionally, you really like this colleague and don't want her to get into trouble. If she loses her job, her personal problems will compound enormously. You may want to make a record of the time that she is on the phone, and the number of clients she is seeing relative to other social workers in the agency. Again, you would not use the record to confront her: it would just help you to determine that your observations are accurate prior to discussing your concerns with her.

You are a first year Master's level student at an agency where caseloads are large and workers appear overwhelmed.. Your field instructor has assigned 2/5 of a regular MSW caseload to you during the second week of your placement, with the rationale that you are there two days a week, and should thus be able to carry that percentage of client load. You might want to check school policy, talk with other students and ask about their caseloads, or read your agency's contract with your school before determining a course of action.

Your work in a crisis intervention agency with suicidal clients. The agency's policy is that clients are given worker's home numbers to use if they are feeling suicidal so that emergency measures can be undertaken. One of your clients has begun to "check in" with you to let you know how he is doing almost every night. This is beginning to impinge on your personal time, and is concerning you. You wonder if you should raise the issue in supervision, or if your field instructor will think you are not dedicated if you express concern with being called so frequently for nonemergencies at home. You will need to determine agency practice. Casual inquiry to colleagues, a general perusal of the policy manual, and reading former clients' charts will assist you to determine if your problem is with an accepted agency practice or an individual abuse of your personal privacy. Both may require attention and intervention — but different approaches are appropriate for these different circumstances!

The information you will need to address your problem in a thoughtful manner may come from many sources, such as your field instructor, agency policy, colleagues, clients, charts, fellow students, your liaison, and other places. Think about what you need to know, and be creative!

Appropriate information will assist you to determine if there is a problem, the nature and extent of the problem, possible options and courses of action, and resources for you to turn to in addressing it.

C. Considering Your Values, Priorities, and Resources

A part of every problem determination relates to the way in which you perceive it. Your perception is affected by your personal values, your experience, your intuition, and your relationship with the people or things that are involved in the problem.

When problems come up in field placement, students find themselves immediately up against some important questions: how will this problem, and any actions I take, impact upon my field work placement? upon my relationship with my field instructor? upon my evaluation? upon my grade in field work?

In other words, what are the costs of this problem? There are some costs if I do nothing, others if I choose to act. Which costs am I willing to bear?

One student became aware early in her field work placement that she just could not work well with her field instructor. She liked to be organized, to plan her work ahead of time, and to stay ahead in her assignments. Her field instructor was much more casual: things got done when they got done, field instruction occurred regularly but not necessarily when scheduled, agenda were not reviewed and reflected upon, but were often examined during supervisory conferences. Papers were sometimes misplaced but not lost, reports to school were a week late. She worried constantly about her problem: should she say something? Should she just "grin and bear it?" Would she get in trouble with the school about the late evaluations?

Eventually, she decided to just accept the problem and do her best to work within it. She was concerned about upsetting the field instructor-student relationship by sharing her feelings with the field instructor. She decided it was the field instructor's style, and that it would be very difficult to change it.

Other students, in other situations, may decide to act because the problem is harming clients, violating professional codes, or is intolerable for them personally.

It is important also to consider the resources available to you to assist you with resolving the problem. Can you turn to your field instructor, your liaison, your adviser? Do you have a good friend who will listen, and whose advice you respect? Is there another student at your agency, who is aware of the problem that concerns you? All of these are wonderful resources and can provide suggestions, support, and a willing ear.

As you proceed with a cost-benefit analysis of your problem you may want to consider some of the following. Do the costs of doing nothing outweigh the potential benefits of action? Are some actions more risky, more costly, than others? There may be little potential risk to confiding your problem to your adviser, but a much greater risk to calling in the media. How much risk are you willing to take?

This self-examination which must occur before you determine a course of action can teach you a great deal about yourself!

D. Weigh Alternatives, Determine a Course of Action

Once you have decided to act, you need to consider all of the potential options open to you. Let your mind range over all of the possibilities that occur to you. Write these down on a sheet of paper, even the most improbable choices.

List the advantages and disadvantages of each choice. As you do this, you will find yourself eliminating some of your options, and perhaps focusing more closely on several others. What do those options you have chosen have in common? How are they different? Which alternative seems best, given the specifics of your problem, your own values and choices, your position as a student, your relationship with your field instructor and with others on your field education team, the agency, and the resources open to assist you?

Which choice suits your character and personality the best? Which is most expedient? Which will resolve the issue fastest?

Approaches to similar problems often vary. Your choice may not be the same as that of a fellow student. Two students: both had concerns about confidentiality issues in their agencies. Both addressed their problems successfully; however, their methods were quite different.

One student noticed that a colleague was frequently violating client confidentiality by discussing client problems with another colleague in the hall outside the students' office, where she could not help overhearing and becoming concerned. She did not know the colleague well, and it was uncomfortable to approach her. Over a period of weeks, the student made an effort to get to know this colleague. When she felt more comfortable, she approached the colleague with her problem. The colleague was embarrassed — but grateful that this behavior had been pointed out to her. It turned out that the colleague was appropriate in discussing her cases with the other colleague — who was her supervisor. She just was not appropriate in discussing clients in the hallway, and the behavior stopped immediately and did not resume.

Another student, concerned about confidentiality issues at his agency, took a different approach. He had been asked to prepare an in-service on the subject of his choice, and to lead a discussion about the subject afterward. He chose the Code of Ethics as his subject and focused particularly on confidentiality. He suggested during the discussion period that the staff think about how confidentiality was protected in their agency, and explore any areas that might need closer attention. From the discussion, a committee was appointed to draw up guidelines for intra-agency sharing of information, and he was asked to be a member of the committee!

Another example of students choosing different alternatives involves fearfulness:

A student was placed in a mental hospital and informed that she would be working regularly with violent patients. She was petite and shy, and was very frightened at the idea of being confronted and attacked by her patients. She was somewhat embarrassed about her fears, since the two other students placed with her did not seem to express any concerns and her field instructor did not raise any either.

She contacted her field liaison, and raised her fears with her. The field liaison suggested that the hospital might have a self-defense or safety program that she could take to prepare herself and suggested she check with her field instructor. She validated the student's right to be concerned. When the student tentatively shared her fears with the field instructor, she was pleased to learn that her field instructor was very supportive, and that the hospital did indeed have a special program for anyone interested. She signed up for the program. When she shared this with the other two students, they quickly signed up as well. All three students successfully completed the program, and their placement, without incident.

Another student was placed in an agency in a moderately high crime area. She too was afraid, and hesitant to express her fear of visiting clients in the field to her field instructor, concerned that she would assume that she was not appropriate for social work. She dreaded going to her placement, and became angry with both school and field for having placed her in this difficult situation. She finally contacted the Field Work office and requested a change in placement. The Director suggested that she take the free self-defense course offered through the campus police, and also request that someone accompany her on field visits if she was concerned about her safety. The Director also offered to ask the liaison to meet with her and with her field instructor to discuss her concerns. The student refused any help, became tearful, and begged for a change in placement. After a month of pleading, her request was granted, and she was placed in a school setting which did not require field visits in the same area as her previous placement. She adjusted well and completed her placement successfully.

A third student, placed in a hospice, was fearful about death. Her fear translated itself into fear of having interviews with clients, and she successfully avoided this until her mid-semester liaison visit. When asked about her caseload, she was forced to admit that she had not yet interviewed a client, though she had participated in many meetings and training sessions. In the discussion that ensued, it seemed that she was partially fearful about all kinds of interviews, but also especially fearful to interview people who were terminally ill. The liaison suggested that she might feel better if she could just get her feet wet, and also reviewed the school's requirements. She asked the student to call her in a week and let her know that she had had her first interview. The student complied. The issue was not raised again, but she saw as few clients as possible during the course of her field placement. Her field instructor sympathized with her and did not assign many interviews. She was able to complete her field placement successfully — but decided to change to a macro area in which interviewing clients directly would not be necessary.

In order to develop a plan of action, and to choose the alternative which best meets your needs, addresses the problem, and has the greatest degree of potential for success, it is important to follow several steps:

Raising the Awareness of Others

Once you have reflected upon your problem, and determined that some action is needed you must decide with whom you will share your concerns. Logical choices include any member of your field work team, but also instructors, fellow students, and others.

Begin with one person, and continue to share your problem until you have reached enough people to affect change. Some problems will require that you share them with only one person. Many of the problems you might encounter with your field instructor, for example, can be resolved by sharing them only with him or her. Others, such as problems with agency policy, may require a much broader base of awareness before effective consideration of change can occur.

Gaining Support and Cooperation

Change will occur more easily if there is a base of support, and cooperation and discussion of possible courses of action. Your goal here is to move from "my problem" to "our problem" — to encourage whose with whom you share your concern to feel an active commitment to addressing the issues. Establishing an alliance with others will be very helpful in resolving problematic issues. Even with delicate issues, such as the comportment of a colleague, establishing an alliance with him or her will establish an open communication to enable discussion.

Developing a Plan

Together with others with whom you have shared your problem or concern, develop a plan to effectively address the situation. You may find here that the issue has taken on a life of its own, and that others are committed equally with you in working toward a resolution. If your problem involves the actions of another person, such as a field instructor or a colleague, assist them to develop an appropriate plan that is comfortable for them. If it is your plan alone, the chances for success will be much smaller!

Resolving the Problem

You will, in all likelihood, have an important role to play in the resolution of the problem you have identified. Be sure that you consistently follow the agreed-upon plan, and that you are encouraging and supportive of others who are also taking action. Teamwork generally works best in many of these kinds of issues.

Moving On

Once your problem has been addressed, and action has been taken, you must be able to let it go, and to move on. It is generally not helpful to continue to dwell on a past problem or situation. If your field instructor is now holding all phone calls during supervision, you will not need to refer to this issue again. If your co-worker has initiated therapy for personal problems, any future action will depend upon those involved — the colleague and the therapist — and not you. If your agency is holding a series of meeting to reconsider a policy, the agency's organizational hierarchy is now responsible for leadership in effecting change.

The primary goal in your field placement is the achievement of professional competence. If problems occur along the way that impact upon this goal, they must of course be addressed. However, focusing too much attention on such problems per se will detract from your potential learning.

Remember:

- Choose the course of action with the greatest ratio of benefit to risk.
- Choose the course of action with the least potential for destructive effect.
- Begin with the smallest scale of action possible: talking with one person about the problem should be considered before calling in the news media!
- Always be certain that the course of action that you choose is in consonance with your professional values and ethical code.

It is important to recognize that learning how to address the problems that you might encounter at your field placement appropriately is also a vital part of your learning. Problems need to be addressed carefully, sensitively, and professionally, and some experience with various kinds of issues may be beneficial to your professional development. Often, your practice class is a good place to go for help.

Most of the problems that you will encounter in field are not unique to you, but are experienced by other students as well. Therefore, they are a good source of learning for your class. Your Practice instructor may have developed a mechanism in class for the presentation and discussion of problems encountered in your field placement. You can always turn to your classmates for advice, certain that your agreement about maintaining the confidentiality of material discussed in class will support and protect your own confidences regarding problems you are experiencing in the field as well.

The last chapter will offer some suggestions for addressing an important issue in many field work placements: personal safety. While some students feel uncomfortable or unsafe at times, they generally hesitate to raise these kinds of issues, feeling that it undermines their stated commitment to the profession in some manner. Because of the at-risk populations traditionally served by social work, problems do sometimes occur. Careful planning will minimize risk and ensure comfort.

CHAPTER TWENTY-FOUR

PERSONAL SAFETY AND SECURITY

All of us risk our personal safety at times. Using subways at hours when they are likely to be almost empty, driving in an unfamiliar neighborhood, or walking to the corner grocery store late at night are only three of the most common examples. Some of the risks we take are obvious, like those listed here; others are unexpected, and catch us unprepared and unaware. In an instant, circumstances that have always appeared comfortable and safe are no longer so.

Circumstances that pose a potential for danger and harm are difficult to define and categorize completely, for, in addition to the external circumstances, individual perception plays an important role in determining which kinds of situations appear potentially risky to us. Variants might include strength, habit, frequency of exposure, personal attitude, life experiences, and many others.

If you have lived in a city for a period of time, you may have developed a set of "street smarts" — patterns of behavior that keep you always wary and conscious of risk. These protective behavior patterns help you to be aware of danger, and to assess the potential for personal harm. If you are entering a social work program from a small town or suburban area, or are coming from another country, you may not always be immediately aware of the signs of danger.

This chapter is dedicated to helping you to adopt the protective behaviors and thought processes that you will need in negotiating city life in general, and your field placement in particular. Suggestions will be focused primarily on your field work experience, but are easily adaptable to your personal life as well.

While the suggestions below are meant to assist you to remain safe, they are not meant to overly alarm you and cause you to fear your field placement, your clients, or the communities you will be visiting. Incidents are very rare. However, whenever you work with populations that are experiencing life stressors, poverty, oppression, alienation, crisis, or other serious problems, there is a potential for impulsive, uncontrolled, or aggressive behavior in certain circumstances.

A. The School's Role

Your school is, of course, very much concerned with your safety and well-being. The Office of Field has visited your field work placement, and safety issues have been assessed and addressed as needed. Schools of social work do not use field placements which expose students to undue risks either in going to and from the agency or during the course of their work.

During orientation, you may have received safety information specific to your school. Safety may have been discussed in your Field Seminar, in Field Orientation, or in your Foundation Practice course. Some schools provide a safety manual, or include material on safety in other school packets.

A good source of information and advice is the Campus Security Office. They are familiar with the areas in which you are living, working, and attending school. They will be able to provide advice on safe routes, use of campus facilities at night, and other questions of concern. Many campus security programs also include classes in self-defense and preparedness for students. They will be happy to assist you in developing a personal security plan.

B. Your Field Work Placement's Role

Your field instructor and your agency's director are the persons in your agency who are most directly concerned with your learning and general well-being. This includes issues of personal safety. Care will be exercised in selecting clients for your caseload, and in determining where you will go during the course of your field work. Your field work agency will always attempt to shield you from undue exposure to personal risk.

Some field work agencies or settings are riskier than others, but you can reduce the risk of harm in any setting in which you are placed. Remember, you are not alone there: colleagues and other staff members will be exposed to a similar risk, and will always work to ensure safety for everyone.

If your agency views the nature of its client population or problems as potentially dangerous to workers, it may have an in-service program which addresses such issues as defusing a potentially dangerous situation with a client, techniques and strategies for working with difficult, violent, or criminal clients, and personal protection during interviews and field visits. Don't be uncomfortable about inquiring about such a program, and signing up to take it!

C. Your Own Role

Ultimately, your personal safety is your responsibility. Don't undermine or underestimate your own ability to judge or intuit whether a situation is potentially dangerous!

The suggestions included here are not an exhaustive list — please add to them any ideas of your own for preparing yourself and minimizing risk. If you believe that your idea would help others, please send it to the editors of this book so that it may be included in a future edition.

Increase Awareness of Risk Factors

Preparedness includes learning all of the potential risk factors in relation to your field work placement, and developing a plan to minimize them, or deal with them safely and successfully. You should:

- take your agency's safety training, if one is offered
- discuss safety issues with your field instructor early in your relationship
- incorporate the development of a personal safety plan into your learning contract as an objective
- develop an ongoing personal risk assessment program

Getting to and from Your Field Placement Agency

Your field placement agency may be located in an area that is unsafe at night, or you may need to travel through an unsafe area to reach your field placement. Although these circumstances are not necessarily a part of your field work placement itself, it is necessary for you to include them in your risk awareness, and plan a system for minimizing risk in traveling to and from placement.

You may find that you have late hours, and that you remain at your field placement during evenings when there are few people in the building, and fewer still outside. Parking lots which are safe during daylight hours may be less so at night, and you may feel uncomfortable in leaving your agency and getting to your car. Planning ahead is helpful when such situations occur.

Your agency may have a security officer, maintenance personnel, or others who are routinely available after normal working hours to escort you to your car, to the bus, or to the subway. You may want to arrange with another worker to walk outside together. You may prefer to have a friend or relative pick you up. Any of these, however, requires some advance planning!

The local Police Department is always on hand to help you with your planning. They are very aware of areas that are more or less dangerous than others. If you need to get from point A to point B, they can assist you to find the safest and most comfortable route. The Police Department can assist you in planning a good route to work, and also in planning the best route to a field visit. Have dates, times, and locations on hand when you call them: circumstances may vary according to day of the week, time of the day, and area to be visited.

When making arrangements for getting to and from your agency, remember to:

- plan a safe route to and from your field placement
- plan how you will leave if you have late hours
- do not walk unaccompanied in unsafe circumstances

In Your Agency

Personal safety factors will vary greatly with setting and population. All can be potentially dangerous, and all can be safe. Again, careful planning and thought will minimize any risks. Your field instructor is familiar with your agency's setting, populations, and problems, and will be able to assist you to structure the times when there is a potential for risk to best ensure your safety and that of others.

Careful attention will reduce your exposure to risk when working with clients with a potential for violence or other behaviors that would place you at risk. You will need to pay particular attention to:

- time and location of interviews
- office arrangements (how desk is placed, who sits where, access to door)
- access to help (location of others who can aid you — having your field instructor nearby is often a big help!)
- emergency plan (press a button, pick up a phone, shout, run from room)

One of the common problems encountered in planning to minimize risk is the necessity of always considering issues of client confidentiality and safety. You will need to balance the two carefully. For example, an open door would protect you best, a closed door ensures confidentiality. Can the door and the office furniture be arranged in such a way that it can be left ajar, with only you or no one visible? Placing your desk, and the client, between you and the door increases risk and lessens your access to help in an emergency.

Even clients whose potential for violence and aggressive behavior is regarded as relatively low can get upset and potentially dangerous in certain situations. Telling a client he or she must be institutionalized against his or her will, for example, may provoke aggressive and angry behavior. Knowing that there will be such a potential in advance will enable you to plan carefully both how the client will be given the information, and how you will respond should a potentially dangerous situation ensue. Preparing for the interview carefully with your field instructor will help you to develop the best possible plan, and also allow your field instructor to be prepared to assist you if needed.

In the Field

Planning for field visits incorporates elements of both of the prior circumstances. As you will be traveling, planning may include the steps you took in developing your route to and from work. Because, during most of your field visits, you will also be seeing clients, you must plan for safety while you are with them in their home, school, or place of employment.

When you visit a client's home, you are "on their turf," instead of your own. In Chapter 8, we discussed some basic guidelines for home visits. These are meant to enable you and your client to be comfortable with your visit, and will also tend to deter potential for harm. However, care should be exercised to ensure that you are safe while visiting in clients' homes.

Visiting clients in other settings, such as school, place of employment, or other outside setting presents less exposure to potential danger. However, plan to minimize any difficult circumstances as possible.

At minimum, you should always:

- schedule field visits during daylight hours
- plan a safe route, and review it with your field instructor
- let your agency know when you are leaving, where you are going, and when you will be back
- ensure that your field instructor is also aware of your plan
- "check in" if there is a change in plan
- always take someone (from your agency) with you if you feel unsafe. This person may accompany you on your visit, or may wait outside or in the car as needed. Plan ahead where the person will be during your visit.

It is hoped that these suggestions will assist you in planning for a safe and secure field placement experience. If you should ever feel uncomfortable, or concerned about your safety, you should not hesitate to discuss this with your field instructor, your liaison, your practice instructor, or your adviser. Better to discuss the problem, and plan to reduce any potential, than to proceed with discomfort and fear. Remember, your personal safety is your responsibility!

D. Sexual Harassment or Other Improper Conduct

There has been much attention and interest in issues of sexual harassment in the workplace. These are especially of concern where there is an imbalance of power and authority between the person who is harassing, teasing, or making derogatory remarks and the receiver of such actions and behavior. As a student, there is such an imbalance between you and your field instructor, other supervisors, professionals at your agency, and others. You have the absolute right not to be exposed to unwanted physical contact, remarks, or otherwise objectionable behavior, including, but not limited to:

- unwanted physical contact, such as touching, brushing against, or rubbing
- unwanted solicitation of dates or physical contact
- comments or remarks about your physical appearance, clothing, makeup, etc.
- unwanted gestures, comments, notes, or messages of a physical, sexual, or objectionably affectionate nature

A single incident does not necessarily constitute such improper conduct; generally, such actions and behavior occur again and again, leaving you angry, uncomfortable, and afraid.

If incidents like these occur in your field placement, you may be afraid to address them as you might outside of the agency, for fear of repercussions which might embarrass you, humiliate you, or affect your educational standing. The sooner these kinds of problems are addressed, the better. Ignoring them, hoping they will disappear, avoiding the person involved, or mutely allowing them to occur will not make them go away!

Your first recourse is always your field instructor, followed by your liaison or the agency director. Obviously, if the problem is with your field instructor, you need to move beyond her or him to ask for assistance. Once you have expressed your concern, you should be assured that the matter will be handled with tact and confidentiality to all parties concerned.

The NASW Code of Ethics proscribes dual relationships between students and field instructors and educators for your protection, due to the power imbalances inherent in such relationships and the potential for harm to the weaker member.

UNIT SUMMARY

Unit Five has attempted to address some of the kinds of problems often experienced by students in field placements. We must recognize that the possibilities for difficulty are almost limitless: we have explored several of the areas in which difficulties are often experienced, offered examples, and some suggestions for resolution.

Chapter 17 examined some of the realities of field work placements at the turn of the century: budget cuts, managed care, and the increase in for-profits used as field placements have changed the landscape permanently, and created new conditions and problems for students to address. Some of the old ones, such as personalities and places, and the needs of organizations, have remained with us as well.

Chapter 18 took a closer look at field placement agencies in the context of student placements. Considerations such as space, agency perceptions of the student role, and the effects of staff overload on students are presented. We explored problems with caseloads and clients in Chapter 18. The all-important relationship with the field instructor is often an area of problems for students' infield work placements: problems with supervision, personality clashes, ethical issues, and others can impact forcefully upon students' experiences and were discussed in Chapter 19.

Although the student relationship with the field instructor is almost always the primary one in a field placement, relationships with colleagues are important as well. These also can be sources of problems for students, and some of these are discussed in Chapter 21. Chapter 22 included some of the difficulties students can encounter with agency policies and practices, as well as the tension and stress that is engendered by difficult agency politics.

A plan for addressing problems is suggested in Chapter 23. Students need to reflect carefully and explore various sources of information and support, such as the Code of Ethics, agency resources, and personal choices in methodologies. The last chapter addresses safety and security, an important consideration in many social work settings.

This Unit has been placed at the end of the book because an over-concern for possible problems, and undue worry over minor, resolvable issues can mar the energy and enthusiasm which is such an essential part of the field work experience. Problems may occur, it is true. When and if they do, they will need to be addressed. It is hoped that the suggestions here will be of assistance to you if you feel that a problem you are experiencing is negatively impacting upon your field work experience and affecting your learning.

A Final Word

As your field placement draws to a close, you will have the time to look back and reflect on all that you have learned, and upon all that you have experienced. In every ending, there is a new beginning, and so you will also be looking ahead — ahead to a productive summer of work, a new semester of classes, a new job, time with loved ones — a whole new world will be opening its doors to you.

You will walk through those doors quite a different person than the one who walked through other doors — those of your agency — some months ago. Your field work placement will have changed you in a profound and foundational way, and these changes, this new you, will remain a part of the person you have become — a professional person, with knowledge and skill and the confidence to use them in the service of others.

May the newly emerged professional you remain true to the values of our profession, and to your own in choosing to enter it, throughout your lifetime.

REFERENCES AND SUGGESTIONS FOR FURTHER READING

Chapter One

Alperin, D.E. (1995) Factors associated with social work student satisfaction with field placements in child welfare. Doctoral Dissertation, Florida International University.

Blake, R., & Peterman, P. (1985) *Social Work Field Instruction: The Undergraduate Experience*. NY: University Press of America

Bogo, M., Michalski, J., Raphael, D., & Roberts, R. (1995) Practice interests and self-identification among social work students: changes over the course of graduate social work education. *Journal of Social Work Education* 31(2), Spring/Summer.

Commission on Accreditation, Council on Social Work Education (1994) *Handbook of Accreditation Standards and Procedures* (4th ed.). Alexandria, VA: Council on Social Work Education

Council on Social Work Education (1994) *Handbook of Accreditation Standards and Procedures*. Alexandria, VA: Author.

Cuzzi, L., Holden, G., Chernack, P., Rutter, S., & Rosenberg, G. (1997) Evaluating social work field instruction: rotations versus year-long placements. *Research on Social Work Practice* 7(3): 402-414, July.

Fortune, A.E. Field Education. In Reamer, F. (1994) *The Foundations of Social Work Knowledge*. NY: Columbia University Press.

George, A. (1982) A history of social work field instruction: apprenticeship to instruction. In Sheafor, B.W., & Jenkins, L.E., Eds. *Quality Field Instruction in Social Work*. White Plains, NY: Longman.

Holden, G., Cuzzi, L., Rutter, S., Rosenberg, G., & Chernack, P. (1996) The hospital social work self-efficacy scale: initial development. *Research on Social Work Practice* 6(3) 353-65, July.

Jenkins, L.E., & Sheafor, B.W., An overview of social work field instruction. In Sheafor, B.W., & Jenkins, L.E., Eds. (1982) *Quality Field Instruction in Social Work*. White Plains, NY: Longman.

Meyer, C.H., & Mattaini, M.A. (1995) *The Foundations of Social Work Practice*. Washington, D.C.: NASW Press .

Raskin, M.S. (1981) Factors associated with student satisfaction in undergraduate social work field placements. Doctoral Dissertation.

Reamer, F. (1994) *The Foundations of Social Work Knowledge*. NY: Columbia University Press.

Rompf, E.L., Royse, D., & Dhooper, S.S. (1993) Anxiety preceding field work: what students worry about. *Journal of Teaching in Social Work* 72(2): 81-95.

Skolnick, L. (1989) Field instruction in the 1980s: Realities, issues, and problem-solving strategies. *Empirical Studies in Field Instruction*. NY: Haworth Press.

Tolson, E.R., & Kopp, J. (1988) The practicum: clients, problems, interventions, and influences on student practice. *Journal of Social Work Education* 24(2): 123-134 Spring/Summer.

Urbanowski, M.L., & Dwyer, M.M. (1988) *Learning through Field Instruction*. Milwaukee, WI: Family Service of America.

Chapter Two

Abramson, J.S., & Fortune, A.E. (1990) Improving field instruction: an evaluation of a seminar for new field instructors. *Journal of Social Work in Education* 26(3): 373-386.

Alperin, D.E. (1989) Confidentiality and the BSW field work placement process. *Journal of Social Work Education* 25(2): 98-108. Spring/Summer.

Conroy, K. (1993) Field advising by full and part-time faculty in social work education. Doctoral Dissertation, City University of New York.

Gelman, S.R. (1990) The crafting of field work training agreements. *Journal of Social Work Education*

26(1): 65-75.

Gladstein, M., & Mailick, M. (1986) An affirmative approach to ethnic diversity in field work. *Journal of Social Work Education* 22(1): 41-49.

Gordon, N. (1982) Orgnizational change in a medical setting: a field work curriculum for direct practice students. Doctoral Disseration, C.U.N.Y.

Kahn, S. (1981) An analysis of the relationship between social work schools and field placement agencies in their joint task of educating social workers. Doctoral Dissertation, Columbia University.

Marshack, E.F. (1988) Ethics in field work. *The Jewish Social Work Forum* 24: 41-44, Spring.

Patti, R.J. (1980) Field education at the crossroads: exploring alternatives for administrative practice. *Administration in Social Work* 4(2): 61-104.

Ruffolo, M.C., & Miller, P. (1994) An advocacy/empowerment model of organizing: developing university-agency partnerships. *Journal of Social Work Education* 30(3): 310-316, Fall.

Showers, N., & Cuzzi, L. (1991) What field instructors of social work students need from hospital field work programs. *Social Work in Health Care* 16(1): 39-52.

Welsh, B.L. (1979) The initial phase of field work placement: an educational process. *School Social Work Quarterly* 1(2): 117-127.

Zakutansky, T.J., & Sirles, E.A. (1993) Ethical and legal issues in field education: shared responsibility and risk. *Journal of Social Work Education* 29(3): 338-347, Fall.

Chapter Three

Abbott, A. A. Professional conduct. In Beebe, L., Ed. (1995) *The Encyclopedia of Social Work*. 19th Edition. Washington, D.C.: NASW Press.

Bisman, C. (1994) *Social Work Practice*. Pacific Grove, CA: Brooks/Cole, Chapter 2, Becoming a social worker: major concepts of the profession, and Chapter 3, Professional values and social work ethical code.

Corey, G., Corey, M.S., & Callanan, P. (1998) *Issues and Ethics in the Helping Professions*. Pacific Grove, CA: Brooks/Cole, Chapter 2, The counselor as a person and as a professional.

National Association of Social Workers (1996) *Code of Ethics*. Washington, DC: Author.

Rothman, J.C. (1999) *The Self-Awareness Workbook for Social Workers*. Boston: Allyn & Bacon.

Simon, B.L. (1995) The profession of social work. In Meyer, C.H., & Mattaini, M.A. *The Foundations of Social Work Practice*. Washington, D.C.: NASW Press.

Chapter Four

Besharov, D.J. (1985) *The Vulnerable Social Worker: Liability for Serving Children and Families*. Washington, D.C.: NASW Press.

Beauchamp, T.L., & Childress, J.F. (1994) *Principles of Biomedical Ethics*. NY: Oxford University Press, Chapter Three, The Respect for Autonomy.

Bullis, R.K. (1995) *Clinical Social Worker Misconduct*. Chicago: Nelson Hall.

Congress, E.P. (1993) Teaching ethical decision-making to a diverse community of students: bringing practice into the classroom. *Journal of Teaching in Social Work* 7(2): 23-36.

Gambrill, E., & Pruger, R. (1997) *Controversial Issues in Social Work Ethics, Values, and Obligations*. Boston: Allyn & Bacon.

Loewenberg, F.M., & Dolgoff, R., (1996) *Ethical Decisions for Social Work Practice*. Itasca, IL: F.E. Peacock, Chapter 1, Ethical Choices in the Helping Professions, Chapter 2, Values and professional ethics; Chapter 4, Confidentiality and informed consent.

National Association of Social Workers (1996) *Code of Ethics*. Washington, D.C.:Author.

Reamer, F. (1994) *Ethical Dilemmas in Social Service*. NY: Oxford University Press, Chapter 2, Fundamental ethical issues in social work; Chapter 3, Ethical dilemmas in service to individuals and families; Chapter 4, Ethical issues in social planning and policy.

Reamer, F. (1994) *Social Work Malpractice and Liability*. NY: Columbia University Press.

Rothman, J. (1998) *From the Front Lines: Student Cases in Social Work Ethics*. Boston: Allyn & Bacon. Introduction.

Santangelo, A.C. (1992) The 1991 class of entering graduate students in California's ten schools and departments of social work: a study of student attitudes toward the poor, the social work field, and characteristics influencing career decisions. Doctoral Dissertation, University of California at Berkeley,

Wilson, S. (1978) *Confidentiality in Social Work: Issues and Principles*. NY: Free Press.

Chapter Five

Donner, S. (1996) Field work crisis: dilemmas, dangers, and opportunities. *Smith College Studies in Social Work* 66(3): 317-331, June.

Kay, G. (1989) The MSW field practicum: replicating socio-economic inequality. *The Social Worker — Le Travailleur Social* 57(4): 205-206. Winter.

Hancock, T.U. (1992) Field placements in for-profit organizations: policies and practices of graduate programs. *Journal of Social Work in Education* 28(3): 330-340, Fall.

Kamerman, S. B., Fields of Practice. In Meyer, C.H., & Mattaini, M.A. (1995) *The Foundations of Social Work Practice*. Washington, D.C.: NASW Press.

Kettner, P.M. (1979) A conceptual framework for developing learning modules for field education. *Journal of Education for Social Work* 15(1): 51-58.

Munson, C.E. (1987) Field instruction in social work education. *Journal of Teaching in Social Work* 1(1): 91-109, Spring/Summer.

Netting, F.E., Kettner, P.M., & McMurtry, S.L. (1998) *Social Work Macro Practice* 2d Ed. NY: Addison Wesley Longman, Chapter 7, Understanding organizations; Chapter 8, Analyzing human service organizations.

Rothman, J., & Sager, J.S. (1998) *Case Management*. Boston: Allyn and Bacon. Chapter 4, Resource identification and intervention planning; Chapter 12, Implementing case management plans: program design and development.

Siu, S.F. (1991) Providing opportunities for macro practice in direct service agencies: one undergraduate program's experience. *Arete* 16(2): 46-51, Winter.

Starr, R., & Haffey, M. (1987) Teaching work-study students: curriculum delivery and design issues. *Journal of Teaching in Social Work* 1(2): 141-153, Fall/Winter.

Chapter Six

Alperin, D.E. (1996) Empirical research on student assessment infield education: what have we learned? *The Clinical Supervisor* 14(1): 149-61.

Berger, S.S., & Bucholz, E.S. (1993) On becoming a supervisee: preparation for learning in a supervisory relationship. *Psychotherapy* 30: 86-92.

Bisman, C. (1994) *Social Work Practice: Cases and Principles*. Pacific Grove, CA: Brooks/Cole. Chapter 6, Communication in social work defined, process recording.

Bogo, M. (1993) The student/field instructor relationship: the critical factor in field education. *The Clinical Supervisor* 11: 23-36.

Burns, C.I., & Holloway, E.L. (1989) Therapy in supervision: an unresolved issue. *The Clinical Supervisor* 7(4): 47-60.

Cimino, D., Cimino, F., Neuhring, E., Raybin, L., & Wisler-Waldock, B. (1982) Student satisfaction with field work. *Contemporary Social Work Education* 5(1): 68-75.

Coe, S.J. (1994) Role satisfaction of social work field instructors. Doctoral Dissertation, University of

Illinois at Chicago.

Cohen, M.B., & Garrett, K.J. (1995) Helping field instructors become more effective group work educators. *Social Work with Groups* 18(2/3): 135-48.

Conrad, A.P. (1988) The role of field instructors in the transmission of social justice values. *Journal of Teaching in Social Work* 2(2): 63-82.

Gelman, S.R. (1988) Who's responsible? The field liability dilemma. *Journal of Social Work Education* 24(1): 70-78, Winter.

Glassman, U., & Kates, L. (1988) Strategies for group work field instruction. *Social Work with Groups* 11(1/2): 111-124.

Goldmeier, J. (1983) Educational assessment, teaching style, and case assignment in clinical field work. *Arete* 8(1): 1-12.

Graybeal, C.T., & Ruff, E. (1995) Process recording: it's more than you think. *Journal of Social Work Education* 31(2): 169-181, Spring/Summer.

Haj-Yahia, M.M. (1997) Culturally sensitive supervision of Arab social work students in western universities. *Social Work* 42(2): 166-174, March.

Hanley, B., Cooper, S., & Dick, G.L. (1994) Videotaping as a teaching tool in social work training. *Journal of Continuing Social Work Education* 6(2): 10-14.

Johnston, N., Rooney, R., & Reitmeir, M.A. Sharing power: Student feedback to field supervisors. In Schneck, D., Grossman, B., & Glassman, U., Eds. (1991) *Field Education in Social Work: Contemporary Issues and Trends*. Dubuque, IA: Kendall/Hunt.

Joslyn, C.P. (August 1978) First-year social work students and their educational environment. Doctoral Dissertation.

Katz, D. (1982) Preparing public agency field instructors. Doctoral Dissertation.

Kurland, R., & Salmon, R. (1992) When problems seem overwhelming: emphases in teaching, supervision, and consultation. *Social Work* 37(3): 240-244, May.

Norman, K.M., & Friedman, B.D. (1997) Process recording: fine tuning an old instrument. *Journal of Social Work Education* 33(2): 237-243.

Meltzer, R. (1977) School and agency cooperation in using videotape in social work education. *Journal of Education for Social Work* 13(1): 90-95.

Perlman, A. (1989) Creativity and the field work performance of graduate social work students. Doctoral Dissertation.

Reamer, F.G. (1989) Liability issues in social work supervision. *Social Work* 34(5): 445-448, September.

Richan, W.C. (1989) Empowering students to empower others: a community-based field practicum. *Journal of Social Work Education* 25(3): 276-283, Fall.

Rohrer, G.E., Smith, W.C., & Peterson, V.J. (1992) Field instructor benefits in education: a national survey. *Journal of Social Work Education* 28(3): 363-369, Fall.

Rose, S., & Finn, J. (1980) Videotape laboratory approach to group work training for undergraduates. *Social Work with Groups* 16(4): 23-30.

Swain, P.A. (1994) But what happens if . . . ? Quasi-legal considerations for social work student placements. *Australian Social Work* 47(2): 13-23, June.

Wayne, J., & Garland, J. (1990) Group work education in the field: the state of the art. *Social Work with Groups* 13(2): 95-109.

Wilson, J., & Moore, D. (1989) Developing and using evaluation guidelines for final practicum. *Australian Social Work* 42(1): 21-28, March.

Wilson, S. (1980) *Recording Guidelines for Social Workers*. NY: Free Press.

Chapter Seven

Bisman, C. (1994) *Direct Social Work Practice*. Pacific Grove, CA: Brooks/Cole, Chapter 2, Becoming a Social Worker.

National Association of Social Workers (1996) *Code of Ethics*. Washington, D.C.: Author.

Chapter Eight

Abramson, J. (1989) Making teams work. *Social Work with Groups* 12(4): 45-63.

Austin, M.J., & Lowe, J.I. (1994) *Controversial Issues in Communities and Organizations*. Boston: Allyn & Bacon

Bisman, C. (1994) *Social Work Practice: Cases and Principles*. Pacific Grove, CA: Brooks/Cole.

Brill, M., & Nahmani, N. (1990) The professional relationship as perceived by welfare clients in Israel. *International Social Work* 33(1): 75-83, January.

Compton, B.R., & Galaway, B. (1994) *Social Work Processes*. Pacific Grove, CA: Brooks/Cole.

Cox, F.M., Erlich, J.I., Rothman, J., & Tropman, J.E. (1987) *Strategies of Community Organization*. Itasca, IL: F.E. Peacock.

Germain, C.H., & Gitterman, A. (1980) *The Life Model of Social Work Practice*. NY: Columbia University Press.

Hartford, M. (1964) Frame of reference for social group work. In *Papers toward a frame of reference for Social Group Work*. NY: NASW Press.

Hellenbrand, S.C. (1978) Integration takes time. *Social Service Review* 52(3): 456-467.

Hepworth, D.H., & Larsen, J.A. (1990) *Direct Social Work Practice*. Belmont, CA: Wadsworth.

Johnson, L.C. (1995) *Social Work Practice: A Generalist Approach*. Boston: Allyn & Bacon.

Kadushin, A. (1990) *The Social Work Interview, Third Ed.* NY: Columbia University Press.

Meyer, C.H., & Mattaini, M.A. (1995) *The Foundations of Social Work Practice*. Washington, D.C.: NASW Press.

Moore, S.T., & Kelly, M.J. (1996) Quality now: moving human services organizations towards a consumer orientation in service quality. *Social Work* 41(1): 33-40.

Netting, F.E., Kettner, P.M., & McMurtry, S.L. (1998) *Social Work Macro Practice*. NY: Longman Publishing.

Patti, R. (1985) In search of purpose for social welfare administration. *Administration in SocialWork* 9(3): 1-14.

Reamer, F.G. (1994) *Social Work Malpractice and Liability*. NY: Columbia University Press.

Sheafor, B.W., & Horejsi, G.A. (1994) *Techniques and Guidelines for Social Work Practice*. Boston: Allyn & Bacon.

Simon, H.A. (1965) *Administrative Behavior*. NY::Macmillan.

Toseland, R.W., & Rivas, R.F. (1995) *An Introduction to Group Work Practice*. Boston: Allyn & Bacon.

Wortman, J. (1989) Empathy and social work: the capacity of students for cognitive and emotional empathy as it relates to field instruction evaluations. Doctoral Dissertation, Fordham University.

Chapter Nine

Abbott, A.A. (1986) The field placement contract: Its use in maintaining comparability between employment-related and traditional field placements. *Journal of Social Work Education* 22(1): 57-66.

Gelman, S.R. (1990) The crafting of field work training agreements. *Journal of Social Work Education* 26(1): 65-75.

Greene, G.J. (1989) Using the written contract for evaluating and enhancing practice effectiveness. *Journal of Independent Social Work* 4: 135-155.

Hepworth, D.H., Rooney, R.H., & Larsen, J.A. (1997) *Direct Social Work Practice*. Pacific Grove, CA:

Brooks/Cole, Chapter 12, Negotiating goals and formulating a contract.

Maluccio, A., & Marlow, W.D. (1974) The case for the contract. *Social Work* 19(1): 28-36.

Rothman, J. (1998) *Contracting in Clinical Social Work*. Chicago: Nelson Hall.

Seabury, B. (1976) The contract: uses, abuses, and limitations. *Social Work* 21(1): 16-21.

Chapter Ten

Berson, M., & Geron, Y. (1996) Theory and practice in teaching evaluation of intervention outcomes. *Social Work Education* 15(3): 98-107.

Haffey, M., Salmon, R., Blau, S., & Johnson, D. (1993) The potential for staff development through work-study programs. *Journal of Continuing Social Work Education* 5(4): 23-28.

Fleming, R. (1994) Self-esteem and self-confidence among female master of social work students: effects of re-entry status. Doctoral Dissertation, California State University at Long Beach.

Kates, L.B. (1980) Group formation and curriculum development in second year social group work field work practice: a pilot project in program development, initiation, and evaluation in social work education. Doctoral Dissertation, City University of New York.

Kazmerski, K.J. (1979) Experiential exercises in social work education for administrative practice. Doctoral Dissertation, City University of New York.

Walter, C.A., & Grief, G.L. (1988) To do or not to do: social work education for private practice.*Journal of Independent Social Work* 2(3): 17-24, Spring.

Chapter Eleven

Faria, G. Brownstein, C., & Smith, H.Y. (1988) A survey of field instructors' perceptions of the liaison role. *Journal of Social Service Education* 24(2): 135-144.

Rosenblum, A.F. & Raphael, F.B. (1983) The role and function of the faculty field liaison. *Journal of Education for Social Work* 19(1): 67-73.

Chapter Twelve

Koerin, B., & Miller, J. (1995) Gatekeeping policies: terminating students for non-academic reasons. *Journal of Social Work Education* 31(2): 247-259.

National Association of Social Workers (1996) *Code of Ethics*. Washington, D.C.: Author.

Chapter Thirteen

Greene, G.J. (1989) Using the written contract for evaluating and enhancing practice effectiveness. *Journal of Independent Social Work* 4: 135-155.

Seabury, B. (1976) The contract: Uses, abuses, and limitations. *Social Work* 21(1): 16-21.

Chapter Fourteen

Bisman, C. (1994) *Social Work Practice: Cases and Principles*. Pacific Grove, CA: Brooks/Cole.

Fortune, A. E. (1985) Planning duration and termination of treatment. *Social Service Review* 59(4): 647-651.

Fortune, A.E. (1987) Grief only? Client and social worker reactions to termination. *Clinical Social Work Journal* 15(2): 159-171.

Fortune, A.E., Pearlingi, B., & Rochelle, C. (1992) Reactions to termination of individual treatment.*Social Work* 37(2): 171-178.

Gutheil, I.A. (1993) Rituals and termination procedures. *Smith College Studies in Social Work* 63(2): 163-76.

Hepworth, D., & Larsen, J.A. (1997) *Direct Social Work Practice*, 4th Ed. Pacific Grove, CA: Brooks/Cole, Part 4, The Termination and Evaluation Phase.

Kauff, P.F. (1977) The termination process: its relationship to the separation-individuation phase of development. *The International Journal of Group Psychotherapy* 28(3): 3-18.

Lum, D. (1996) *Social Work Practice with People of Color* Pacific Grove, CA: Brooks/Cole, Chapter 8, Termination.

National Association of Social Workers (1996) *Code of Ethics*. Washington, D.C.: Author.

Sheafor, B W., Horejsi, C.R., & Horejsi, G.A. (1994) *Techniques and Guidelines for Social Work Practice.* Boston: Allyn & Bacon. Chapter 14, Evaluation and termination.

Siebold, C. (1992) Forced termination: reconsidering theory and technique. *Smith College Studies in Social Work* 63: 323-341.

Chapter Fifteen

Fortune, A.E., Feathers, C.E., Rook, S.R., Scrimenti, R., Smollen, O., Stemerman, B., & Tucker, E. (1985) Student satisfaction with field placement. *Journal of Social Work Education* 21(3): 92-104.

Johnston, N., Rooney, R., & Reitmeir, M.A. Sharing power: student feedback to field supervisors. In Schneck, D., Grossman, B., & Glasman, U., Eds. (1991) *Field Education in Social Work: Contemporary Issues and Trends*. Dubuque, IA: Kendall/Hunt.

Martin, E.S., & Shurtman, R. (1985) Termination anxiety as it affects the therapist. *Psychotherapy*, 22: 92-96.

McRoy, R.G., Freeman, E.M., & Logan, S. (1986) Strategies for teaching students about termination. *The Clinical Supervisor* 4(4): 45-56.

Wilson, J., & Moore, D. (1989) Developing and using evaluation guidelines for final practicum. *Australian Social Work* 42(1): 21-28, March.

Wortman, J. (1989) Empathy and social work: the capacity of students for cognitive and emotional empathy as it relates to field instruction evaluations. Doctoral Dissertation, Fordham University.

Chapter Sixteen

Blumenfield, S., & Lowe, J.I. (1987) A template for analyzing ethical dilemmas in discharge planning. *Health and Social Work* 12(1): 47-56.

Conte, H.R., Plutchik, R., Picard, S., & Karasu, T.B. (1989) Ethics in the practice of psychotherapy. *American Journal of Psychotherapy* 43: 32-42. 1989.

Loewenberg, F., & Dolgoff, R. (1992) *Ethical Decisions for Social Work Practice*. Itasca, IL: F.E. Peacock Publishers, Inc.

Reamer, F.G. (1994) *Social Work Malpractice and Liability*. NY: Columbia University Press, Chapter 8, Termination of Service.

Reamer, F.G. (1990) *Ethical Dilemmas in Social Service*. NY: Columbia University Press, Section on The Limits of Obligation.

Chapter Seventeen

Gambrill, E., & Pruger, R., Eds. (1992) *Controversial Issues in Social Work*. Boston: Allyn & Bacon,

Debate 2, Should social workers work for for-profit firms?; Debate 17, Should a minimum, mandatory percentage of funds be set aside for prevention in all social welfare program areas?

Germain, C.B., & Gitterman, A. (1980) *The Life Model of Social Work Practice*. NY: Columbia University Press, Chapter 1, Introduction to the life model.

Goodman, M., Brown, J., & Dietz, P. (1992) *Managing Managed Care: A Mental Health Practitioner's Survival Guide*. Washington, D.C.: American Psychiatric Association.

Hancock, T.U. (1992) Field placements in for-profit agencies: Policies and practices of graduate programs. *Journal of Social Work Education* 28(3): 330-340.

Loewenberg, F.M., & Dolgoff, R. (1996) *Ethical Decisions for Social Work Practice*. Itasca, IL: F.E. Peacock.

National Association of Social Workers (1996) *Code of Ethics*. Washington, D.C.: Author.

Packard, T. (1991) Participation in decision-making, performance, and job satisfaction in a social work bureaucracy. *Administration in Social Work* 13(1): 59-73.

Popple, P.R., & Leighninger, L.H. (1990) *Social work, social welfare, and American society*. Boston: Allyn & Bacon.

Reamer, F.G. (1990) *Ethical Dilemmas in Social Service*. NY: Columbia University Press.

Rothman, J. (1998) *From the Front Lines: Student Cases in Social Work Ethics*. Boston: Allyn & Bacon, Case 3.5, An employee assistance counselor's dilemma; Case Study 5.4, "Discharge her to a hospice *now*!" — a conflict of professional loyalties.

Wilson, S. (1978) *Confidentiality in Social Work: Issues and Principles*. NY: Free Press.

Chapter Eighteen

Bisman, C. (1994) *Social Work Practice: Cases and Principles*. Pacific Grove, CA: Brooks/Cole, Chapters One and Two.

Netting, F.E., Ketner, P.M., & McMurtry, S.L. (1998) *Social Work Macro Practice*. NY: Addison Wesley Longman, Inc., Chapter 7, Understanding Organizations.

Chapter Nineteen

Rothman, J.C. (1998) *From the Front Lines: Student Cases in Social Work Ethics*. Boston: Allyn & Bacon, Case 4.3, Motivation or Consequence: when "help" *may* result in dishonesty, fraud, or deception; Case 6.2, Dealing drugs: can confidentiality ever be justified?

Chapter Twenty

Brashears, F. (1995) Supervision as social work practice: a reconceptualization. *Social Work* 40(5): 677-720.

Chapter Twenty-One

Gambrill, E., & Pruger, R., Eds. (1992) *Controversial Issues in Social Work* Boston: Allyn & Bacon, Debate Five, Should Social Workers Blow the Whistle on Incompetent Colleagues?

Chapter Twenty-Two

Loewenberg, F., & Dolgoff, R. (1996) *Ethical Decisions for Social Work Practice*. Itasca, IL: F.E. Peacock, Chapter 7, Equality, inequality and limited resources; Chapter 9, Bureauocratic and work relationships.

Gambrill, E., & Pruger, R. (1992) *Controversial Issues in Social Work.* Boston: Allyn & Bacon, Debate 10, Should social workers use the DSM-III?

NASW (1996) *The NASW Code of Ethics.* Washington, D.C.: Author.

Netting, F.E., Kettner, P.M., & McMurtry, S.L. (1997) *Social Work Macro Practice.* NY: Longman.

Reamer, F.G. (1990) *Ethical Dilemmas in Social Service.* NY: Columbia University Press, Chapter 4, Ethical dilemmas in social planning and policy.

Rothman, J. (1998) *From the Front Lines: Student Cases in Social Work Ethics.* Boston: Allyn & Bacon, Cases 3.1 and 3.2.

Wells, C.C. (1999) *Social Work Day to Day: The Experience of Generalist Social Work Practice.* NY: Addison Wesley Longman Publishers, Part Four, Policy Issues.

Chapter Twenty-Three

Gambrill, E., & Pruger, R. (1992) *Controversial Issues in Social Work.* Boston: Allyn & Bacon.

Loewenberg, F., & Dolgoff, R. (1996) *Ethical Decisions for Social Work Practice.* Itasca, IL: F.E. Peacock, Chapter 3, Guidelines for ethical decisionmaking.

Netting, F.E., Kettner, P.M., & McMurtry, S.L. (1997) *Social Work Macro Practice* NY: Longman, Part 3, The organization as the arena of change.

Reamer, F.G. (1990) *Ethical Dilemmas in Social Service.* NY: Columbia University Press, Chapter 2, Fundamental ethical issues in social work.

Rothman, J. (1998) *From the Front Lines: Student Cases in Social Work Ethics.* Boston: Allyn & Bacon, Introduction: elements of ethical decision-making.

Chapter Twenty-Four

Dhooper, S.S., Huff, M.B., & Schultz, C.M. (1989) Social work and sexual harassment. *Journal of Sociology and Social Welfare* 16(3): 125-138.

Jacobs, C. (1991) Violations of the supervisory relationship: An ethical and educational blind spot. *Social Work* 36(2): 130-135.

Kagle, J.D., & Giebelhausen, P.N. (1994) Dual relationships and professional boundaries. *Social Work* 39: 213-220, March.

Maypole, D.E., & Skaine, R. (1983) Sexual harassment in the workplace. *Social Work* 28(5): 385-390.

National Association of Social Workers (1997) *NASW Code of Ethics.* Washington, D.C.: NASW.

Code of Ethics
of the NATIONAL ASSOCIATION OF SOCIAL WORKERS
As Adopted by the Delegate Assembly of August 1996

Overview

The National Association of Social Workers Code of Ethics is intended to serve as a guide to the everyday professional conduct of social workers. This code includes four sections.

- <u>Section one</u> *Preamble* summarizes the social work profession's mission and core values.
- <u>Section two</u> *Purpose of the Code of Ethics* provides an overview of the Code's main functions and a brief guide for dealing with ethical issues or dilemmas in social work practice.
- <u>Section three</u> *Ethical Principles* presents broad ethical principles, based on social work's core values, that inform social work practice.
  - <u>Service</u>
  - <u>Social Justice</u>
  - <u>Dignity and Worth of the Person</u>
  - <u>Importance of Human Relationships</u>
  - <u>Integrity</u>
  - <u>Competence</u>
- <u>The final section</u> *Ethical Standards* includes specific ethical standards to guide social workers' conduct and to provide a basis for adjudication.
  - <u>social workers' ethical responsibilities to clients,</u>
  - <u>social workers' ethical responsibilities to colleagues,</u>
  - <u>social workers' ethical responsibilities in practice settings,</u>
  - <u>social workers' ethical responsibilities as professionals,</u>
  - <u>social workers' ethical responsibilities to the social work profession,</u> and
  - <u>social workers' ethical responsibilities to the broader society.</u>

Preamble

The primary mission of the social work profession is to enhance human well-being and help meet the basic human needs of all people, with particular attention to the needs and empowerment of people who are vulnerable, oppressed, and living in poverty. A historic and defining feature of social work is the profession's focus on individual well-being in a social context and the well-being of society. Fundamental to social work is attention to the environmental forces that create, contribute to, and address problems in living.

Social workers promote social justice and social change with and on behalf of clients. 'Clients' is used inclusively to refer to individuals, families, groups, organizations, and communities. Social workers are sensitive to cultural and ethnic diversity and strive to end discrimination, oppression, poverty, and other forms of social injustice. These activities may be in the form of direct practice, community organizing, supervision, consultation, administration, advocacy, social and political action, policy development and implementation, education, and research and evaluation. Social workers seek to enhance the capacity of people to address their own needs. Social workers also seek to promote the responsiveness of organizations, communities, and other social institutions to individuals' needs and social problems.

The mission of the social work profession is rooted in a set of core values. These core values, embraced by social workers throughout the profession's history, are the foundation of social work's unique purpose and perspective:

- Service
- Social justice
- Dignity and worth of the person
- Importance of human relationships
- Integrity
- Competence

This constellation of core values reflects what is unique to the social work profession. Core values, and the principles that flow from them, must be balanced within the context and complexity of the human experience.

Purpose of the NASW Code of Ethics

Professional ethics are at the core of social work. The profession has an obligation to articulate its basic values, ethical principles, and ethical standards. The *NASW Code of Ethics* sets forth these values, principles, and standards to guide social workers' conduct. The *Code* is relevant to all social workers and social work students, regardless of their professional functions, the settings in which they work, or the populations they serve.
The *NASW Code of Ethics* serves six purposes:

- The *Code* identifies core values on which social work's mission is based.
- The *Code* summarizes broad ethical principles that reflect the profession's core values and establishes a set of specific ethical standards that should be used to guide social work practice.
- The *Code* is designed to help social workers identify relevant considerations

when professional obligations conflict or ethical uncertainties arise.

- The *Code* provides ethical standards to which the general public can hold the social work profession accountable.

- The *Code* socializes practitioners new to the field to social work's mission, values, ethical principles, and ethical standards.
- The *Code* articulates standards that the social work profession itself can use to assess whether social workers have engaged in unethical conduct. NASW has formal procedures to adjudicate ethics complaints filed against its members. (For information on NASW adjudication procedures, see *NASW Procedures for the Adjudication of Grievances*.) In subscribing to this *Code,* social workers are required to cooperate in its implementation, participate in NASW adjudication proceedings, and abide by any NASW disciplinary rulings or sanctions based on it.

The *Code* offers a set of values, principles, and standards to guide decision making and conduct when ethical issues arise. It does not provide a set of rules that prescribe how social workers should act in all situations. Specific applications of the *Code* must take into account the context in which it is being considered and the possibility of conflicts among the *Code*'s values, principles, and standards. Ethical responsibilities flow from all human relationships, from the personal and familial to the social and professional.

Further, the *NASW Code of Ethics* does not specify which values, principles, and standards are most important and ought to outweigh others in instances when they conflict. Reasonable differences of opinion can and do exist among social workers with respect to the ways in which values, ethical principles, and ethical standards should be rank ordered when they conflict. Ethical decision making in a given situation must apply the informed judgment of the individual social worker and should also consider how the issues would be judged in a peer review process where the ethical standards of the profession would be applied.

Ethical decision making is a process. There are many instances in social work where simple answers are not available to resolve complex ethical issues. Social workers should take into consideration all the values, principles, and standards in this *Code* that are relevant to any situation in which ethical judgment is warranted. Social workers' decisions and actions should be consistent with the spirit as well as the letter of this *Code.*

In addition to this *Code,* there are many other sources of information about ethical thinking that may be useful. Social workers should consider ethical theory and principles generally, social work theory and research, laws, regulations, agency policies, and other relevant codes of ethics, recognizing that among codes of ethics social workers should consider the *NASW Code of Ethics* as their primary source. Social workers also should be aware of the impact on ethical decision making of their clients' and their own personal values and cultural and religious beliefs and practices. They should be aware of any conflicts between personal and professional values and deal with them responsibly. For additional guidance social workers should consult the relevant literature on professional ethics and ethical decision making and seek appropriate consultation when faced with ethical dilemmas. This may involve consultation with an agency-based or social work organization's ethics committee, a regulatory body, knowledgeable colleagues, supervisors, or legal counsel.

Instances may arise when social workers' ethical obligations conflict with agency policies or relevant laws or regulations. When such conflicts occur, social workers must make a responsible effort to resolve the conflict in a manner that is consistent with the values, principles, and standards expressed in this *Code*. If a reasonable resolution of the conflict does not appear possible, social workers should seek proper consultation before making a decision.

The *NASW Code of Ethics* is to be used by NASW and by individuals, agencies, organizations, and bodies (such as licensing and regulatory boards, professional liability insurance providers, courts of law, agency boards of directors, government agencies, and other professional groups) that choose to adopt it or use it as a frame of reference. Violation of standards in this *Code* does not automatically imply legal liability or violation of the law. Such determination can only be made in the context of legal and judicial proceedings. Alleged violations of the *Code* would be subject to a peer review process. Such processes are generally separate from legal or administrative procedures and insulated from legal review or proceedings to allow the profession to counsel and discipline its own members.

A code of ethics cannot guarantee ethical behavior. Moreover, a code of ethics cannot resolve all ethical issues or disputes or capture the richness and complexity involved in striving to make responsible choices within a moral community. Rather, a code of ethics sets forth values, ethical principles, and ethical standards to which professionals aspire and by which their actions can be judged. Social workers' ethical behavior should result from their personal commitment to engage in ethical practice. The *NASW Code of Ethics* reflects the commitment of all social workers to uphold the profession's values and to act ethically. Principles and standards must be applied by individuals of good character who discern moral questions and, in good faith, seek to make reliable ethical judgments.

Ethical Principles

The following broad ethical principles are based on social work's core values of service, social justice, dignity and worth of the person, importance of human relationships, integrity, and competence. These principles set forth ideals to which all social workers should aspire.

VALUE: *Service*
Ethical Principle: *Social workers' primary goal is to help people in need and to address social problems.* Social workers elevate service to others above self-interest. Social workers draw on their knowledge, values, and skills to help

people in need and to address social problems. Social workers are encouraged to volunteer some portion of their professional skills with no expectation of significant financial return (pro bono service).

VALUE: *Social Justice*
Ethical Principle: *Social workers challenge social injustice.* Social workers pursue social change, particularly with and on behalf of vulnerable and oppressed individuals and groups of people. Social workers' social change efforts are focused primarily on issues of poverty, unemployment, discrimination, and other forms of social injustice. These activities seek to promote sensitivity to and knowledge about oppression and cultural and ethnic diversity. Social workers strive to ensure access to needed information, services, and resources; equality of opportunity; and meaningful participation in decision making for all people.

VALUE: *Dignity and Worth of the Person*
Ethical Principle: *Social workers respect the inherent dignity and worth of the person.* Social workers treat each person in a caring and respectful fashion, mindful of individual differences and cultural and ethnic diversity. Social workers promote clients' socially responsible self-determination. Social workers seek to enhance clients' capacity and opportunity to change and to address their own needs. Social workers are cognizant of their dual responsibility to clients and to the broader society. They seek to resolve conflicts between clients' interests and the broader society's interests in a socially responsible manner consistent with the values, ethical principles, and ethical standards of the profession.

VALUE: *Importance of Human Relationships*
Ethical Principle: *Social workers recognize the central importance of human relationships.* Social workers understand that relationships between and among people are an important vehicle for change. Social workers engage people as partners in the helping process. Social workers seek to strengthen relationships among people in a purposeful effort to promote, restore, maintain, and enhance the well-being of individuals, families, social groups, organizations, and communities.

VALUE: *Integrity*
Ethical Principle: *Social workers behave in a trustworthy manner.* Social workers are continually aware of the profession's mission, values, ethical principles, and ethical standards and practice in a manner consistent with them. Social workers act honestly and responsibly and promote ethical practices on the part of the organizations with which they are affiliated.

VALUE: *Competence*
Ethical Principle: *Social workers practice within their areas of competence and develop and enhance their professional expertise.* Social workers continually strive

to increase their professional knowledge and skills and to apply them in practice. Social workers should aspire to contribute to the knowledge base of the profession.

Ethical Standards

The following ethical standards are relevant to the professional activities of all social workers. These standards concern:
1. social workers' ethical responsibilities to clients,
2. social workers' ethical responsibilities to colleagues,
3. social workers' ethical responsibilities in practice settings,
4. social workers' ethical responsibilities as professionals,
5. social workers' ethical responsibilities to the social work profession,
6. social workers' ethical responsibilities to the broader society

Some of the standards that follow are enforceable guidelines for professional conduct, and some are aspirational. The extent to which each standard is enforceable is a matter of professional judgment to be exercised by those responsible for reviewing alleged violations of ethical standards.

1. Social Workers' Ethical Responsibilities to Clients

1.01 Commitment to Clients   Social workers' primary responsibility is to promote the well-being of clients. In general, clients' interests are primary. However, social workers' responsibility to the larger society or specific legal obligations may on limited occasions supersede the loyalty owed clients, and clients should be so advised. (Examples include when a social worker is required by law to report that a client has abused a child or has threatened to harm self or others.)

1.02 Self-Determination Social workers respect and promote the right of clients to self-determination and assist clients in their efforts to identify and clarify their goals. Social workers may limit clients' right to self-determination when, in the social workers' professional judgment, clients' actions or potential actions pose a serious, foreseeable, and imminent risk to themselves or others.

1.03 Informed Consent (a) Social workers should provide services to clients only in the context of a professional relationship based, when appropriate, on valid informed consent. Social workers should use clear and understandable language to inform clients of the purpose of the services, risks related to the services, limits to services because of the requirements of a third-party payer, relevant costs, reasonable alternatives, clients' right to refuse or withdraw consent, and the time frame covered by the consent. Social workers should provide clients with an opportunity to ask questions.

(b) In instances when clients are not literate or have difficulty understanding the primary language used in the practice setting, social workers should take steps to ensure clients' comprehension. This may include providing clients with a detailed verbal explanation or arranging for a qualified interpreter or translator whenever possible.

(c) In instances when clients lack the capacity to provide informed consent, social workers should protect clients' interests by seeking permission from an appropriate third party, informing clients consistent with the clients' level of understanding. In such instances social workers should seek to ensure that the third party acts in a manner consistent with clients' wishes and interests. Social workers should take reasonable steps to enhance such clients' ability to give informed consent.

(d) In instances when clients are receiving services involuntarily, social workers should provide information about the nature and extent of services and about the extent of clients' right to refuse service.

(e) Social workers who provide services via electronic media (such as computer, telephone, radio, and television) should inform recipients of the limitations and risks associated with such services.

(f) Social workers should obtain clients' informed consent before audiotaping or videotaping clients or permitting observation of services to clients by a third party.

1.04 Competence (a) Social workers should provide services and represent themselves as competent only within the boundaries of their education, training, license, certification, consultation received, supervised experience, or other relevant professional experience.

(b) Social workers should provide services in substantive areas or use intervention techniques or approaches that are new to them only after engaging in appropriate study, training, consultation, and supervision from people who are competent in those interventions or techniques.

(c) When generally recognized standards do not exist with respect to an emerging area of practice, social workers should exercise careful judgment and take responsible steps (including appropriate education, research, training, consultation, and supervision) to ensure the competence of their work and to protect clients from harm.

1.05 Cultural Competence and Social Diversity (a) Social workers should understand culture and its function in human behavior and society, recognizing the strengths that exist in all cultures.

(b) Social workers should have a knowledge base of their clients' cultures and be able to demonstrate competence in the provision of services that are sensitive to clients' culture and to differences among people and cultural groups.

(c) Social workers should obtain education about and seek to understand the nature of social diversity and oppression with respect to race, ethnicity, national origin, color, sex, sexual orientation, age, marital status, political belief, religion and mental or physical disability.

1.06 Conflicts of Interest (a) Social workers should be alert to and avoid conflicts of interest that interfere with the exercise of professional discretion and impartial judgment. Social workers should inform clients when a real or potential conflict of interest arises and take reasonable steps to resolve the issue in a manner that makes the clients' interests primary and protects clients' interests to the greatest extent possible. Occasionally, protecting clients' interests may require termination of the professional relationship with proper referral of the client.

(b) Social workers should not take unfair advantage of any professional relationship or exploit others to further their personal, political, or business interests.

(c) Social workers should not engage in dual or multiple relationships with clients or former clients in which there is a risk of exploitation or potential harm to the client. In instances when dual or multiple relationships are unavoidable, social workers should take steps to protect clients and are responsible for setting clear, appropriate, and culturally sensitive boundaries. (Dual or multiple relationships occur when social workers relate to clients in more than one relationship, whether professional, social, or business. Dual or multiple relationships can occur simultaneously or consecutively.)

(d) When social workers provide services to two or more people who have a relationship with each other (for example, couples, family members), social workers should clarify with all parties which individuals will be considered clients and the nature of social workers' professional obligations to the various individuals who are receiving services. Social workers who anticipate a conflict of interest among the individuals receiving services or who anticipate having to perform in potentially conflicting roles (for example, when a social worker is asked to testify in a child custody dispute or divorce proceedings involving clients) should clarify their role with the parties involved and take appropriate action to minimize any conflict of interest.

1.07 Privacy and Confidentiality (a) Social workers should respect clients' right to privacy. Social workers should not solicit private information from clients unless it is essential to providing service or conducting social work evaluation or research. Once private information is shared, standards of confidentiality apply.

(b) Social workers may disclose confidential information when appropriate with a valid consent from a client, or a person legally authorized to consent on behalf of a client.

(c) Social workers should protect the confidentiality of all information obtained in the course of professional service, except for compelling professional reasons. The general expectation that social workers will keep information confidential does not apply when disclosure is necessary to prevent serious, foreseeable, and imminent harm to a client or other identifiable person or when laws or regulations require disclosure without a client's consent. In all instances, social workers should disclose the least amount of confidential information necessary to achieve the desired purpose; only information that is directly relevant to the purpose for which the disclosure is made should be revealed.

(d) Social workers should inform clients, to the extent possible, about the disclosure of confidential information and, when feasible, before the disclosure is made. This applies whether social workers disclose confidential information as a result of a legal requirement or based on client consent.

(e) Social workers should discuss with clients and other interested parties the nature of confidentiality and limitations of clients' right to confidentiality. Social workers should review with clients circumstances where confidential information may be requested and where disclosure of confidential information may be legally required. This discussion should occur as soon as possible in the social worker-client relationship and as needed throughout the course of the relationship.

(f) When social workers provide counseling services to families, couples, or groups, social workers should seek agreement among the parties involved concerning each individual's right to confidentiality and obligation to preserve the confidentiality of information shared by others. Social workers should inform participants in family, couples, or group counseling that social workers cannot guarantee that all participants will honor such agreements.

(g) Social workers should inform clients involved in family, couples, marital, or group counseling of the social worker's, employer's, and agency's policy concerning the social worker's disclosure of confidential information among the parties involved in the counseling.

(h) Social workers should not disclose confidential information to third-party payers unless clients have authorized such disclosure.

(i) Social workers should not discuss confidential information in any setting unless privacy can be ensured. Social workers should not discuss confidential information in public or semipublic areas such as hallways, waiting rooms, elevators, and restaurants.

(j) Social workers should protect the confidentiality of clients during legal proceedings to the extent permitted by law. When a court of law or other legally authorized body orders social workers to disclose confidential or privileged information without a client's consent and such disclosure could cause harm to the client, social workers should request that the court withdraw the order or limit the order as narrowly as possible or maintain the records under seal, unavailable for public inspection.

(k) Social workers should protect the confidentiality of clients when responding to requests from members of the media.

(l) Social workers should protect the confidentiality of clients' written and electronic records and other sensitive information. Social workers should take reasonable steps to ensure that clients' records are stored in a secure location and that clients' records are not available to others who are not authorized to have access.

(m) Social workers should take precautions to ensure and maintain the confidentiality of information transmitted to other parties through the use of computers, electronic mail, facsimile machines, telephones and telephone answering machines, and other electronic or computer technology. Disclosure of identifying information should be avoided whenever possible.

(n) Social workers should transfer or dispose of clients' records in a manner that protects clients' confidentiality and is consistent with state statutes governing records and social work licensure.

(o) Social workers should take reasonable precautions to protect client confidentiality in the event of the social worker's termination of practice, incapacitation, or death.

(p) Social workers should not disclose identifying information when discussing clients for teaching or training purposes unless the client has consented to disclosure of confidential information.

(q) Social workers should not disclose identifying information when discussing clients with consultants unless the client has consented to disclosure of confidential information or there is a compelling need for such disclosure.

(r) Social workers should protect the confidentiality of deceased clients consistent with the preceding standards.

1.08 Access to Records (a) Social workers should provide clients with reasonable access to records concerning the clients. Social workers who are concerned that clients' access to their records could cause serious misunderstanding or harm to the client should provide assistance in interpreting the records and consultation with the client regarding the records. Social workers should limit clients' access to their records, or portions of their records, only in exceptional circumstances when there is compelling evidence that such access would cause serious harm to the client. Both clients' requests and the rationale for withholding some or all of the record should be documented in clients' files.

(b) When providing clients with access to their records, social workers should take steps to protect the confidentiality of other individuals identified or discussed in such records.

1.09 Sexual Relationships (a) Social workers should under no circumstances engage in sexual activities or sexual contact with current clients, whether such contact is consensual or forced.

(b) Social workers should not engage in sexual activities or sexual contact with clients' relatives or other individuals with whom clients maintain a close personal relationship when there is a risk of exploitation or potential harm to the client. Sexual activity or sexual contact with clients' relatives or other individuals with whom clients maintain a personal relationship has the potential to be harmful to the client and may make it difficult for the social worker and client to maintain appropriate professional boundaries. Social workers -- not their clients, their clients' relatives, or other individuals with whom the client maintains a personal relationship -- assume the full burden for setting clear, appropriate, and culturally sensitive boundaries.

(c) Social workers should not engage in sexual activities or sexual contact with former clients because of the potential for harm to the client. If social workers engage in conduct contrary to this prohibition or claim that an exception to this prohibition is warranted because of extraordinary circumstances, it is social workers -- not their clients -- who assume the full burden of demonstrating that the former client has not been exploited, coerced, or manipulated, intentionally or unintentionally.

(d) Social workers should not provide clinical services to individuals with whom they have had a prior sexual relationship. Providing clinical services to a former sexual partner has the potential to be harmful to the individual and is likely to make it difficult for the social worker and individual to maintain appropriate professional boundaries.

1.10 Physical Contact Social workers should not engage in physical contact with clients when there is a possibility of psychological harm to the client as a result of the contact (such as cradling or caressing clients). Social workers who engage in appropriate physical contact with clients are responsible for setting clear, appropriate, and culturally sensitive boundaries that govern such physical contact.

1.11 Sexual Harassment Social workers should not sexually harass clients. Sexual harassment includes advances, sexual solicitation, requests for sexual favors, and other verbal or physical conduct of a sexual nature.

1.12 Derogatory Language Social workers should not use derogatory language in their written or verbal communications to or about clients. Social workers should use accurate and respectful language in all communications to and about clients.

1.13 Payment for Services (a) When setting fees, social workers should ensure that the fees are fair, reasonable, and commensurate with the service performed. Consideration should be given to the client's ability to pay.

(b) Social workers should avoid accepting goods or services from clients as payment for professional services. Bartering arrangements, particularly involving services, create the potential for conflicts of interest, exploitation, and inappropriate boundaries in social workers' relationships with clients. Social workers should explore and may participate in bartering only in very limited circumstances when it can be demonstrated that such arrangements are an accepted practice among professionals in the local community, considered to be essential for the provision of services, negotiated without coercion, and entered into at the client's initiative and with the client's informed consent. Social workers who accept goods or services from clients as payment for professional services assume the full burden of demonstrating that this arrangement will not be detrimental to the client or the professional relationship.

(c) Social workers should not solicit a private fee or other remuneration for providing services to clients who are entitled to such available services through the social workers' employer or agency.

1.14 Clients Who Lack Decision-Making Capacity When social workers act on behalf of clients who lack the capacity to make informed decisions, social workers should take reasonable steps to safeguard the interests and rights of those clients.

1.15 Interruption of Services Social workers should make reasonable efforts to ensure continuity of services in the event that services are interrupted by factors such as unavailability, relocation, illness, disability, or death.

1.16 Termination of Services (a) Social workers should terminate services to clients, and professional relationships with them, when such services and relationships are no longer required or no longer serve the clients' needs or interests.

(b) Social workers should take reasonable steps to avoid abandoning clients who are still in need of services. Social workers should withdraw services precipitously only under unusual circumstances, giving careful consideration to all factors in the situation and taking care to minimize possible adverse effects. Social workers should assist in making appropriate arrangements for continuation of services when necessary.

(c) Social workers in fee-for-service settings may terminate services to clients who are not paying an overdue balance if the financial contractual arrangements have been made clear to the client, if the client does not pose an imminent danger to self or others, and if the clinical and other consequences of the current nonpayment have been addressed and discussed with the client.

(d) Social workers should not terminate services to pursue a social, financial, or sexual relationship with a client.

(e) Social workers who anticipate the termination or interruption of services to clients should notify clients promptly and seek the transfer, referral, or continuation of services in relation to the clients' needs and preferences.

(f) Social workers who are leaving an employment setting should inform clients of all available options for the continuation of service and their benefits and risks.

2. Social Workers' Ethical Responsibilities to Colleagues

2.01 Respect (a) Social workers should treat colleagues with respect and represent accurately and fairly the qualifications, views, and obligations of colleagues.

(b) Social workers should avoid unwarranted negative criticism of colleagues with clients or with other professionals. Unwarranted negative criticism may include demeaning comments that refer to colleagues' level of competence or to individuals' attributes such as race, ethnicity, national origin, color, age, religion, sex, sexual orientation, marital status, political belief, mental or physical disability, or any other preference, personal characteristic, or status.

(c) Social workers should cooperate with social work colleagues and with colleagues of other professions when it serves the well-being of clients.

2.02 Confidentiality with Colleagues Social workers should respect confidential information shared by colleagues in the course of their professional relationships and transactions. Social workers should ensure that such colleagues understand social workers' obligation to respect confidentiality and any exceptions related to it.

2.03 Interdisciplinary Collaboration (a) Social workers who are members of an interdisciplinary team should participate in and contribute to decisions that affect the well-being of clients by drawing on the perspectives, values, and experiences of the social work profession. Professional and ethical obligations of the interdisciplinary team as a whole and of its individual members should be clearly established.

(b) Social workers for whom a team decision raises ethical concerns should attempt to resolve the disagreement through appropriate channels. If the disagreement cannot be resolved social workers should pursue other avenues to address their concerns, consistent with client well-being.

2.04 Disputes Involving Colleagues (a) Social workers should not take advantage of a dispute between a colleague and employer to obtain a position or otherwise advance the social workers own interests.

(b) Social workers should not exploit clients in disputes with colleagues or engage clients in any inappropriate discussion of conflicts between social workers and their colleagues.

2.05 Consultation (a) Social workers should seek advice and counsel of colleagues whenever such consultation is in the best interests of clients.

(b) Social workers should keep informed of colleagues' areas of expertise and competencies. Social workers should seek consultation only from colleagues who have demonstrated knowledge, and competence related to the subject of the consultation.

(c) When consulting with colleagues about clients, social workers should disclose the least amount of information to achieve the purposes of the consultation.

2.06 Referral for Services (a) Social workers should refer clients to other professionals when other professionals' specialized knowledge or expertise is needed to serve clients fully, or when social workers believe they are not being effective or making reasonable progress with clients and additional service is required.

(b) Social workers who refer clients to other professionals should take appropriate steps to facilitate an orderly transfer of responsibility. Social workers who refer clients to other professionals should disclose, with clients' consent, all pertinent information to the new service providers.

(c) Social workers are prohibited from giving or receiving payment for a referral when no professional service is provided by the referring social worker.

2.07 Sexual Relationships (a) Social workers who function as supervisors or educators should not engage in sexual activities or contact with current supervisees, students, trainees, or other colleagues over whom they exercise professional authority.

(b) Social workers should avoid engaging in sexual relationships with colleagues where there is potential for a conflict of interest. Social workers who become involved in, or anticipate becoming involved in, a sexual relationship with a colleague have a duty to transfer professional responsibilities, when necessary, in order to avoid a conflict of interest.

2.08 Sexual Harassment Social workers should not engage in any sexual harassment of supervisees, students, trainees, or colleagues. Sexual harassment includes sexual advances, sexual solicitation, requests for sexual favors, and other verbal or physical conduct of a sexual nature.

2.09 Impairment of Colleagues (a) Social workers who have direct knowledge of a social work colleague's impairment which is due to personal problems, psychosocial distress, substance abuse, or mental health difficulties, and which interferes with practice effectiveness, should consult with that colleague and assist the colleague in taking remedial action.

(b) Social workers who believe that a social work colleague's impairment interferes with practice effectiveness and that the colleague has not taken adequate steps to address the impairment should take action through appropriate channels established by employers, agencies, NASW, licensing and regulatory bodies, and other professional organizations.

2.10 Incompetence of Colleagues (a) Social workers who have direct knowledge of a social work colleague's incompetence should consult with that colleague when feasible and assist the colleague in taking remedial action.

(b) Social workers who believe that a social work colleague is incompetent and has not taken adequate steps to address the incompetence should take action through appropriate channels established by employers, agencies, NASW, licensing and regulatory bodies, and other professional organizations.

2.11 Reporting Unethical Conduct (a) Social workers should take adequate measures to discourage, prevent, expose, and correct the unethical conduct of colleagues.

(b) Social workers should be knowledgeable about established policies and procedures for handling concerns about colleagues' unethical behavior. Social workers should be familiar with national, state, and local procedures for handling ethics complaints. These include policies and procedures created by NASW, licensing and regulatory bodies, employers, agencies, and other professional organizations.

(c) Social workers who believe that a colleague has acted unethically should seek resolution by discussing their concerns with the colleague when feasible and when such discussion is likely to be productive.

(d) Social workers should defend and assist colleagues who are unjustly charged with unethical conduct.

3. Social Workers' Ethical Responsibilities in Practice Settings

3.01 Supervision and Consultation (a) Social workers who provide supervision or consultation should have the necessary knowledge and skill to supervise or consult appropriately and should do so only within their areas of knowledge and competence.

(b) Social workers who provide supervision or consultation are responsible for setting clear, appropriate, and culturally sensitive boundaries.

(c) Social workers should not engage in any dual or multiple relationships with supervisees in which there is a risk of exploitation of or potential harm to the supervisee. (d) Social workers who provide supervision should evaluate supervisees' performance in a manner that is fair and respectful.

3.02 Education and Training (a) Social workers who function as educators, field instructors for students, or trainers should provide instruction only within their areas of knowledge and competence and should provide instruction based on the most current information and knowledge available in the profession.

(b) Social workers who function as educators or field instructors for students should evaluate students' performance in a manner that is fair and respectful.

(c) Social workers who function as educators or field instructors for students should take reasonable steps to ensure that clients are routinely informed when services are being provided by students.

(d) Social workers who function as educators or field instructors for students should not engage in any dual or multiple relationships with students in which there is a risk of exploitation or potential harm to the student. Social work educators and field instructors are responsible for setting clear, appropriate, and culturally sensitive boundaries.

3.03 Performance Evaluation Social workers who have responsibility for evaluating the performance of others should fulfill such responsibility in a fair and considerate manner and on the basis of clearly stated criteria.

3.04 Client Records (a) Social workers should take reasonable steps to ensure that documentation in records is accurate and reflects the services provided.

(b) Social workers should include sufficient and timely documentation in records to facilitate the delivery of services and to ensure continuity of services provided to clients in the future.

(c) Social workers' documentation should protect clients' privacy to the extent that is possible and appropriate and should include only information that is directly relevant to the delivery of services.

(d) Social workers should store records following the termination of service to ensure reasonable future access. Records should be maintained for the number of years required by state statutes or relevant contracts.

3.05 Billing Social workers should establish and maintain billing practices that accurately reflect the nature and extent of services provided, and specifically by whom the service was provided in the practice setting.

3.06 Client Transfer (a) When an individual who is receiving services from another agency or colleague contacts a social worker for services, the social worker should carefully consider the client's needs before agreeing to provide services. In order to minimize possible confusion and conflict, social workers should discuss with potential clients the nature of their current relationship with other service providers and the implications, including possible benefits or risks, of entering into a relationship with a new service provider.

(b) If a new client has been served by another agency or colleague, social workers should discuss whether consultation with the previous service provider is in the client's best interest.

3.07 Administration (a) Social work administrators should advocate within and outside their agencies for adequate resources to meet clients' needs.

(b) Social workers should advocate for resource allocation procedures that are open and fair. When not all clients' needs can be met, an allocation procedure should be developed that is nondiscriminatory and based on appropriate and consistently applied principles.

(c) Social workers who are administrators should take reasonable steps to ensure that adequate agency or organizational resources are available to provide appropriate staff supervision.

(d) Social work administrators should take reasonable steps to ensure that the working environment for which they are responsible is consistent with and encourages compliance with the *NASW Code of Ethics*. Social work administrators should take reasonable steps to eliminate any conditions in their organizations that violate, interfere with, or discourage compliance with the *Code of Ethics*.

3.08 Continuing Education and Staff Development Social work administrators and supervisors should take reasonable steps to provide or arrange for continuing education and staff development for all staff for whom they are responsible. Continuing education and staff development should address current knowledge and emerging developments related to social work practice and ethics.

3.09 Commitments to Employers (a) Social workers generally should adhere to commitments made to employers and employing organizations.

(b) Social workers should work to improve employing agencies' policies and procedures, and the efficiency and effectiveness of their services.

(c) Social workers should take reasonable steps to ensure that employers are aware of social workers' ethical obligations as set forth in the *NASW Code of Ethics* and of the implications of those obligations for social work practice.

(d) Social workers should not allow an employing organization's policies, procedures, regulations, or administrative orders to interfere with their ethical practice of social work. Social workers should take reasonable steps to ensure that their employing organization's practices are consistent with the *NASW Code of Ethics*.

(e) Social workers should act to prevent and eliminate discrimination in the employing organization's work assignments and in its employment policies and practices.

(f) Social workers should accept employment or arrange student field placements only in organizations that exercise fair personnel practices.

(g) Social workers should be diligent stewards of the resources of their employing organizations, wisely conserving funds where appropriate and never misappropriating funds for unintended purposes.

3.10 Labor-Management Disputes (a) Social workers may engage in organized action, including the formation of and participation in labor unions, to improve services to clients and working conditions.

(b) The actions of social workers who are involved in labor-management disputes, job actions, or labor strikes should be guided by the profession's values, ethical principles, and ethical standards. Reasonable differences of opinion exist among social workers concerning their primary obligation as professionals during an actual or threatened labor strike or job action. Social workers should carefully examine relevant issues and their possible impact on clients before deciding on a course of action.

4. Social Workers' Ethical Responsibilities as Professionals

4.01 Competence (a) Social workers should accept responsibility or employment only on the basis of existing competence or the intention to acquire the necessary competence.

(b) Social workers should strive to become and remain proficient in professional practice and the performance of professional functions. Social workers should critically examine, and keep current with, emerging knowledge relevant to social work. Social workers should routinely review professional literature and participate in continuing education relevant to social work practice and social work ethics.

(c) Social workers should base practice on recognized knowledge, including empirically based knowledge, relevant to social work and social work ethics.

4.02 Discrimination Social workers should not practice, condone, facilitate, or collaborate with any form of discrimination on the basis of race, ethnicity, national origin, color, age, religion, sex, sexual orientation, marital status, political belief, or mental or physical disability.

4.03 Private Conduct Social workers should not permit their private conduct to interfere with their ability to fulfill their professional responsibilities.

4.04 Dishonesty, Fraud, and Deception Social workers should not participate in, condone, or be associated with dishonesty, fraud, or deception.

4.05 Impairment (a) Social workers should not allow their own personal problems, psychosocial distress, legal problems, substance abuse, or mental health difficulties to interfere with their professional judgment and performance or to jeopardize the best interests of people for whom they have a professional responsibility.

(b) Social workers whose personal problems, psychosocial distress, legal problems, substance abuse, or mental health difficulties interfere with their professional judgment and performance should immediately seek consultation and take appropriate remedial action by seeking professional help, making adjustments in workload, terminating practice, or taking any other steps necessary to protect clients and others.

4.06 Misrepresentation (a) Social workers should make clear distinctions between statements made and actions engaged in as a private individual and as a representative of the social work profession, a professional social work organization, or of the social worker's employing agency.

(b) Social workers who speak on behalf of professional social work organizations should accurately represent the official and authorized positions of the organization.

(c) Social workers should ensure that their representations to clients, agencies, and the public of professional qualifications, credentials, education, competence, affiliations, services provided, or results to be achieved are accurate. Social workers should claim only those relevant professional credentials they actually possess and take steps to correct any inaccuracies or misrepresentations of their credentials by others.

4.07 Solicitations (a) Social workers should not engage in uninvited solicitation of potential clients who, because of their circumstances, are vulnerable to undue influence, manipulation or coercion.

(b) Social workers should not engage in solicitation of testimonial endorsements (including solicitation of consent to use a client's prior statement as a testimonial endorsement) from current clients or other persons who, because of their particular circumstances are vulnerable to undue influence.

4.08 Acknowledging Credit (a) Social workers should take responsibility and credit, including authorship credit, only for work they have actually performed and to which they have contributed.

(b) Social workers should honestly acknowledge the work of and the contributions made by others.

5. Social Workers' Ethical Responsibilities to the Social Work Profession

5.01 Integrity of the Profession (a) Social workers should work toward the maintenance and promotion of high standards of practice.

(b) Social workers should uphold and advance the values, ethics, knowledge, and mission of the profession. Social workers should protect, enhance, and improve the integrity of the profession through appropriate study and research, active discussion, and responsible criticism of the profession.

(c) Social workers should contribute time and professional expertise to activities that promote respect for the value, integrity, and competence of the social work profession. These activities may include teaching, research, consultations, service, legislative testimony, presentations in the community and participation in their professional organizations.

(d) Social workers should contribute to the knowledge base of social work and share with colleagues their knowledge related to practice, research, and ethics. Social workers should seek to contribute to the profession's literature and to share their knowledge at professional meetings and conferences.

(e) Social workers should act to prevent the unauthorized and unqualified practice of social work.

5.02 Evaluation and Research (a) Social workers should monitor and evaluate policies, the implementation of programs, and practice interventions.

(b) Social workers should promote and facilitate evaluation and research in order to contribute to the development of knowledge.

(c) Social workers should critically examine and keep current with emerging knowledge relevant to social work and fully utilize evaluation and research evidence in their professional practice.

(d) Social workers engaged in evaluation or research should consider carefully possible consequences and should follow guidelines developed for the protection of evaluation and research participants. Appropriate institutional review boards should be consulted.

(e) Social workers engaged in evaluation or research should obtain voluntary and written informed consent from participants, when appropriate, without any implied or actual deprivation or penalty for refusal to participate; without undue inducement to participate; and with due regard for participants' well-being, privacy, and dignity. Informed consent should include information about the nature, extent, and duration of the participation requested and disclosure of the risks and benefits of participation in the research.

(f)When evaluation or research participants are incapable of giving informed consent, social workers should provide an appropriate explanation to the participants, obtain the participants' assent to the extent they are able, and obtain written consent from an appropriate proxy.

(g) Social workers should never design or conduct evaluation or research that does not use consent procedures, such as certain forms of naturalistic observation and archival research, unless rigorous and responsible review of the research has found it to be justified because of its prospective scientific, educational, or applied value and unless equally effective alternative procedures that do not involve waiver of consent are not feasible.

(h) Social workers should inform participants of their right to withdraw from evaluation and research at any time without penalty.

(i) Social workers should take appropriate steps to ensure that participants in evaluation and research have access to appropriate supportive services.

(j) Social workers engaged in evaluation or research should protect participants from unwarranted physical or mental distress, harm, danger, or deprivation.

(k) Social workers engaged in the evaluation of services should discuss collected information only for professional purposes and only with people professionally concerned with this information.

(l) Social workers engaged in evaluation or research should ensure the anonymity or confidentiality of participants and of the data obtained from them. Social workers should inform participants of any limits of confidentiality, the measures that will be taken to ensure confidentiality, and when any records containing research data will be destroyed.

(m) Social workers who report evaluation and research results should protect participants' confidentiality by omitting identifying information unless proper consent has been obtained authorizing disclosure.

(n) Social workers should report evaluation and research findings accurately. They should not fabricate or falsify results and should take steps to correct any errors later found in published data using standard publication methods.

(o) Social workers engaged in evaluation or research should be alert to and avoid conflicts of interest and dual relationships with participants, should inform participants when a real or potential conflict of interest arises, and should take steps to resolve the issue in a manner that makes participants' interests primary.

(p) Social workers should educate themselves, their students, and their colleagues about responsible research practices.

6. Social Workers' Ethical Responsibilities to the Broader Society.

6.01 General Welfare Social workers should promote the general welfare of society, from local to global levels, and the development of people, their communities, and their environments. Social workers should advocate for living conditions conducive to the fulfillment of basic human needs and should promote social, economic, political, and cultural values and institutions that are compatible with the realization of social justice.

6.02 Public Participation Social workers should facilitate informed participation by the public in shaping social policies and institutions.

6.03 Public Emergencies Social workers should provide appropriate professional services in public emergencies, to the greatest extent possible.

6.04 Social and Political Action (a) Social workers should engage in social and political action that seeks to ensure that all people have equal access to the resources, employment, services, and opportunities they require to meet their basic human needs and to develop fully. Social workers should be aware of the impact of the political arena on practice and should advocate for changes in policy and legislation to improve social conditions in order to meet basic human needs and promote social justice.

(b) Social workers should act to expand choice and opportunity for all persons, with special regard for vulnerable, disadvantaged, oppressed, and exploited persons and groups.

(c) Social workers should promote conditions that encourage respect for cultural and social diversity within the United States and globally. Social workers should promote policies and practices that demonstrate respect for difference, support the expansion of cultural knowledge and resources, advocate for programs and institutions that demonstrate cultural competence, and promote policies that safeguard the rights of and confirm equity and social justice for all people.

(d) Social workers should act to prevent and eliminate domination of, exploitation of, and discrimination against any person, group, or class on the basis of race, ethnicity, national origin, color, sex, sexual orientation, age, marital status, political belief, religion, or mental or physical disability.